SCOTLAND'S GIFT
GOLF

Copyright © 2021 Coventry House Publishing

All rights reserved.

ISBN: 1736696165
ISBN-13: 978-1736696163

First Published, 1928 by Charles Scribner's Sons

Contents

I. Introduction to St. Andrews 1

II. Early Golf at St. Andrews and My Early Golfing Records 17

III. Early Implements, Clubs, Balls; Also Links 33

IV. The Dark Ages, 1875-1892 49

V. Beginning of American Golf 59

VI. Beginning of U.S.G.A.—Bogey 75

VII. Personal Golf, 1894-1906 89

VIII. Activities of U.S.G.A., 1902-1912 107

IX. Inception of Ideal Golf Course 129

X. History of National Golf Links of America 143

XI. Tournaments, 1911-1924 157

XII. Lido—Yale—Bermuda 171

XIII. Activities of U.S.G.A., 1911-1927 189

XIV. Standardization 201

XV. Architecture 219

XVI. Rambling Thoughts 231

Appendix 245

Illustrations

Charles Blair Macdonald................................... ix
    From the painting by Gari Melchers presented to the Links Club by Henry C. Frick

Lord Macdonald of the isles and his brother Sir James Macdonald of Sleat................................... x

Ruins of the Castle, St. Andrews................................... 3

Ruins of the Cathedral and St. Regulus' Tower, St. Andrews........... 4

An etching by De Hooghe showing *Kolf* of the seventeenth century.... 7

A plaque from the author's collection showing the Dutch game *Kolf*... 8

Delft tiles from the author's collection................................... 9

John Gray, Esq., Clerk to the Betts of the Honorable Company of Edinburgh Golfers................................... 11

Singin' Jamie Balfour, Secretary and Treasurer of the Honorable Company of Edinburgh Golfers................................... 13

Old Tom and Jamie Morris in the old workshop................................... 22

Allan Robertson................................... 24

Mr. Henry Callender, Captain General of the Royal Blackheath Golf Club, 1807................................... 25
    From the painting by Lemuel Francis Abbott, R. A.

Grand Golf Tournament by professional players on Leith Links, May 17, 1867................................... 29

The club house and the home green at St. Andrews................................... 34

Clubs used by Charles B. Macdonald and made by Tom Morris
    in 1873 and 1874..38

Tom Morris, Jr. 51

Andrew Kirkcaldy and a friend on the old bridge over Swilcan Burn...54

A lost ball beyond the home hole at the original Chicago Golf
    Course, 1894..67

The author in 1895 at the top of his swing.........................68

Facsimile of the signatures of the founders of the Amateur Golf
    Association of the United States, later the U.S.G.A...............77

Theodore A. Havemeyer, donor of the U.S.G.A. Championship Cup .. 82

The first American Championship Cup, won by Charles B.
    Macdonald in Newport, 1895......................................93

Travis, Macdonald, Douglas, and Harriman at Onwentsia in 1899 97

Charles B. Macdonald, James Blackwell, and William T. Linskill,
    taken in 1906 at St. Andrews 103

Messrs. Macdonald, Jacques, Morgan, Clark, Bob Watson, and
    George Watson at Chicago, in 1909..............................113

Horace Hutchinson...130
    From the drawing by Sargent

Approaching the fourth, Redan, at the National Golf Links..........145

First green at the National Golf Links 149

The sixth, twelfth, and thirteenth greens at the National Golf Links...154

Harold Hilton driving. Old Tom Morris and Johnny Low in the
    background...158

Jerry Travers...162

Francis Ouimet about to hole final putt in play-off with Vardon
    and Ray in the Open Championship, 1913.........................165

The teams of the Walker Tournament held at the National Golf
   Links, 1922..167

Robert Gardner and Cyril Tolley 169

Bobby Jones and Roger Wethered 170

The fifth hole at the Mid-Ocean Club, Bermuda 172

The eighteenth hole from the tee at the Mid-Ocean Club 174

Score-card of the Mid-Ocean Club................................175

Map of the Mid-Ocean Club course.............................. 176

The First-Prize Design in the *Country Life* Competition for the
   Lido two-shot hole...179

The Second-Prize Design in the *Country Life* Competition for
   the Lido two-shot hole.....................................181

The fourth hole at the Lido Golf Club 182

Score-card of the Lido Country Club............................ 183

The first tee at Yale 185

Map of the Ray Tompkins Memorial Yale Golf Club course 186

Score-card of the Ray Tompkins Memorial Yale Golf Club.......... 187

Jerome D. Travers holing final putt to win the Open Championship,
   June 18, 1915, at the Baltusrol Golf Club 191

Francis Ouimet 193

T. Suffern Tailer's "Ocean Links," Newport 221

Prince Paul Troubetzkoy at work on statue of Charles B. Macdonald,
   August 2, 1915, in Mrs. Willie Astor Chanler's studio........... 223

Map of the nine-hole practice course on the Payne Whitney
   estate at Manhasset..228

Bobby Jones 234

Fred Herreshoff 236

Jim Whigham 238

Bobby Jones and the author at Atlanta, Georgia, 1926 240

The Honorable Morgan J. O'Brien and the author, 1924 243

CHARLES BLAIR MACDONALD
From the painting by Gari Melchers presented to the Links Club
by Henry C. Frick.

MASTER ALEXANDER MACDONALD OF MACDONALD, AFTERWARD
FIRST LORD MACDONALD OF THE ISLES, AND HIS BROTHER
SIR JAMES MACDONALD OF SLEAT.
From "A Golfer's Gallery by Old Masters."

Chapter I

Introduction to St. Andrews

"Far and Sure."—Motto of John Patersone, The Cobbler-Partner of James VI.

It was early in August in 1872 when I was first introduced to golf. I was then sixteen years old. My father desired that I should go to my grandfather in St. Andrews, Scotland, and there complete my education at the university, the United Colleges of St. Salvador and St. Leonard's. I left Chicago in July, placed in the care of an old family friend, Mr. Kirkwood. We crossed the Atlantic in the *Scotia*, a side-wheel steamer of the Cunard Line, the last of its character that ever crossed the Atlantic. We arrived in Queenstown after a nine-days' voyage. From Cork we drove to the Lakes of Killarney, and I must confess I climbed up the castle and kissed the Blarney Stone; hence my readers will understand any excessive praise I may bestow on any one whom fortune has permitted me to meet on the links. After visiting Dublin we crossed to Glasgow, then by train to Edinburgh, where I was duly delivered in good health and spirits to my grandfather, William Macdonald, of Ballyshear.

Mr. Kirkwood hailed from Musselburgh, a town five miles to the east of Edinburgh. I was permitted to go with Mr. Kirkwood to Musselburgh and spend the night at his aged mother's home. Here it was I first heard of golf. I was much interested in seeing the red coats of the players and watching the leisurely way in which they lounged about the Musselburgh common—"common" to me, but "links" to them, as I soon learned. It seemed to me a form of tiddle-de-winks, stupid and silly, for never in my life had I known a sport that was not strenuous or violent. Musselburgh, too, seemed most unattractive, and that night I wondered if I was to be immured in as uninteresting a place.

We left Edinburgh the next afternoon at three from Waverly Station reaching St. Andrews about six. It was then a weary journey. We first took the train to Granton, then the steamer across the Firth of Forth to Burnt Island. I can recall a blind man fiddling all the way over. Next a train to the junction, Luchars, where we changed carriages again for a run of six miles to dear old St. Andrews. The train in those days ran alongside the third, fourth, fifteenth, and sixteenth holes of the old course into the station, and a friend of my father's who was in the carriage with us, Sir Thomas Moncrieffe, of the well-known golfing family, winner of the silver cross in 1856 with a 95, the lowest score since 1836, tried to explain at some length the fascination of the game. I couldn't see it. My day had yet to come.

Much to my surprise, the town of St. Andrews charmed me at once. It was so quaint and venerable. As I look back now, I see that it had every chance to impress me, if only by contrast with the life I had known in America. Seven years after the Civil War I had left Chicago, a city of 300,000 inhabitants, recovering slowly from the great fire which had almost destroyed it some nine months before. The contrast St. Andrews presented was extraordinary. Unique in its historic and romantic antiquity, there it stood on its bleak promontory, remotely situated and difficult of access, cut off on the south by the Firth of Forth and on the north by the Firth of Tay. Here every one seemed to move along absorbed in the past, while in America every one was absorbed in the future. The contrast reminded me of Handel's "Funeral March" compared with "Marching Through Georgia." It was not long before I became acclimated. Soon I fell in step with this leisurely, delightful life.

Never will I forget my first Sabbath in St. Andrews. My grandfather's house—20 Queen Street—was opposite the Church of England. Sitting in the window, I watched the parishioners on their way to worship. You can imagine my astonishment when I saw boys down to six years of age dressed in Eton jackets and tall hats—"stove pipe" or "plug" hats in Chicago. This gave me my first burst of merriment in Scotland.

One could do nothing on the Sabbath but go to Church (Anglican, of course) or Kirk (Presbyterian), or stroll on the links or the sands, or through the ruins. My only interesting Sunday diversion, at first, was to

RUINS OF THE CASTLE, ST. ANDREWS.

explore the ruins of the castle, the ruins of the cathedral, and the transept of Blackfriars Chapel, or to climb St. Regulus' Tower—then to read of them in the evening as directed by my grandfather.

I found I was living in a city of ancient times, founded some six or seven hundred years before America was discovered, and I was enrolled in a university established before the birth of Columbus. Legendary history conflicts as to the repository of the bones of St. Andrew, the patron saint of Scotland, but it is generally conceded that they were brought by Regulus in the eighth century to the town that now bears his name. The fact that one legend of Regulus makes him an Irishman has emboldened my friend, the Honorable Morgan J. O'Brien, to claim that the good saint brought golf from Ireland to Scotland along with the bones.

For many years St. Andrews was the battle-ground between the Church of Rome, the English Church, and the Presbyterian Church of John Knox. Its history is largely legendary, and its beginnings, like the beginnings of golf, are lost in antiquity. Andrew Lang—devoted to St. Andrews and golf, as well as to fairy tales—tells the story of the old town delightfully and at length in his book "St. Andrews," published in 1893.

Interwoven with the history and the antiquity of St. Andrews are the history and the antiquity of golf. The beginnings of both are hidden beyond remembrance. There is no evidence as to when St. Andrews was founded, and there is no evidence as to when golf was first played. We do

RUINS OF THE CATHEDRAL AND ST. REGULUS' TOWER, ST. ANDREWS.

know that golf is the national game of Scotland, and that the links of St. Andrews are and always have been one of its inspirations.

At St. Andrews I found plenty of evidence of the ancient popularity of the game. Novelists long dead and lawgivers centuries gone have testified to the passion that kings and commoners alike had for golf. It was in truth a "royal and ancient" game. A hundred years before I came to St. Andrews, Smollett was so struck by the popularity of golf that he wrote in "Humphrey Clinker":

"I never saw such a concourse of genteel company at any races in England as appeared on the course of Leith. Hardby, in the fields called the Links, the citizens of Edinburgh divert themselves at a game called Golf, in which they use a curious kind of bats tipt with horn, and small elastic balls of leather stuffed with feathers, rather less than tennis balls, but of a much harder consistence. This they strike with such force and dexterity from one hole to another that they will fly an incredible distance. Of this diversion the Scotch are so fond, that, when the weather will permit, you may see a multitude of all ranks, from the senator of justice to the lowest tradesman, mingled together in their shirts, and following the balls with the utmost eagerness. Among others, I was shown one particular set of Golfers, the youngest of whom was turned of fourscore. They were all gentlemen of independent fortunes, who had amused

themselves with this pastime for the best part of a century, without having ever felt the least alarm from sickness or disgust, and they never went to bed without having each the best part of a gallon of claret in his belly. Such uninterrupted exercise, cooperating with the keen air from the sea, must, without all doubt, keep the appetite always on edge, and steel the constitution against all the common attacks of distemper."

The democracy of golf even in the sixteenth century is attested by a passage in *The Scot's Magazine* describing the game a century before:

"Then the greatest and wisest of the land were to be seen on the Links of Leith, mingling freely with the humblest mechanics in pursuit of their common and beloved amusement. All distinctions of rank were levelled by the joyous spirit of the game. Lords of Sessions and cobblers, knights, baronets and tailors might be seen earnestly contesting for the palms of superior dexterity and vehemently, but good humoredly, discussing moot points of the game, as they arose in the course of the play."

The royal house of Stuart was devoted to golf. When James VI of Scotland became James I of England he eased his absence from his native links by founding in 1608, so tradition says, the Blackheath Club on the outskirts of London. If no document can be found to date Blackheath earlier than 1787, unless we go by the evidence of a silver golf club that was played for there in 1776, at least we have the satisfaction of knowing that in 1567 Mary Queen of Scots sought solace in golf the day after the murder of Darnley. Charles I played golf on the Links of Leith and it was while thus engaged that he received news of the Irish Rebellion. James II was likewise a golfer, and on one occasion he chose a cobbler for a partner to aid him in winning a wager from two English noblemen who had challenged him to a foursome. Winning the match, he gave the money to his partner, John Patersone, who built himself a house, now to be seen in Cannongate, Edinburgh, with the golfer's motto over the door: "Far and Sure."

The earliest mention of golf springs from the enthusiasm with which artisans as well as gentlemen pursued the game. In the sixteenth century, just as now, the long evenings of North Britain gave the workingmen three or four hours of good play after the day's labor was done. Scotsmen devoted their evenings so thoroughly to golf to the exclusion of archery that the Scottish Parliament, concerned at the greater proficiency of their English enemies with bow and arrow, decreed in 1457 that "ye futball and ye golf be utterly cryt doune," and provided for the setting up of archery butts for popular amusement. Obviously, golf must have been played for many years to become such a popular menace. In May, 1471, an act of Parliament opposing "our auld enimies of England" declared it expedient that "the Fute-ball and Golfe be abusit in tyme coming and the buttis maid up and schutting usit." Again, in 1491 it was ordained "that in na place of the Realme be usit fut bawis, gouff, or uthir sic unproffitable sport's", this likewise, "for common gude and defence of the Realme."

Toward the end of the sixteenth century Church as well as State attacked the game. The Scottish church party got the Town Council of Edinburgh to pass an ordinance forbidding golf on Sundays. Yet neither government nor clergy could stamp out a game so dear to the Scotch heart and so fitted to the Scotch character. Its popularity was as steady as it was inevitable.

Despite the early and continuous enthusiasm with which the game was played in Scotland, many chroniclers have tried to prove that golf originated on the Continent. There is not the slightest scintilla of evidence to support this. Numberless games with club and ball have been played for the past two thousand years, and doubtless for millenniums before; but no game with more than one club and with a separate ball for each player, and no game having as its goal a designated hole in the ground. Caesar came as close as any to modern golf when he played *Paganica* to a mark—but not to a small hole in the ground—with one club and the sort of leather ball stuffed with feathers which Scotchmen used before the discovery of the gutta percha.

There are many other Continental rivals to golf. There is even a resemblance of name in the German word *Kolbe* and the Dutch word *Kolf,* each signifying "club." And Dutch pictures and tiles of the sixteenth and seventeenth centuries show men playing a game which has a superficial resemblance to the Scotch sport so far as the club goes. Actually it resembles golf in no other particular. It is nearly always pictured as a winter game on the ice, with the goal as a post. Later kolf came indoors and was played in a rectangular space sixty by twenty-five feet with a floor as hard and level as a billiard table enclosed by walls two feet high, from which the ball could be made to rebound accurately against posts placed near

AN ETCHING BY DE HOOGHE SHOWING THE *KOLF* OF
THE SEVENTEENTH CENTURY.
By courtesy of the Victoria and Albert Museum, London.

A PLAQUE FROM THE AUTHOR'S COLLECTION SHOWING
THE DUTCH GAME *KOLF.*

either end. The French game of *jeu de mail* comes closer to golf, being played cross-country, with a kind of croquet mallet and to posts or raised marks.

Why so many historians of the game have so persistently interpreted kolf as golf I fail to comprehend. As Andrew Lang says in "Badminton": "Clearly golf is no more kolf than cricket is poker." The only explanation I can see lies in the facility with which Dutch painters turned out pictures of their countrymen playing with kolf club and ball. In the golf collection which I purchased from Doctor W. Laidlaw Purves, a noted Scotch golfer who founded the Royal St. George's Golf Club of Sandwich, there are some twenty pictures of Dutch kolf scenes from paintings and many Delft tiles including one from which the little figures used as insignia of the National Golf Links of America and the Links Golf Club near New York were taken. All of these Doctor Purves collected during some years of residence in Holland, but not one represents a true golfing scene. Yet they can and do lead astray the golf enthusiast who seeks some concrete evidence of the origin of his favorite sport.

In the British Museum there is a tail-piece from an illuminated "Book of Hours" executed at Bruges, 1500-1520, which shows four little men, three of whom have clubs like inverted canes with which they are knocking three balls around a fenced-in plot of ground where there appears to be a hole. Some students of golf believe this to be proof that golf originated in Holland. It would take a tremendous stretch of imagination to make a student consider this as reliable evidence of the origin of golf. The balls are three or four times the size of usual balls, more like a tennis ball, and they are playing in a yard about thirty or forty yards square.

DELFT TILES FROM THE AUTHOR'S COLLECTION

One may wonder why Holland is so full of paintings and engravings of people playing kolf while there is nothing of the sort extant in Scotland to-day showing Scotchmen playing their national game. The answer is simple. The Dutch, as every one knows, were devoted to painting and the graphic arts, and their artists could find no more animated and delightful scene than people skating and playing any game on ice. Kolf must have captivated the painter. The Scotch, on the contrary, were not an artistic people, especially in the sixteenth and seventeenth centuries, and there is nothing from this period in the way of native plastic art. The spirit of the collector, coupled with enthusiasm for golf, has resulted in the gathering together of a large number of Continental pictures of games resembling golf.

To-day hockey in the rink resembles golf on the links as much as Dutch kolf resembles the Scotch game. The same may be said of jeu de mail, pell mell, chole, and cambuco. These games were played with club and ball, but they were not golf. The test is simple. None of these games called for a player to use more than one club. From the beginning each golf player has provided himself with quite a number of clubs; the evidence of this is ancient and unquestionable, for in the accounts of the Lord High Treasurers of Scotland at the beginning of the sixteenth century appears this entry:

"1503-4, Feb. 3. Item to Golf Clubbis and Ballis to the King that he playit with. . . . . ix s."

In golf each player has his own ball, and his opponent may not touch it. Again, golf is played from a teeing ground to holes four and a half inches in diameter ranging from one hundred yards to over a quarter of a mile apart.

When I first became acquainted with golf, historical questions of this sort never came within my ken, much less troubled me. I fell in love with golf immediately, and I made no inquiries into the antecedents or forebears of my mistress. Her charms were evident and overpowering.

Golf was so simple at St. Andrews. You may ask what was the particular simplicity of the game in those days, and wherein lay its hidden charm. This was due partly, I think, to the charm of St. Andrews itself, the remoteness of the links amid antiquated surroundings, and the dour

JOHN GRAY, ESQ.
Clerk to the Betts of the Honorable Company of Edinburgh Golfers.
From an engraving by G. Dawe, after a painting by Raeburn.

character of the Scotch, and partly to the strict and Spartan rules of the game in those days.

The earlier rules of play always suggested a code of honor. One rule alone governed the play after driving off: the player must play the ball as it lay and not interfere with his opponent's ball. The ball was not to be touched with anything but a club until it was holed out. There were only two exceptions—a lost ball or ball in water. In each case there was a penalty.

There are only thirteen rules in the oldest surviving code, "Articles and Code of Playing Golf, St. Andrews, 1754." In May, 1857, St. Andrews approved a code of twenty-two rules, decreeing for the first time that one round of the links, or eighteen holes, should be reckoned a match, unless otherwise stipulated. It has been so ever since. Compare these codes with the code of 1908, which had forty-five rules for match-play and fifteen special rules for medal play, not to mention the local rules which each club made to suit its own environment.

You must realize that every time you add a rule to golf you make the entire code more intricate. For instance, if you played a game of golf according to the thirteen rules originally adopted by St. Andrews in 1754 there would be few interpretations needed. On the other hand, during the three years after the 1908 code was adopted the Rules of Golf Committee made 309 decisions, and it has been making decisions ever since.

It is interesting to note that of the 309 decisions 215 were for English clubs; 45 for Scotch; 24, foreign; 17, Irish; and 8, Welsh. There was not a single question asked by any club of outstanding prominence, such as Prestwick, Royal Liverpool, or St. George's. This only proves that where they play the game of golf in the right spirit there is never any controversy as to what is right or wrong. *The spirit of the game prevails.*

As for the simple charm of the St. Andrews links itself, it was in my day the most entrancing course in the world besides being the finest test of golfing ability. The hazards were all natural sandpits, or bunkers as the golfers call them, heather, whins (tough old bushes), and bent. All combined in endless variety to give an unsurpassed golfing terrain. Mr. James Balfour, three times holder of the Royal and Ancient Golf Medal, and father of Leslie Balfour-Melville, amateur champion in 1895, writes of the links in 1887:

SINGIN' JAMIE BALFOUR
Secretary and Treasurer of the Honorable Company of Edinburgh Golfers.
Died in 1795. From an engraving by J. Jones, after a painting by Raeburn.

"If there be added to its golfing charms the charms of all its surroundings—the grand history of St. Andrews and its sacred memories—its delightful air—the song of its numberless larks, which nestle among the whins—the scream of the sea-birds flying overhead—the blue sea dotted with a few fishing boats—the noise of its wave—the bay of Eden as seen from the high hole when the tide is full—the venerable towers and the broken outline of the ancient city, and in the distance the Forfarshire coast, with the range of the Sidlaws, and, further off, the Grampian Hills, it may be truly said that, probably, no portion of ground of the same size on the whole surface of the globe has afforded so much innocent enjoyment to so many people of all ages from two to eighty-nine, and during so many generations."

Here is a description of golf at St. Andrews as printed in *Chambers' Edinburgh Journal*, Saturday, October 8, 1842:

Gossip About Golf

"It is curious to observe how even such a matter as sport is determined by local circumstances. Cricket may be said to be a natural result of the existence of the village greens of England. In like manner Golf exists in Scotland by virtue of the previous existence of a certain peculiar kind of waste ground called Links. Links are chiefly found along the shores of the Firth of Forth and the neighbouring coasts, being low undulating tracts composed of sand which has been blown up from the sea and covered with a slight herbage, varied here and there by patches of broom and furze. They are generally common to the inhabitants of the nearest town, by whom they are devoted statedly to the feeding of a few sheep or geese and occasionally to purposes of recreation and amusement. Thus there are links at Leith, Musselburgh, and Gullane, on the south side of the Firth, and at Kirkaldy, Dunbarnie, Crail, and St. Andrew's on the north side—all of them, but especially the last, being fine open cheerful expanses of ground, albeit of little more than nominal value in the eye of the rural economist. On these prairies of the north, the game of golf, which is said to be of Dutch extraction, has been naturalised for hundreds of years, without spreading to other places, and this simply because in no other places is there ground adapted for the sport. A links

(there is no distinct singular for the word) and golf go, it may be said, hand in hand together. Where there is no links there can properly be no golf; and where there is a links, there golf is as sure to be as a public-house by the side of a stable-lane, or the dandelion and groundsil where there is nothing else."

It has seemed to me imperative to say something of the early history of St. Andrews and the early history of golf, as the genii of both pervaded the very atmosphere of the place when I was a boy. It is necessary to do this so that others may understand a St. Andrews man's feeling and reverence for the game of golf as guiding his association with it through life. It cast a glamour over the links. It instilled the true spirit of the game. So strong was the influence of my associations with St. Andrews that for many years touching the ball in play without penalty was anathema to me, a kind of sacrilegious profanity. The impression of the true old game of golf is indescribable. It was like the dawn or the twilight of a brilliant day. It can only be felt. The charm, the fascination of it all, cannot be conveyed in words.

Would that I could hand on unimpaired the great game as it was my good fortune to know it! The iconoclast and the bolshevik, knowing nothing of golfing law or golfing sin, may mar its spirit, but I have faith in its supremacy.

Chapter II

Early Golf at St. Andrews and My Early Golfing Records

"And I haid my necessaire honestlie aneuch of my father, but nocht else; for archerie and goff, I haid bow, arrose, glub and balls, but nocht a purs for catchpoll and tavern, sic was his fatherlie wisdom for my weill."—From the "Autobiography of Melvill," a student at St. Andrews in 1574.

The day after I arrived in St. Andrews my grandfather took me to genial and much-beloved old Tom Morris and bought me three or four clubs. He also secured me a locker in Tom's shop, for juniors were not permitted in the Royal and Ancient Club, to which both my grandfather and my uncle, Colonel William Macdonald, belonged. Then I sallied forth with Charles Chambers, who was some two years my junior, to be initiated into the mysteries of the game. Chambers's father, Robert Chambers, of the eminent publishing family, and my grandfather followed us around as a gallery. I cannot recall my sensations after so long a time, but I do remember my astonishment when my grandfather always found my ball and I could not.

There was nothing to do in St. Andrews but play golf and bathe. So until college began I was a regular attendant on the links. I soon learned that batting a baseball and driving a golf ball were totally different strokes. I persevered through the long days of summer until I could feel my way toward better things.

One must remember that in summer in that latitude it is light from three in the morning until eleven at night, while in winter the days are correspondingly short. A large part of the college year it was dark until nine or nine-thirty in the morning and again at three or three-thirty. So the only opportunity the students had to play golf when the college was in session came on Saturdays. Sundays, of course, were strictly consecrated to the Kirk or Church, constitutional walks, or the reading of approved books like "Pilgrim's Progress." Naturally, July, August, and September were and still are the height of the season at St. Andrews. Then the links were full of players and the sands crowded with bathers.

St. Andrews was a charming and exclusive watering place. Its inaccessibility made it difficult for week-end trips and excluded casual visitors. On the other hand, many people prominent in scholarship, letters, and art lived in St. Andrews or spent a longer or shorter time there each season. Pervading the city was an atmosphere of spiritual and intellectual refinement given to it by these people. During the period of my short career at St. Andrews I met many of them who were friends of my grandfather's and I heard the names of many more. Among these were Dean Stanley, Lord Rector of the University; Principal Tulloch, of St. Mary's College, Minister to the Queen in Scotland; Principal Sharp, of the United College of San Salvador and St. Leonard's; John White Melville, father of George, the distinguished novelist who died shortly before I went to St. Andrews.

Publishers in particular seemed to delight in golf. Many spent their summers at St. Andrews; notably, John Blackwood, Robert Chambers, and William Longmans. Among authors can be named Carlyle, Andrew Lang, John Stuart Mill, Froude, the historian, Charles Kingsley, Anthony Trollope, Mrs. Oliphant, Thomas Hughes, author of "Tom Brown's School Days," and Martin Tupper. Among the great artists were Sir Edwin Landseer and Millais. Besides these were James Ballantine, author of the Scotch song "Castles in the Air," and many other songs; Lord Cockburn and Sergeant Ballantine, who was in the Orton-Tichborne case, and others without number; Charles Wordsworth, Bishop of St. Andrews diocese, who was a nephew of the poet and an eminent scholar. It was Bishop Wordsworth who confirmed me in the attractive Church of England opposite my grandfather's home. St. Andrews was so small and its diversions so limited that these visitors could be seen on the links almost any day.

Besides these scholars and literary men there were noted gentlemen golfers of that period, leading members of the Royal and Ancient Golf Club, names to conjure with for those who love golf: Robert Clark, Sir Thomas Moncrieffe, Gilbert Mitchell-Innes, Doctor Douglass Robertson, Sir Robert Anstruther, Captain Maitland Dougall, Thomas Hodge, H. S. C. Everhard, Sir Robert Hay, George Glennie, and a host of others. These all played excellently well and were nearly all medal winners at different periods of their lives. I was always much interested in watching their games when not absorbed in my own futile efforts at imitation.

In recalling some of the matches played when I first went to St. Andrews, I can remember Sir Robert Anstruther and young Tom playing a foursome with D. D. Whigham of Prestwick and Robert Clark of Edinburgh. Little did I think then that I was witnessing the play of the father of H. J. Whigham, twice champion of the United States, and now my son-in-law.

Among the golfers whom I met and played with were Doctor J. H. Blackwell's family. Doctor Blackwell was a retired sergeant-major of the old East India Company, serving in the Indian army. He was now residing in St. Andrews, an ardent devotee of the game, a good golfer, and a picturesque figure on the links. His four sons have all been noted golfers. James and Colin were about my own age; Walter, Edward (Ted), and Ernley were much younger. From Colin and James I learned much of the game. Colin was called to India and, sad to relate, never returned.

My other playmates at this period were William T. Linskill, now Dean of the Guild; a New York boy who was at college at the same time, Edward R. Burgess, and the Bairnsfathers, Kenneth and Tommy, the latter the father of Bruce Bairnsfather, the noted caricaturist of the war. William T. Linskill has been a conspicuous figure in golf more owing to his devotion than to his preeminence as a player in the game, though he was a fine foursome partner. Later, going to Cambridge, he founded the Cambridge University Golf Club in 1875 on Coldham Common. He was secretary of the Club for many years and later, until 1895, president. Linskill was notably an excellent putter. Many hours Linskill and I spent of an evening on the ladies' putting links. Horace Hutchinson refers to him in "Badminton":

> "The best putters we have seen, he writes, used their wrists greatly—Jamie Allan, in his best days, Mr. A. F. MacFie, and Mr. W. T. Linskill, are the names that, among a host of fine putters, occur to us. All these players putted almost exclusively with the wrist, and let the club swing very far through after the ball. In driving Linskill was noted for his 'double-joined' style. Its individuality consists in a tremendously exaggerated length of back swing—so much so that Mr. W. T. Linskill, perhaps its chief exponent, is said to have sometimes knocked his ball from the tee with the club-head as it swung round until it became quite vertical again behind his back."

I can recall now how on Sunday afternoons and fast days Linskill and I would stroll nonchalantly over the links to where we had hidden our putters the day before. Then we would putt to improvised holes made between the high whins where we could not be detected.

It was with Edward R. Burgess that I first played *at* golf in America when, on returning to Chicago, we took our clubs out to Camp Douglass and drove and putted to old tin cans sunk in the ground.

Besides the brilliant group of gentlemen who played golf at St. Andrews during my college days there was an equally brilliant group of professionals. At their head stood old Tom Morris. Old Tom was the Grand Old Man of golf, the philosopher and friend of all youthful, aspiring golfers. Horace Hutchinson calls him "The High Priest of the Hierarchy of Professional Golf." He was always equable in temper, always courteous, much beloved by every one. Here is a bit of his talk and his philosophy from an article in "Badminton" by the Right Hon. A. J. Balfour, M. P., who conversed with old Tom on New Year's day, 1886:

> "A gude new year t'ye, Maister Alexander, an' mony o' them! An' it's come weel in, the year has; for it's just a braw day for a mautch. Lod, sir, it aye seems to me the years, as they rise, skelp fester the tane after t'ither; they'll sune be makin' auld men o've a'. Hoo auld am I, d'ye ask, sir? Weel I was born June 16, 1821; and ye can calc'late that for yoursel'. Aye! as ye say, sir, born and bred in St. Andrews, an' a gowffer a' ma days. The vera first time, I think, I hae mind o' mysel' I was toddlin' about at the short holes, wi' a putter uneath ma bot oxter.

"I was made 'prentice to Allan as a ba'macker at eighteen, and wrocht wi' him eliven years. We played, Allan and me the-gither, some geyan big mautches—ane in parteecler wi' the twa Dunns, Willie and Jamie, graund players baith, nane better—over fower greens. It was a' through a braw fecht atweens—green and green—but we snoddit 'em bonnie ere the end o't. I canna ca' to mind Allan an me was iver sae sair teckled as that time; though a wheen richt gude pair o' them did their best to pit oor twa noses oot o' joint. But it was na to be dune wi' Allan an' me. An awfu' player, puir Allan! the cunningest bit body o' a player, I dae think, that iver haun'led cleek an' putter. An' a kindly body tae, as it weel fits me to say, sir, an' wi' a walth a' slee pawky fun aboot him.

"I left Allan to keep the Green at Prestwick, and was there fourteen years. Three years after Allan deed I cam to keep the Green here; an' here I hae been sin syne. Na! sir, I niver weary a the gemm; an' I'm as ready noo to play any gentleman as I was in ma best days. I think I can play aboot as weel yet as I did in ma prime. No, may be, drive jist sae lang a ba'; but there's no muckle odds e'en in that yet. Jist the day I was sixty-four, I gaed roon' in a single wi' Mr. H. in 81. No that ill for the 'Auld Horse' as they ca' me—it'll tak' the best of the young ones, I reckon, to be mony shots better than that.

"An it had na been for gowff, I'm no sure that at this day, sir, I wad hae been a leevin' man. I've had ma troubles an' ma trials, like the lave; an', whiles, I thocht they wad hae clean wauved me, sae that to 'lay me down an' dee'—as the song says—lookit aboot a' that was left in life for puir Tom. It was like as if ma vera sowle was a' thegither gane oot a' me. But there's naething like a ticht gude-gowing mautch to soop yer brain clear a' that kin' o' thing; and wi' the help a' ma God an' o' gowff, I've gotten warsled through somehow or ither. The tae thing ta'en wi' the tither, I hae no had an ill time o't. I dinna mind that iver I had an unpleasant ward frae ony o' the many gentlemen I've played wi'. I've aye tried—as ma business was, sir—to mak masel' pleesant to them; an' they've aye been awfu' pleesant to me.

"An' noo, sir, to end a long and, maybe, a silly crack—bein' maistly about masel'—ye'll jist come wi' me, and ye'll hae a glass a' gude brandy, and I'll have ma pint o' black strap, an' we'll drink a gude New Year to ane anither, an' the like to a' gude gowffers."

OLD TOM AND JAMIE MORRIS IN THE OLD WORKSHOP.

Old Tom learned to make clubs and balls with Allan Robertson and was associated with him until the gutta came in. Although Allan died in 1859 at the early age of forty-four, I found his name was a household word in 1872. He was the best known golfer of his generation and generally thought to have been the greatest player of his day. His marvellous record of 79, made in 1858, was not equalled until young Tom made a 77 in 1869, ten years later. I cannot but believe young Tom's meteoric career from 1867 to 1872 rather dimmed Allan's escutcheon. It is said that Allan was never beaten. That may be so, but one recalls the fact that old Tom left St. Andrews in 1852 to go to Prestwick, and consequently Allan had the links to himself. Old Tom was known to remark once: "I could cope wi' Allan mysel' but never wi' Tommy." It is recalled Allan repeatedly refused Willie Park's challenges.

Allan did not approve of the gutta ball. He had practically the exclusive making of feather balls in St. Andrews, turning out 2,456 in one year, and, Scotchlike, he wanted the "bawbies" that he made on the balls. He got Tom to promise never to play with a gutta, and Tom himself has described in the English weekly, *Golf Illustrated*, how he inadvertently broke his pledge:

"One day, and it is one that will always be clearly stamped upon my memory, I had been out playing golf with a Mr. Campbell of Saddell, and I had the misfortune to lose all my supply of balls, which were, you can well understand, very much easier lost in those days, as the fairway of the course was ever so much narrower then than it is now, and with thick, bushy whins close in at the side. But to return to my story. I had, as I said, run short of balls, and Mr. Campbell kindly gave me a gutta one to try. I took to it at once, and, as we were playing in, it so happened that we met Allan Robertson coming out, and someone told him that I was playing a very good game with one of the new gutta balls, and I could see fine, from the expression of his face, that he did not like it at all, and, when we met afterwards in his shop, we had some high words about the matter, and there and then we parted company, I leaving his employment."

Besides old Tom at St. Andrews there were his two sons, young Tom and Jimmy (J. O. F.). Young Tom was the Nestor of professional golfers. He was without a peer among them all. His championship record was unique. The championship belt which was played for at Prestwick, first in 1861, and which was to become the property of the player who won it three times in succession, was won four times by old Tom, but not consecutively, and three times by Willie Park, but not consecutively. Young Tom won it in 1868, 1869, and 1870; consequently, the championship belt became his property. His three scores were 154, 157, and 149, an average well under 80 for eighteen holes, a miraculous performance when one considers the condition of the links in those days. In 1871 there was no championship held, but in 1872 he again won it. I think these performances place him in the Hall of Fame as an unexcelled golfer despite his brief career.

ALLAN ROBERTSON FROM THE GOLFERS ANNUAL FOR 1869-1870.
COMPILED BY CHARLES MACARTHUR AYR.

MR. HENRY CALLENDER, CAPTAIN GENERAL OF THE
ROYAL BLACKHEATH GOLF CLUB, 1807.
Painted by Lemuel Francis Abbott, R. A.

There was David Strath, Tom's most redoubtable competitor. In many ways David Strath was a more sound golfer. He had the old St. Andrews full swing; young Tom had a dashing style and a comparatively short swing, but he possessed an unconquerable spirit, and, when it came to a tight place, he always mastered the situation. Young Tom invariably wore a Scotch bonnet, and after making a stroke he had a way of shaking his head. It was even betting you could put a peg in the ground and his Balmoral bonnet would fall on the peg.

Naturally I always followed the matches of Strath and young Tom intently. Besides these professionals, there were also at St. Andrews in my time, Jimmy Anderson, who later won the open championship three times; Tom Kidd, who won it once in 1873; Andrew Kirkaldy, who tied with Willie Park, Jr., in 1889, and Bob Martin, a club-maker in old Tom's shop, who won it in 1876. One can see by all this what a remarkable galaxy of golfers there was at St. Andrews in the early '70s. I doubt if in any one country they have ever been matched in brilliance of play, devotion to the principles of the game, and personal integrity.

Nearly all of these professionals were willing to caddy for gentlemen in their great matches, and some of them, like Tom Kidd and James Fenton, "The Skipper," always caddied. The caddy was an institution in early golfing days and an excellent mentor. Rarely did one have to choose one's own club. So well versed were the caddies in the game and so acquainted with your own weaknesses, that they would hand you the club you ought to play with, and should you refuse it and take one of your own choice, you would usually make a bad shot. The refusal to take the club your caddy chose seemed to have a psychological influence over you.

I can recall when I went to North Berwick in 1906 to study the character of the best holes there, a friend of H. J. Whigham's with whom I was going down, disappointed me owing to a family bereavement. I was all alone, with out any one to play with, so I chose their oldest and best caddy. Of course, I asked him numerous questions about the fairway and different holes—Point Garry, Perfection, and particularly the Redan. Arriving at the tee of the Redan, the fifteenth hole, I saw my old caddy stoop down and pick up a bunch of dry grass, which he threw in the air, watching the way the wind blew it. I asked him what that was for. "Did ye not see the way the grass blew?" I said "Yes." He said: "Tak' your cleek." The way the wind blew determined which club he would hand you; possibly the driver, possibly the spoon, possibly a light iron, possibly a cleek. This demonstrates the homely golfing intelligence of the old caddies.

There is a story of a famous caddy at St. Andrews named Lang Willie. He was much taken out as an instructor of beginners, and, when one met him and asked him how his pupil was getting on, he had always the same stereotyped answer, "Jist surprisin'," which might mean very well or very ill. On one occasion he was teaching one of the professors of the University the noble game. The professor was not a promising pupil. As he hammered away, sometimes "missing the globe," sometimes topping the ball, or cutting up large divots of turf, Willie fairly got out of patience and said to him: "Ye see, Professor, as long as ye are learning thae lads at the college Latin and Greek it is easy work, but when ye come to play golf ye maun hae a heid!"

When I went to St. Andrews nearly all of the players wore red coats. Against the green grass they made a very picturesque scene. For more than a century the red coat was the distinctive insignia of the pastime, and as late as 1892 the conservators of Wimbledon, in an effort to prevent the public from being taken unawares by flying golf balls, issued an order that golfers on Wimbledon Common should wear "an outer garment of red." Gradually, however, the red coat disappeared, due to the great increase in the number of players who were satisfied to play in old coats taken apparently from their discarded wardrobes. The picturesque red coat in time was seen no more, and great is the pity.

When we first played golf in America in the early '90s the players wore the traditional red coats, particularly at the Chicago Golf Club. However, one can understand why not only red coats but all coats have been generally discarded in America. In summer weather they are too hot, while on colder days a sweater is apt to be preferred because it gives more freedom to the arms. I remember a story I heard in St. Andrews of how a nattily dressed English golfer approached an old Highlander and asked him why it was all the St. Andrews players did not wear red coats. The Highlander, drawing himself up, replied: "We in the Highlands have always been taught to shoot at a red coat."

With the spring of 1874 I first won recognition as a real golfer. In the early part of that year I played around St. Andrews in from 90 to 100, while just before leaving in September I was frequently breaking 90, which was the score usually winning the various Royal and Ancient medals. A correspondent of the London *Field* began to record my matches on March 28, 1874, and continued to do so until I was obliged to say goodbye to the dearest playground I have ever known. Often I have been asked if I played a better game at the time I won the first championship in this country than I did when I left Scotland. Looking over the items in the *Field*, you can get a pretty good line on my game during my last summer at St. Andrews. You will see by this that I was playing regularly with the best golfers of the day, young Tom Morris, David Strath, Tom Kidd, et al. With pardonable pride I hereby append the record from the London *Field*, with a few comments of my own:

"March 28, 1874. Mr. C. B. Macdonald and Mr. Burgess, playing one ball against James Beveridge, lost by six and four to play. The bye was halved. A return match likewise resulted in favor of Beveridge by six and five to play. He took the round with a low score of 83—regular professional play. Mr. Macdonald and young Tom Morris beat Tom Kidd and J. Beveridge by one. Mr. Burgess and Mr. M'Lauchlan lost a round to Mr. Macdonald and Mr. Alfred by two and one to play. The same day Mr. Edward and J. O. F. Morris defeated Mr. Burgess and Mr. Macdonald by one hole.

"April 11, 1874. A capital match was played between Mr. C. Macdonald (a young player of much promise) and Tom Morris, Jr., against Tom Kidd and James Beveridge; one round was played which the former couple won by two; their score was 86.

"May 9, 1874. An interesting match came off between Messrs. Macdonald, Rutherford, and Beveridge against Tom Morris, Jr., the latter playing against the best ball of the other three. Tom won by two and one to play.

"May 16, 1874. On the afternoon of the same day a rather peculiar match was played. The two men above mentioned (Young Tom and David Strath) encountered Messrs. Burgess, Beveridge, Macdonald, Rutherford and J. O. F. Morris. Each played one ball, Tom and Strath playing the best of theirs against the better score for each hole of the other five. After an exciting contest Tom and Strath won the match by four and three to play and also the bye by one hole. The former played a remarkably fine game, going the round in 81 strokes, 44 out and 37 in; taking the best of his and Strath's score the total amounted to 76. In the evening the

GRAND GOLF TOURNAMENT BY PROFESSIONAL PLAYERS ON LEITH LINKS, MAY 17, 1867. From left to right the players are: James Dunn, George Morris, Alexander Greig, A. Strath, David Park, W. Dunn, Tom Morris, Tom Morris, Jr., Bob Kirk, W. Dow James Anderson.

vanquished five on the same terms played Tom himself and succeeded in defeating him by two at the 'burn.' "

It was hard to convince us boys at college that we could not get the better of these two great players. But when we found that all our allowances were gone and our resources mortgaged for some time to come, we woke up. Incidentally, the Royal and Ancient forbade us to play in such numbers, even though it was in the evening, when the links was more or less deserted.

"June 13, 1874. Tom Morris, Sen. played against the best ball of Messrs. Macdonald and Rutherford and lost by one. A return match was played on Monday night, the couple again proving successful by two at the 'burn,' the last hole was halved. The scores were: Tom 88, Rutherford 88, Macdonald 91.

"July 4, 1874. On Wednesday, last week, Messrs. Linskill and Tom Morris, Jr. played Messrs. Macdonald and Burgess two rounds. At the end of the first, the latter were three up, and they got the match in the second by one. On Saturday Mr. Macdonald had a tussle with Mr. Linskill and Tom, Jr. In the first round the couple got a third and lost by three, but in the afternoon, with a half, they won by one.

"July 18, 1874. Mr. W. T. Linskill and Tom Morris, Jr., against Mr. C. B. Macdonald and Mr. E. R. Burgess played two rounds, winning the first by two and halving the second.

"August 1, 1874. Mr. Macdonald and Mr. R. Balfour (Glasgow) playing the best of their balls against J. O. F. Morris were worsted by two and one to play. The following day, playing the same match, the couple won by three holes. The match was gained by Mr. Macdonald holeing the last hole with his 'tee' shot from the 'burn,' a feat unprecedented in the annals of the links."

Owing to the excessive drought prevailing in July burning up the turf and threatening to make a bunker of the eighteenth green, the last hole had been placed close to the "Old Brig" over the burn. I believe the hole was about 170 to 180 yards in length. There was a foursome ahead of us, with Major Boothby and David Lamb among the players, and they witnessed the ball go into the hole. Of course I took pleasure in buying the traditional bottle of Scotch whiskey for the caddies, which they evidently enjoyed. I remember the drive perfectly, for I had teed my ball a little ahead of the whitewashed marks, which always indicated the teeing grounds in those days, and Jamie Morris, having made a very good shot, called my ball back, and I was obliged to re-tee it, with the happy result I have recorded. Fifty-two years elapsed before I made another hole in one. This was last year, in 1926, when I holed out my tee shot at the sixth hole at the National, 130 yards.

"August 8, 1874. Mr. C. B. Macdonald and J. Beveridge playing the best of their balls, halved a match with J. O. F. Morris; a short match of eight holes was played to decide, when the couple won by four and three to play.

"August 22, 1874. Mr. Macdonald, getting five strokes, played J. O. F. Morris a round, and won by one.

These are my last recorded matches at St. Andrews.

One of the most interesting golfing stunts of that last year was when Davie Strath backed himself to go round in 120, starting at midnight and playing by the light of the May moon. Wagers were made and he won them by going round in 113. The following night, wagering he could beat 113, he made the round in 108 strokes. Of course, the flag could not be seen from a distance, but the forecaddies went ahead to mark the hole and find the ball. It was always located by the thud on the turf. If I recall correctly, not a ball was lost. This will convey to my readers what wonderful nights we had to play golf.

One of my own stunts of that year was to drive a ball off my watch, wagering that it would go 100 yards or more and not damage the watch. I did this very successfully for some time, but one day I topped the ball and my small hunting case silver watch was consigned to oblivion.

Recalling the great part golf has played in the happiness of my life, I feel impelled here to urge any man engaged in the struggle for human existence to encourage devotion to an outdoor sport. Remember how closely interwoven with the highest civilization the world has ever known were the Olympian and Pythian games in Greece. Nothing has a greater influence in moulding the character than public contests. An outdoor sport will mean everything in the healthy development of all that is interesting in life. Golf is the best of outdoor games, I believe, but any is better than none. I don't know how I would ever have been able to look into the past with any degree of pleasure or enjoy the present with any degree of contentment if it had not been for the extraordinary influence the game of golf has had upon my welfare.

In September I bade farewell to St. Andrews to return to America, shedding more tears at leaving the dear old city than I had breathed sighs on leaving my home in Chicago.

Chapter III

Early Implements, Clubs, Balls: Also Links

"Hail, gutta percha priceless gum!"—Graham, 1848

Golf was a more difficult game in 1872 than the game of to-day. The difference for even the best of players was roughly ten strokes. The reason for this did not lie in the players. No golfer of to-day, except it be Bobby Jones, is the equal of young Tom Morris; yet young Tom usually averaged over 80 at St. Andrews. Golf is an easier game to-day partly because the courses are well kept up as against no upkeep whatever; the rubber-cored ball has done the rest, the improvement in clubs being of small importance.

St. Andrews, with its unrolled greens, its rabbit scrapes, and its tough whins and its narrow fairways, was difficult enough when I first played. But imagine what it was like before 1857, when every fairway was played both forward and backward to provide the eighteen holes. At that time St. Andrews had only ten putting greens and on each green only one hole. The players played to the same holes and over the same fairways on the homeward journey that they had played on the outward journey. This made their eighteen holes of golf. The party first on the green had the right to putt out before a match from the opposite direction could play. Furthermore, there was no special teeing-ground; it was merely ruled that the players should tee up not less than four nor more than eight club-lengths from the hole. You can imagine the confusion and inconvenience that this arrangement would occasion on a crowded day. There must have been a mutual "giving and forgiving" for golf to exist at all. With the advent of the gutta ball in 1850, the number of golfers increased

THE CLUB HOUSE AND THE HOME GREEN AT ST. ANDREWS.

enormously, and the situation became intolerable. From what I can gather, it was about 1857 that two holes as widely separated as the space permitted, were cut in each putting green. The course has been much widened since then, but this early method of play in and out to the same holes accounts for the putting greens and fairways lying parallel to-day at St. Andrews.

The golf courses in the United Kingdom in the seventies were very different in the main from the courses we are familiar with throughout most of the United States. Many of them—the best in Scotland—were built on true links land among the dunes. St. Andrews lies, of course, on this character of ground, and it is probable that the links were at one time under water. In a pamphlet issued in 1863, "Historical Gossip About Golf and Golfers," by "A Golfer," the writer says: "Links and golf, it may be said, go hand in hand; where there is no links there can be no golf." I wonder what he would say if he could see the Lido course which was built on a marsh with a lake some four to six feet deep covering ten to fifteen acres. The marsh and the lake were filled up according to a topographical map with valleys and hills, bunkers and water-hazards, all costing some $750,000. The Yale course was built through woods and a very rocky country at a cost of $440,000. The Mid-Ocean course in Bermuda, built over coral rock and through semi-tropical valleys, cost some $300,000. Certainly the writer of 1863 would marvel and cry: "Crazy! Crazy!" And from his point of view I am inclined to think he would be right.

The golf courses throughout the United Kingdom before my arrival in St. Andrews had various numbers of holes—some five, some seven, some nine, some twelve. A few had eighteen. In the rules of 1857 St. Andrews had decreed this number as a round of golf in match-play. This lead was followed by all the important golf clubs, and by 1872 nearly all had adopted the same rule. The two leading golf clubs of England, Westward Ho! and Wimbledon, had courses of eighteen holes by 1872. On courses which consisted of six holes, it was decreed that they play three rounds, and on those courses which had nine holes, two rounds of the links.

Old Tom laid out eighteen holes at Westward Ho! in 1869 but altered them in 1873. It is interesting to note the number of crossings from tee to hole. At St. Andrews there are only two holes that cross, the seventh and the eleventh. In view of the lamentations one hears at the nineteenth hole regarding the danger of being killed by a golf ball where two fairways cross, these timid golfers should have played at Westward Ho! with its twelve crossings. To this day, St. Andrews men like to tell the story that in all the years golf has been played there nothing has been killed except a "cuddy." Jameson's Scottish Dictionary gives the definition: Cuddy—An ass; most probably a cant term.

> *"Then hey the ass, the dainty ass,*
> *That cocks aboon them a'—*
> *Any mony ane will get a bite,*
> *Or cuddy, gangs awa."*
> —Jacobite Relics, i, 83.

> *"His courage fail'd him a' at length,*
> *His very heart maist left its hole!*
> *But what think ye was at the last,*
> *Just simply cuddy and her foal!"*
> —Duff's "Poems," p. 96.

Clubs have changed somewhat in my fifty-five years of golf, but not so much as courses and balls. One may truthfully say that the age of wood has departed, and we are living in the iron age.

When I left St. Andrews my clubs were the driver, the grass club, the long spoon, the middle spoon, the short spoon or baffy, the wooden niblick, the cleek, the midiron, the lofter, the iron niblick, and the wooden putter—seven wooden clubs to four of iron. The grass club had a thin face, well-spooned back; it was used in the soft grass of the hollows, on the downward slope of a hillock, or when there was a dangerous hazard to play immediately in front of you. The wooden niblick had a short, stocky head with a concave face, and it was used for cuppy lies and divot marks. Later the wooden niblick was soled with brass where it was played on courses that had "break clubs." Thus originated the brassy.

To-day these wooden clubs are practically discarded. I now play with a cross between a driver and a brassy, which, like all the best play-clubs nowadays, is made with a slight bulge. I have a driving iron, a light iron, a mashie, a niblick, and a putter—six clubs, only one of them wooden. If you carry more clubs, you are always in doubt which to take, and while you are musing and trying to determine the right club, you have begun to lose your confidence as well as your concentration. Scylla and Charybdis stare you out of countenance. I am very much in favor of using only one driving club. Johnny Ball always used a brassy for his play-club, and I think J. E. Laidlay did the same. I have often heard it said—and I believe it—that it is wise to be wedded to one club, one that you have absolute confidence in. I believe this is particularly true of the play-club and the putter.

As for the clubs of 1872 compared with those of 1927, I may say that there is a distinction without a difference—at least the difference is relatively so slight as to distance gained, that it would be hard to prove that the later clubs accomplish much more than the older clubs. The shape of the wooden club is somewhat different. The head in 1872 was more swanlike, with a whippy shaft, while the present modified bulger is more bulldog, with a stiff shaft.

I have carefully preserved the clubs with which I played at St. Andrews in 1874. They certainly are much better looking clubs than those made to-day. The head is beautifully curved. The face is longer and much thinner. The weight is about the same, certainly not less. The shafts are wonderfully preserved and far more whippy. The grips are distinctly larger. Using the long St. Andrews swing, I do not believe any one could hold this whippy old club in his hands with the thin grip in vogue to-day. Many golfers contend that the overlapping grip which was used by Johnny Laidlay long before it was made fashionable by Vardon necessitates a much thinner wrapping than the older method. One must remember this difference in the whippiness of the old clubs when considering the various playing tests made between the gutta and the rubber-cored ball. The old club was suited to the guttie, the new club to the rubber-cored ball.

The parklike fairways of to-day have eliminated the long, middle, and short or baffy spoon. Irons have taken their places. In 1872 we had a cleek, a heavy iron, a light or midiron, a lofter, and a niblick. To-day, without the slightest improving effect on one's game, except possibly psychology, we have a myriad of irons with such different names and different parentage that one might call them "mongrel" clubs. It is not to any of these changes in our clubs that we must credit the lower scores of to-day, but rather to improved upkeep of courses, and more particularly to the longer-driving ball.

There have been two great changes in the ball; first, the introduction of the gutta-percha ball, replacing the feather-stuffed ball about 1850; and second, the Haskell or rubber-cored ball of half a century later. Each change improved the driving-power of the clubs, increased the number of players enormously, and affected many things from courses to rules.

The old feather balls had been played with from time immemorial. They were constructed with great trouble to the maker and great expense to the player. They cost two shillings and sixpence, while the guttas sold for one shilling, and the best rubber-cored balls in England now sell for two and six. The manufacture of the feather ball constituted a distinct trade in golfing communities. The leather was cut in three pieces, softened with alum and water, and sewn together with waxed thread. Through a small hole left in the side the maker stuffed an incredible quantity of soft-boiled feathers by means of a kind of awl. The hole was then sewn up, the case hammered round and painted, and the ball was ready for use. These balls were extraordinarily hard, but seldom round. They were easily cut, and in wet weather they became sodden and likely to burst and moult their feathers.

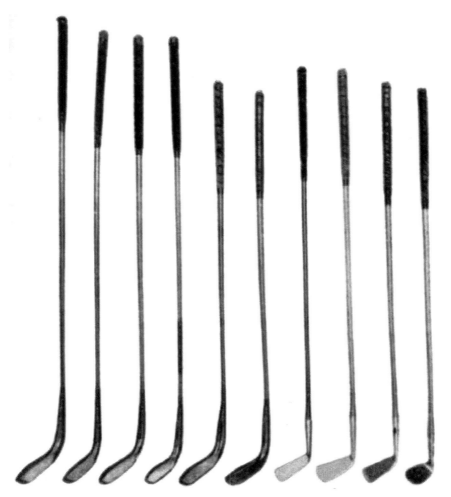

CLUBS USED BY CHARLES B. MACDONALD AND MADE
BY TOM MORRIS IN 1873 AND 1874.
The putter is a duplicate of that used by Young Tom.

In 1848 and 1849 the gutta-percha ball was introduced. Some historians state that Sir Thomas Moncrieffe brought the gutta-percha from London in 1848 and had a ball-maker hammer out a sphere from some of it. Others state that John Campbell of Saddell from the Mull of Kintyre (where my forebears came from) first introduced the gutta ball at St. Andrews. James Balfour writes that he remembers commencing to play with them perfectly. On a very wet day his brother-in-law, Admiral Maitland Dougall, played a double match at Blackheath with the late Sir Ralph Anstruther and Will Adam of Blair-Adam, and another friend, using the gutta balls. He quotes Sir Ralph as saying after dinner: "A most curious thing? Here is a golf ball of gutta-percha. Maitland and I have played with it all day in the rain, and it flies better at the end of the day than it did at the beginning."

Neither the opposition of professional feather-ball makers like Allan Robertson nor certain early defects in the gutta-percha balls could stand in the way of their success. The first balls, being perfectly smooth, had a trick of ducking after they had flown some distance. Presently it was discovered that after the balls had been cut by the irons they flew much better. It then occurred to an ingenious saddle-maker to hammer them all around with the sharp end of a dull chisel. The experiment was successful, and from then on the use of the gutta became universal. The feather ball is only to be found in museums.

During my time at St. Andrews all the gutties were marked with a dull chisel. Later they were put in moulds with various indentations. The Thornton and the Silvertown were the best known in early days. They were marked with little squares. For the next twenty years a wide variety of markings appeared—I have a list of no less than 166 makes—and you bought the ball which suited your fancy. The Eclipse became very popular in 1886 and the Agrippa in 1890.

In 1898 Coburn Haskell of Cleveland conceived the idea of putting a rubber-wound core inside a gutta cover. He got the idea from the old lively baseball with its rubber core string winding and leather jacket. His difficulty was to get a machine that would wind the rubber evenly in the centre and tautly, and to cover the ball with the gutta-percha. Haskell went to a great friend of his, Bertram Work, of the Goodrich Company, and they collaborated. Finally the ball was put on the market about 1899 or 1900. Then history repeated itself. While the early balls were stamped with a slight Silvertown marking, the paint on the cover was so heavy that it closed up the indentations, and the ball ducked just as the original gutta had done.

Haskell was a friend of mine, and while I was visiting his aunt, Mrs. Jay Morse of Thomasville, Fla., he was visiting his father-in-law, Melville Hanna. Coburn showed me the ball and asked me if I would take an interest in it, and help put it on the market. I told him I would be happy to do anything in the world that I could to help him get the ball on the market if it proved the success in actual use that it promised to be. Declining an interest, I told him I made it a principle never to receive any profit, either directly or indirectly, from my association with the game of golf. She was a mistress whom I adored, and I could do nothing that would taint the relationship with commercialism.

My old friend, Eliphalet W. Cramer, has just given me a most entertaining account of the successful introduction of the Haskell ball at the Chicago Golf Club. Here is his letter:

"My Dear Charles:

"The credit of the remade Haskell ball is primarily due to you who gave me the hint as to what was the matter with the original Haskell ball. It seems in the old days, so you told me, when they played with the gutta ball that the experience was, after they had been nicked a bit, the flight was longer. My experience with the Haskell was that it would go a certain distance and then duck, so I took one of these into the shop and had David Foulis put it in an Agrippa mould. It, of course, came out black, and just as I was about to try the effect James Foulis came across with a driver in his hand. I asked him to try this ball and see if he could hit it. He took his full swing, and then an explosion of holy oaths ending up with 'What is it?' I then told him what we had done and asked him to keep it a secret for a time and make me a dozen of them. This he did and I found, of course, the length of my drive tremendously improved. The first one I worked it on was your own dear self, and I said to you one day: 'Charley, my game is improving and I will play you a game for a box of balls at the same odds that you are giving'—you had always been winning heretofore. The first ball I drove was beyond yours and I remember distinctly you saying, 'You have improved.' At the second hole the same thing happened and you went and looked at the ball. It seemed all right to you and I said nothing. When we finished the game, and I for the first time had won, I told you what we had done and I ordered a dozen balls made for you and I think also for Jim Whigham. You were both going to some tournament, perhaps it was Newport.

"At the time of my discovery I told the Foulis brothers to buy up all the Haskell balls they could get and remold them, which they did. Haskell finally got on to it and tried to stop them, but, of course, they were per-

fectly within their rights and nothing was done to prevent them. The Foulis brothers made quite a bit of money.

*"Yours sincerely,
Liph.
Chicago, July 18, 1927"*

The patent of the Haskell ball, while it was supported by the American courts, was by the English courts denied in a decision by Mr. Justice Buckley because it "lacked novelty." Being appealed, the House of Lords sustained the verdict of the lower courts in 1906. It is said that the cost of this litigation was more than £20,000.

In the amateur championship held at the Country Club at Atlantic City in 1901, I used the Haskell ball. I remember well Walter J. Travis the day before the championship, having been the recipient of two or three of the Haskell balls made in the Agrippa mould, went out on the putting green near the club house and practiced for some considerable time. He realized that the rubber-cored ball would go from fifteen to twenty yards farther than the gutta, but he was very dubious about the putting, and as putting was his metier, he did not want to fall down where he ordinarily excelled so greatly. He told me at the time that he wished to test the resilience of the ball on the putting green. I think he found there was little or no difference on the short putts, but on the long putts the new ball seemed to go farther than the gutta with less effort.

Some said about the Haskell ball exactly what was said about the gutta when it displaced the feather ball—that it marred the traditional, aristocratic mien of the game with all its deliberateness and caused a rush of new and unskilled players to the links, thereby overcrowding the courses. There is something to be said on both sides. Certainly the Haskell ball contributed mightily to the happiness of the greater number. Jim Whigham told me the other day that in his opinion there would never have been the present great spread of golf in America if it had not been for the discovery of the Haskell ball, just as he was confident England would not have taken up golf in the last half of the past century if it had not been for the gutta. In John L. Low's book, "Concerning Golf," he speaks of one important disadvantage of the Haskell:

"It was a man's job to drive a gutta-percha ball the requisite one hundred eighty yards; a lad may easily do it now. But did the loss only lie in the athletic side of the game, there would be some excuse for the players, who, having been dug out of their graves by the new balls, advocated their use as good for golf. But the worst feature of the new balls is the distance they travel from a mis-hit. Not only had the old ball to be hit hard, but it had to be hit accurately, or it would not go at all."

All golfers have frequently heard discussions of what was the relative distance of a drive with the old feather ball compared with the gutta ball, and also the comparative distance of the gutta and the Haskell. In 1813 it is recorded in the "Chronicles of Blackheath Golfers" that a Mr. Lang made a wager that he would drive a ball 500 feet, giving him the choice of ten strokes to accomplish it and the choice of ground. What were Mr. Lang's driving-powers one can only conjecture, but it is reasonable to suppose that if an amateur in 1813 would wager he could drive 166 yards under those conditions, it is not unlikely that the best drivers would be able under favorable conditions to drive 180 yards. Thus it is fair to assume that the feather ball was some twenty to thirty yards short of the gutta ball.

The same difference between the gutta and the Haskell was proven by professionals in England a few years ago at Sandy Lodge, when Vardon and Duncan played Braid and Taylor, one couple using the gutta and the other the Haskell in the morning and then changing about in the afternoon. The rubber-cored ball won, Braid averaging about twenty-five yards less with the gutta than with the Haskell.

Probably one of the most interesting competitions showing the comparison between the two balls took place in England in 1923 between two teams of amateurs called the "Hasbeens" and the "Neverwasers." Bernard Darwin took part in this match. Here is a letter from him:

"The match took place at Woking, Surrey, on October 13, 1923. First there were four-ball matches—Hasbeens, that is, those brought up on guttas, vs. Neverwasers, those brought up on the rubber-cored. Both sides played with guttas. Result, two matches won by each side and two halved. Anyway, the whole match was halved for the young 'uns, Wethered and Holderness, Storey and Hezlet, who were the best known, and

the old ones, Harris, Ted Blackwell, de Zoete, Torrance, Hoomans, self and various others.

"Then in the afternoon there was a scoring competition. Wethered won with 76, Harris 79, Hoomans and Holderness 80, Darwin 82, Tolley and Willie Murray, 84 and Hezlet 85. Wethered played easily the best of all. In the morning he would have had a 74, but had a disastrous hole and took 76. He drove with an astounding springy old club, which had a rubber face and most of us had our ordinary, modern heads which were all too hard for the very stoney balls we had.

"It was noticeable that those who could normally drive the rubber ball farthest showed equal superiority in driving the gutta. That was very clear. There was evidently no secret of gutta driving which the young ones did not possess. Such a notion is all stuff.

"Always yours,
Bernard Darwin."

You will note that Wethered took a 76. We must assume that if he had had the rubber-cored ball he would not have made less than a 72. What I want to call your attention to is that he drove with an "astounding springy old club." I have pointed out that all the clubs of 1874 were very springy and with steely shafts and thick grips. The stroke with the gutta was entirely different from the stroke with the rubber-cored ball. One was a sweep and the other is a hit. The gutta had to be swept from the tee with a long follow-through, whereas the rubber-cored ball wants to be hit with a stiff shaft and a bullet-headed club. This shows you how difficult it is to compare the two balls so far as long driving is concerned. I know that Ted Blackwell never got the percentage of greater length with the new ball that most players secured, and the same was true of Hugo Johnston, one of America's longest drivers. While I could get about eighteen yards farther, Johnston did not increase his driving more than ten yards.

To my mind one hears more nonsense about long driving than about any other feature in the game of golf. Fishermen are not in it. The discussion arrives nowhere and probably does more to lead young players astray than any other description of the game. I have known personally all the longest drivers in the world, notably Ted Blackwell, Roger Wethered, and Cyril Tolley on the other side, and Guilford, Jones, and others in America. My judgment is that not one of them at their best can drive a rubber-cored ball more than 280 yards on a day when *there is no wind* and *on a level piece of fairway when the coarse is reasonably moist* and *on links proper*, which implies a sandy subsoil. In making this statement I do not doubt that balls, both gutta and Haskell, have been driven over 300 yards under unusual circumstances. By that I mean on a dried-up clay fairway and with a following wind or downhill.

About 1906, finding I had a number of boxes of gutta balls left over, I invited eight or ten men to play with them at the Garden City Golf Club eighteen holes medal play. Fred Herreshoff made an 82 with the gutta, which was within two or three strokes of his usual round with the Haskell ball. I made an 86. Herreshoff won the Scratch Cup and Joe Knapp won the Handicap Cup. The same was true of most of the other men who played. This demonstrated to us that there was not such a tremendous difference between the two balls. One must realize that the gutta was very much easier to approach with and quite as easy if not easier to putt with. Assuming a player takes eighty strokes as his average round, one must realize that there are not more than twenty full wooden shots, including driver and brassy; the other sixty shots can best be played with balls of less resilience.

I remember some years ago a friend of mine telling me about extraordinary driving that he had witnessed. He seemed astonished that he did not impress me at all and wished to know why I was contemptuous. I told him that, under circumstances which I would name, I would agree to take a putter and drive a mile. A wager having been made, he asked what the circumstances were. I told him that Lake Michigan, which is sixty miles wide at Chicago, was sometimes frozen over and that with no snow on the ice, and with a strong west wind I would putt a ball off a pier on the lake front and that the wind would certainly blow it a mile and I was not sure about the sixty. He paid the wager without asking me to prove it, and it probably resulted in a bottle of wine, as in the primitive days when all golfing bets were paid in that happy fashion.

Samuel L. Parrish, former president and first secretary of the Shinnecock Hills Golf Club, tells the following story of a similar wager:

"We were at the north end of Lake Agawam, Southampton, N. Y., looking south toward the ocean. There was a strong north wind blowing

down the lake at the time, and, as I was able to steady myself on a patch of snow, the drive was a fair success, so that the ball went sailing down the lake until it struck the ice, and then kept on with but little diminution in its velocity. Had the ice and wind held out the ball would doubtless still be going, but it finally struck a snow bank on the shore of the lake and stopped. Morton then solemnly paced off the drive and reported its length to have been four hundred eighty-nine and a half yards, being very particular about the extra half yard. He then posted up in the club house a statement to the effect that I, 'under favorable conditions' (no particulars being given) had made a drive of four hundred eighty-nine and a half yards. The result was that for a short time, until the facts became known, I enjoyed a tremendous reputation as a driver, my fame having penetrated to Boston, and I was the recipient of many congratulations."

Ted Blackwell, in an article of his, "Great Golfers in the Making," states that the longest drive he ever made was from the seventeenth tee at St. Andrews. He drove almost to the first hole. Marking the spot, he and his father measured the distance the next morning, and it was 366 yards. He also tells the story of having driven from the eighteenth tee and hit the steps going up to the club house in St. Andrews, which must be a distance of over 350 yards. Such drives as those must have been made when the course was baked and half a gale blowing. The fifth hole at St. Andrews is 520 yards and the thirteenth, paralleling it, about 500. It is well known that Ted Blackwell did drive the fifth going out and the thirteenth coming in, each in two strokes in the same round. That is certainly marvellous driving with a gutta ball, because the wind could not have been with him both ways. It is stated the wind was slightly against him coming in.

The following letter, published in the British weekly, *Golf*, May 20, 1892, records a fairly accurate test of the gutta ball:

"It may possibly be of some interest to your readers to know the approximate length of the tee-shots driven this afternoon by Mr. John Ball and by Douglas Rolland in the Amateur v. Professional foursome match at Sandwich. I say 'approximate length' with some diffidence, though no little trouble was taken to secure as much accuracy as was possible. I append the distances in paces:

HOLE	MR. BALL	ROLLAND
Second	242	227
Fourth	205	216
Eighth	180	209
Tenth	199	234
Fourteenth	193	216
Sixteenth	<u>217</u>	<u>175</u>
Total	1236	1277
Average	206	213

"On the preceding evening Rolland, playing a single with Hugh Kirkaldy, drove two hundred seventy-two paces from the eighteenth tee and was on the thirteenth green (four hundred sixty-five yards, with a bunker fifteen yards short of the hole) in 2. There was not a breath of wind at the time.

"I am, Sir, etc.,
Oxon.
St. George's Golf Club, 14th May."

Now to come again to the Haskell ball, in the driving competition at the open championship meeting at Troon in 1923 in which all the best amateur and professional drivers entered, the longest drive was 278 yards 8 inches, made by Roger Wethered. The drives registered were from 247 yards to 278. In 1919 James Braid, George Duncan, Sandy Herd, and W. Watt made a test of driving at Woodcote Park, Epsom, playing five fairways with a variety of wind and slope. For morning and afternoon combined the averages were: Braid, 235 ½; Duncan, 229 ¼; Herd, 227 ¼; Watt, 220 ¾.

Coming to myself, I won the amateur driving competition, all carry, no wind, in 1898. Playing with a gutta ball, I carried 190 yards 6 inches. I have taken the figures from the cup given me by the Onwentsia Club, which is now among the trophies at the National Golf Links of America. To-day I am very much pleased when I carry 200 yards with the rubber-cored ball, but I don't consider that I can drive within thirty yards of what I could thirty years ago.

I pay no attention to records of long driving unless the conditions are absolutely known. A great friend of mine by the name of Fred Young belonged to the Ardsley Golf Club, on which there was a hole about 310 yards long, all down-hill. He told me that with another friend he went out well wrapped up one cold November day to get a little fresh air. His friend teed his ball on a snow-tee at this hole, took a mighty swipe at it; missing the globe, the vacuum created by the swish of the clubhead, plus the wind behind, caused the ball to fall off the tee and sent it down-hill over the icy ground. Finally, it lay dead at the hole. Young was tremendously offended at my incredulity, but I can easily believe it may have been true.

My general conclusion is that under normal conditions a 280-yard drive with the present ball is about a record and some thirty-five or forty yards greater than the average of the longest hitters.

Chapter IV

The Dark Ages, 1875-1892

Adieu to St. Andrews
St. Andrews! they say that thy glories are gone,
That thy streets are deserted, thy castles o'er-thrown;
If thy glories be gone, they are only, methinks,
As it were, by enchantment, transferr'd to thy Links.
Though thy streets be not, as of yore, full of prelates,
Of abbots and monks, and of hot-headed zealots,
Let none judge us rashly, or blame us as scoffers,
When we say that instead there are Links full of Golfers,
With more of good heart and good feeling among them
Than abbots, the monks, and the zealots who sung them—
If golfers and caddies be not better neighbours
Than abbots and soldiers, with crosses and sabres,
Let such fancies remain with the fool who so thinks,
While we toast old St. Andrews, its Golfers, and Links.
—Carnegie

If the contrast between Chicago and St. Andrews in 1872 was great in its exaltation, the contrast between St. Andrews and Chicago was greater still when I returned to my home. In Chicago from 1874 to 1879 it was a question of "root, hog, or die." The great fire of 1871 had devastated the city, and close upon that had come the greatest financial reverse in the history of the United States, the panic of 1873. So it was work from seven in the morning until seven at night. I believe if anybody had been seen playing an out-door game he would have been thought half-witted.

Certainly, bankers would call a loan—if one was fortunate enough to get so rare an accommodation—of any one who attended to anything outside of business. So it surely was the Dark Ages for me.

To add further to the desolation I felt after returning to Chicago, on Christmas Day, 1875, young Tom Morris passed away, in his twenty-fifth year. The following is an extract from Doctor Boyd's "Twenty-five Years of St. Andrews":

"There was a pathetic event here at the beginning of September in this year (1875). The grand old Tom Morris (always so called, in respect and affection, great golfer and best of men) had a son, called for distinction's sake, Tommy Morris, who was a greater golfer than himself. At an early age Tommy won the dignity of Champion of the World and bore it well and meekly. On Thursday, September 2, father and son went together to North Berwick to play a match on the Links there. Tommy left his wife perfectly well. She was a remarkably handsome and healthy young woman; most lovable in every way. Her brother was a great manager and speaker in the Trades Union world. But on Saturday afternoon that fine girl (she was no more) had her first child and at once ran down and died. A telegram was sent to Tom, who told his son they must leave at once; afore yacht was put at their disposal, and without the weary railway journey by Edinburgh, they were brought across the Firth of Forth. Tom did not tell his son that all was over till they were walking up from the harbour. I was in the house when they arrived. What can one say in such an hour? I never forget the poor young man's stony look; stricken was the word; and how, all of a sudden he started up and cried, 'It's not true!' I have seen many sorrowful things; but not many like that Saturday night. Poor Tommy went about for a little while, but his heart was broken. On the morning of Christmas day they found him dead in his bed: and so Tommy and his poor young wife were not long divided."

While I am writing the above, July 15, 1927, a cablegram is shown me from St. Andrews that Bobby Jones has won the open championship with a record score of 285 at St. Andrews. I have always thought that young Tom Morris was the greatest golfer that ever lived; to-day I believe that Bobby Jones is equally wonderful. He is, as it were, the reincarnation of young Tom. I have known both more or less intimately and I am familiar

TOM MORRIS, JR.
Died Christmas, 1875, in his twenty-fifth year.

with the conditions under which each played, conditions to-day and those in the early seventies; young Tom on an unkept, rough course with the gutta ball, Bobby on a smooth, parklike, perfectly kept course with the rubber-cored ball. To my mind, these two are the greatest golfers in history, both as to execution, clean sportsmanship, courtesy, equable temperament, and most attractive personality.

During the Dark Ages I made one fruitless attempt to play golf in America. My friend and fellow student in St. Andrews, Edward R. Burgess, visited me in Chicago in August, 1875. We would take my clubs and balls which I brought from St. Andrews and repair to the vacant land where Camp Douglass was during the Civil War. We cut out three or four holes, putting in them some of the empty cans which the soldiers had left. To these holes we enjoyed driving and approaching, recalling our college days. We were not long left undisturbed. The hoodlums in the vicinity tormented us to death. Evidently they thought we were demented. Burgess soon going home, my golf clubs were stowed away until such time as I could go abroad.

Happily, from that time on till 1892 there were a few oases in this desert. These were the occasions when I was called to Europe on business, which, fortunately for me, were quite frequent.

When I was abroad in 1878 I played golf at the Royal Liverpool Golf Club at Hoylake, my friend, George H. Warren, introducing me. I probably did not have more than three or four afternoons to play at that time. Then again I spent Saturday and Sunday with my friend, W. T. Linskill, at Cambridge. He had established golf there in 1875 under the greatest handicaps. He has lately described to me his pioneering work in the following letter:

"I had an awful job as a golf missionary down there. They laughed at the idea. I taught a few chaps on Col Fen, and Sheeps Green, and then I discovered Coldham Common. There was a rifle range there and they did coursing and pigeon shooting there—all dead up against me, and an unknown and idiotic Scotch game. I had to fight the commoners and explain the game to the unsympathetic town council. They all looked on it as a mad fad. At last I got it started with a few chaps. I cut the holes myself and the greens (?), marked the tees, mended the clubs, and made balls in an outhouse. Then I began to get converts slowly, my father gave the

Linskill cup and other medals followed. Then we got professionals and built a pavilion, and then I managed to start the Oxford and Cambridge match, and Horace at Oxford assisted. I played in the first three varsity matches. Then Cambridge prospered. We built a fine club house and had three resident professionals, drained the big common, laid greens and made it quite a good and very long inland course. Everything must, of course, have a beginning, and mine was a stiff, uphill game in a flat fen country among golf heathens. I was a gardener, a navvy, and a pro and teacher, to start with. In 1869, I learn, six Trinity College men used to dig holes on various fields around Cambridge, and at Royston Heath and play friendly games among themselves occasionally—that was all."

I played golf with Linskill at Coldham Common, which was then probably the poorest excuse for a golf course I have ever seen in my life. It certainly was a great proof of the attraction of the game when college students rose superior to the uninviting grounds. Bernard Darwin writes of it: "I will leave unsung as muddy ditches, its villainous caddies, its most unsavory odors. In the days of Mr. John Low the course was positively crowded, for Mr. Low, by sheer force of his own attractive personality, brought hundreds of his innocent friends to learn the game upon the worst course on which it has probably ever been played."

Again in 1879 I visited England, and then I spent some little time in Liverpool, making my headquarters at the Royal Hotel, Hoylake, kept by Johnny Ball's father. The father (known as John Ball, Jr., while his son was known as John Ball, Tertius) was also an excellent golf player. At this hotel the Royal Liverpool Golf Club maintained its headquarters. At that time, I played every evening after business.

Hoylake has reared more great golfers than any other English green—John Ball, Harold Hilton, A. H. MacFie, John Graham, Charles Hutchins, every one of whom has been amateur champion and two of whom have been open champions. It was in this year I joined the Royal Liverpool Golf Club, which had the same rule prevailing at St. Andrews, namely, that a member who resided away from the country any one year was exempt from dues. We have adopted this rule at the National.

In looking back over *The Field*, I find that at the spring meeting of the Royal Liverpool Golf Club I had a handicap of five and was twelfth in the list of sixty entries. In a handicap competition in 1884 *The Field*

ANDREW KIRKCALDY AND A FRIEND ON THE OLD
BRIDGE OVER SWILCAN BURN.

quotes my handicap at two, A. H. MacFie at plus one, John Ball, Tertius, at plus five.

I can remember perfectly well marvelling at MacFie's putting at Hoylake. MacFie had a house on the Mersey side of the links. I was told that he maintained on a small grass plot back of his house a well-kept-up putting green in which he planted egg cups. He would putt by the hour into these tiny cups. Naturally, when it came to putting into a 4½ inch hole, it looked to him as if he couldn't keep out of a bunker.

I had a few rounds of golf in England in 1880 and also in 1881. It was in 1881 I turned my back on the links for one day and was induced by friends to go with them on a four-in-hand to the "Derby." I was fully repaid, for it was a wonderful sight and I had the pleasure of seeing an American horse win; Pierre Lorillard's Iroquois coming in first, the odds against him were five to one.

There was one incident at this meeting that struck me forcibly. When mixing with the crowd I overheard comments from some hucksters gathered together who remarked, as the Prince of Wales drove by in his phaeton and six horses, "Them's the people we buy corn for," and similar unpatriotic remarks.

Scotland's Gift: Golf

Going to Europe in June, 1883, I spent nearly a year abroad, the better part of the time in London, where I had a house for four months. However, I spent some four or five weeks at the Royal Hotel, Hoylake, playing golf every evening after business. Though I went abroad in 1886 and also in 1888, I had little or no golf, possibly a desultory round here or there. I was never more than a few days in any one place, except London, and when there I played occasionally at Wimbledon with my friend, Alfred Lubbuck.

All this brings me to the end of the Dark Ages and the advent of golf in America. Before I close this chapter I should like, if possible, to describe to the reader my relationship to the game. I have given you the golfing mise-en-scene and the background of St. Andrews together and an attempt to express the spirit which prevailed among the Scotch golfers during my time and which I imbued. My friend, John L. Low, more than any man that I have ever known, has been the greatest advocate of preserving the traditional game in all its pristine excellence, and with his views I am thoroughly in accord. He expresses himself so delightfully that I cannot do better than steal some of his expressed convictions. In his book, "Concerning Golf," he has a quotation from Robert Louis Stevenson which sounds the note of Low's character:

"Those who play by rule will never be more than tolerable players; and you and I would play our game to the noblest and most divine advantage....For no definite precept can be more than illustration, though its truth were resplendent like the sun...and not twenty times or perhaps not twice in the ages shall we find that nice consent of circumstances to which alone it can apply."

Low writes in 1912 an article for the "Royal and Ancient Game of Golf":

"During the past five and twenty years, men have been looking at the rules of the game from two very distinct points of view. We may style the opposing forces as the Conservative Party and the Party of Equity. The doctrine of the Conservative Party is easily understood; it lies round one fundamental principle: it makes golf a game of two sides and two balls and demands that every ball shall be played from the place where it lies.

The Party of Equity holds that golf should be ruled by laws which mete out to each offense an absolutely just and properly proportioned punishment: it cannot bear that a man suffer unjustly or that the wicked appear to prosper while the slightly erring are discomfited. The Conservative Party holds that golf is a game of risks and hazards, a game in which a man distinguishes himself by his steady progress around the course, a progress which should not be needlessly interrupted. We Conservatists hold that a ball which cannot be played should make the rest of its journey holewards in the pocket of the player, some men cannot stand up to big risks or penalties; they are all for giving the golfer a second chance; they do not wish to make the game heroic; they would legislate for the benefit of the weak-kneed, and so humble the game."

I cannot help but feel that the changes in the rules which the English have forced upon the Royal and Ancient, and again some of the changes which America has advocated, have distinctly lowered the morale of the game. But St. Andrews has stood fast by one feature, namely, the stymie, against all the persistency of the English golfers and later the endeavor of the American golfing world. A strong fight to abolish the stymie was made in 1894, ably headed by Horace Hutchinson, who has had and still has a devoted following, a gentleman himself of the old school, twice amateur champion, and, I believe, the only Englishman other than royalty whom the Royal and Ancient honored by electing him captain. St. Andrews stood steadfast, and the stymie still prevails, although four-ball matches have now become so prevalent that stymies are rarely played in America. More's the pity. In the championships both in Great Britain and America stymies must be played.

Before closing this chapter I wish to draw attention to how a golfer was regarded when the game became popular in England. What Horace Hutchinson says about English golfers can be applied to the golfer in America when the game was first introduced:

"It is almost impossible for those who have grown up in the midst of golf-playing in England, such as the country is to-day, to realize what a strange and rare animal a golfer found himself at that time. If you announced yourself a golfer, people stared at you. What did it mean? Oh, yes! that Scotch game—like hockey, was it not, or like polo? Did you play

it on horseback? Travelling from Westward Ho! to Wimbledon and Hoylake, or vice versa, with your golf clubs you were eyed most curiously. In general people had never seen the weapons before, and asked you, with an apology for their inquisitiveness, what their use could be. Many a practical joke was played by the waggishly minded golfer on their ignorance, and they went home with wonderful tales to tell their wives and children. Or if people did know a little of the game, then their regards were no longer curious, but pitiful, as who would say, 'See the poor looney—is he not a sad sight?' It grew common to regard golf as a harmless form of imbecility, holding towards it much the same attitude that the general mind has towards a grown man with a butterfly net and a taste for entomology. Among golfers themselves there was a phrase current a good deal about the 'freemasonry existing among golfers,' meaning thereby that if you happened to be a devotee of this strange and new cult, and saw another golfer awaiting his train at a station and advertising himself as a co-religionist by having some clubs with him, you might, and naturally would, at once approach him with the words: 'I see you are a golfer, sir,' and forthwith you would be as blood brothers. Indeed it was quite rare to hear of a man who was a golfer and whom you did not personally know."

Just how ignorant of the game the people in America were in the Dark Ages you may judge from an article in the Philadelphia *Times*, of February 24, 1889, just one year after the "apple-tree gang" established golf in Yonkers:

"At the beginning of play each player places his ball at the edge of a hole which has been designated as the starting point. When the word has been given to start he bats his ball as accurately as possible towards the next hole, which may be either 100 or 500 yards distant. As soon as it is started in the air he runs forward in the direction which the ball has taken and his servant, who is called a 'caddy', runs after him with all the other nine tools in his arms....His (the player's) purpose is to put the ball in that next hole, spoon it out and drive it forward to the next further one before his opponent can accomplish the same end. The province of the 'caddy' is to follow his master as closely as possible, generally at a dead run, and be ready to hand him whatever implement of the game the mas-

ter calls for, as the play may demand...if one player has his ball in a hole and his opponent has his within an inch or two of it, he must wait before he plays until the first player has gotten his clear of it and thrown it towards the next hole. As a general custom the players make the entire circuit of the circle (of holes) and the one who gets his ball in the hole at which they began first wins the game. Nevertheless it is sometimes agreed that the game shall be won by him who makes the largest number of holes within a given number of minutes, say twenty or thirty."

The above demonstrates the virgin soil golf was destined to take root in; but, once planted, like the acorn it has grown into a mighty oak. One can scarcely believe how primitive were its first beginnings: a thirty-four acre lot at Yonkers, with trees; a seventy-acre cow pasture near Chicago; a lawn at Lake Forest; in Boston seven holes on undulating lawns and park, the hazards consisting of avenues, dumps of trees, bushes, beds of rhododendrons and azaleas, an aviary, green-houses, and an occasional drawing room window pane. When one tries to realize how the game of golf overcame ignorance of the game and such crude conditions in different parts of the States, hundreds of miles apart, one can readily understand how all the edicts of the Scottish Parliament and the Scotch Church had absolutely no effect upon the devotees of the game in Scotland.

Chapter V

Beginning of American Golf

The beginning of golf in America is largely apocryphal. Many unauthenticated stories are told of the game having been played many years back, particularly in Charleston, in Savannah, in Albany, in Florida, and elsewhere.

There is fairly good recorded evidence that Scotchmen played golf in Charleston and Savannah during the last decade of the eighteenth century, if not earlier. History relates that quite a colony of Scotchmen migrated to Charleston and Savannah in 1736. It is reasonable to suppose they carried their favorite home game with them. In colonial days sporting records were rarely kept, so one cannot determine the particular date they first played golf.

Many notices of the South Carolina Golf Club appeared in the Charleston press. The following is the first notice:

"The anniversary of the Golf Club will be held on Saturday next at the Club House on Harleston's Green where the members are requested to attend at one o'clock.

"William Milligan, Secretary"
—Charleston *City Gazette*, October 13, 1795.

About the same time, September 22, 1796, the *Georgia Gazette* printed an advertisement as follows:

"Saturday, the first of October, being the anniversary of the Savannah Golf Club, the members are requested to attend at the Merchants and Planters Coffee House for the purpose of electing officers for the next twelve months and of transacting the necessary business."

For years afterward other advertisements appeared; for instance, from the *Columbian Museum and Savannah Daily Gazette*, of November 4, 1808:

"Golf Club

"The members are requested to meet at the Exchange, this evening, at 6 o'clock, to make arrangements for the season."

Three years later we find in the *Columbian Museum*, of November 25, 1811, this call to the members:

"Golf Club

"The members of the Golf Club are requested to meet at the Exchange this evening at 7 o'clock."

This meeting was of unusual interest. It was called to arrange for a "Golf Club Ball," a great social event, to see out the old and welcome in the New Year. The ball may have been an annual event of that period. Here is the invitation:

"Golf Club Ball

"The honor of Miss Eliza Johnston's company is requested to a Ball, to be given by the members of the Golf Club, of this City, at the Exchange on Tuesday evening, the thirty-first instant, at seven o'clock.

"Managers:
"George Woodruff
"Robert Mackay
"John Craig
"James Dickson

"George Hogarth, Treasurer.
Savannah, 20th December 1811."

The original is a cherished possession of the Johnston family to-day.

In the New Netherland *Register*, of April and May, 1811, under the caption of "Pioneer Founders of New Netherlands," a writer takes the sheriff at Albany called Meuwis Hoogeboom, Gysbert Van Loon (Van Loan), and others to account for playing at golf on the public prayer day. The case was put over, but as there is no later reference to fine or punishment, the officer probably dismissed them with a warning. The incident is important as showing at what an early time golf was played in this country by the Dutch. There is little doubt in my mind that the golf referred to here was nothing more or less than the Dutch game of kolf, and there is nothing to show it was other than that. The game in Albany was played in the streets.

It would seem that the *Rivington Royal Gazette*, published in New York, April 21, 1779, has the first printed record of the Scottish game in America. It was an advertisement to golf players:

"The season for this pleasant and healthy exercise now advancing, gentlemen may be furnished with excellent Clubs and Caledonian Balls by inquiring at the Printers."

There is no evidence to whom the clubs and balls were sold or where they were played with.

There is evidence that in 1881 a couple of miles west of White Sulphur Springs, W. Va., a few holes were laid out and half a dozen men played golf. The Oakhurst holes were finally abandoned when the Green Briar course was laid out.

One of the members of this coterie tells a funny story. Returning from abroad he brought over an unusual supply of clubs and balls for himself and friends. The customs inspectors at New York, being dubious, after an hour's conference insisted that "no one ever played a game with such implements of murder." The owner objected strenuously; nevertheless, he had to leave the clubs in New York and wait six weeks before the customs officials thought the "sticks" were harmless enough to enter the country.

Putting aside numerous instances of sporadic golf played here and there spasmodically in America, I think we can give credit to the St. Andrews Club of Yonkers as the first organized association of golfers in the

United States and as having a distinct bearing on the development of the game to-day. Robert Lockhart, a Scotchman from Dumferline and a New York merchant, had learned his golf at Musselburgh. In 1888 he brought over several sets of clubs and balls, and had interested John Reid, of Yonkers. At Reid's home, November 14, 1888, it was decided to organize the St. Andrews Club of Yonkers for the purpose of engaging in the ancient and honorable game of golf. John Reid was president, and H. O. Talmadge, one of the board of managers. In 1889, J. C. Ten Eyck became a member, and I am indebted to him for the privilege of looking over the minutes of this association. It is rather amusing to note in these minutes that they scored by halves. How they did it, I do not know, but in a case of twenty holes being played Reid's score was 16½ against Putnam's 13½.

They began on H. O. Tallmadge's pasture of twenty to thirty acres on which there were six holes. It was here John Reid first played golf. In 1892 they moved to a thirty-four-acre tract at Palisades Avenue, and there laid out another six holes in an apple orchard. Here it was they became known as the "Apple-tree Gang."

Judge O'Brien's first golfing experience was with this "Apple-tree Gang." He tells a very amusing story, and here it is in his own words:

"My first introduction to golf was in 1892 when with Judge Henry Gildersleeve I went to the St. Andrews Golf Club, then situated on Palisades Avenue on a plot of ground devoted to the raising of apples in which there were innumerable apple trees. Those who were expert could manage fairly well but, for the beginners we were, the Judge and myself found the apple trees an ever-occurring obstacle to our progress. Having struck a tree, the ball either fell at the bottom or rolled into long grass, and the clubs that were most used were the niblick and the lofter. The latter was essential, because usually among the apple trees you had to get over one which was in front, so that in the beginning all of us who were unfamiliar with the game spent most of our available money for the purpose of purchasing niblicks and lofters.

"This was the first and only golf course I had ever seen until I moved down to Good Ground on Long Island—which is now known as Hampton Bays—in the spring of 1894.

"*On the fourth of July of that year I was invited by Judge Horace Russell to a luncheon at which I found a most distinguished company. The Judge presided, and there were present Elihu Root, Judge Howland, Judge Hornblower, General Barber, Charles T. Barney, George C. Clark, and others. Before luncheon I went over the course with Judge Russell. At luncheon I was asked what I thought of it. All will remember who have seen the Shinnecock Hills with their delightful verdure and charming views of bay and ocean, that the one thing lacking is trees of any kind. If you will recall the fact that I had never seen but one course and that was played through the trees at Palisades Avenue in the manner described, you will understand my disappointment over the absence of trees; and therefore, when asked as to my opinion of the course I stated with full confidence of a little and recently gained knowledge of the game, that it was not a golf course at all. This rather disturbed the gathering until I was called upon to explain why I insisted it was not a golf course, and, having in mind the picture of Palisades Avenue, I said it was not a golf course because they had no apple trees over which to loft and play.*

"*I lived to regret that I did not have more of a knowledge of what really constituted a golf course, for in the subsequent gatherings which I had with some of the gentlemen named, the reference was always made to my discomfiture to what I had said at my first luncheon at Shinnecock.*"

In 1894 the Club moved to a hundred-acre tract at Grey Oaks where they had nine holes. Although the Club was organized in 1888, its charter was not taken out until April 12, 1895. Eventually, in the fall of 1897, they took possession of the present course at Mount Hope with eighteen holes.

The Shinnecock Hills Golf Club was incorporated September 22, 1891, and has the proud position of being the first incorporated club in the United States, if not on the western continent, and in many ways it was the first substantial club permanently established. At the start they had twelve holes laid out by Willie Dunn who came from the well-known family of professional golfers in Scotland. Later, owing to the congestion, they laid out an additional nine-hole course constructed for the exclusive use of women players. This discrimination caused dissatisfaction, so the nine-hole course was abandoned in favor of a single eighteen-hole course. The eighteen-hole course was completed in 1895.

The Chicago Golf Club played over their eighteen-hole course before the Shinnecock Hills Golf Club did over theirs; nevertheless, Shinnecock had a larger club membership and owned a handsome club house designed by McKim, Mead & White.

I think Chicago can justly claim to be in the front rank in the introduction of golf in the States. I say "States" because the Royal Montreal Golf Club was established in Canada in 1873, but not incorporated until March, 1896, and the Toronto Golf Club in 1876. In many ways the Chicago Golf Club outstripped Shinnecock and St. Andrews; it had a good eighteen-hole course in 1893, and in 1894 it purchased 200 acres of land, and in 1895 it opened a really first class eighteen-hole course of 6,200 yards. In 1900 at the open championship, J. H. Taylor, Open Champion of Great Britain, in an article pronounced it as good an inland course as he had ever seen.

When I look back over golf in Chicago I can recall how for many weary years I had tried in vain to interest my friends in golf. The late James Deering, of Viscaya, Fla., was one of my closest friends, and I did my utmost to interest him; but he, with the others, looked bored to extinction. After he had joined the Chicago Golf Club in 1893 he confessed to me one evening how insufferably bored he had been with my presence at his house talking golf, and he said that politeness forbade his showing in his own house how bored he was.

"I was always happy to go to your house, Charley, for, thank heaven! I didn't have to listen to your golf chatter. As you were host, I was not obliged to be attentive."

This attitude of James Deering was practically the attitude of every person in Chicago until the approach of the World's Fair. Extraordinary as it may seem, the birth of golf in the States and the conception of the World's Fair in Chicago were simultaneous. One who did not live in Chicago at that time can scarcely believe how lethargic Chicago people were so far as sporting spirit went and the development of physique by outdoor sports. After the World's Fair, Chicago was like a community born again. Of course, I do not wish to convey to the reader that golf did that. The World's Fair did it with its wonderful artistic development. Architecture, painting, sculpture, landscape gardening, and in fact all the fine arts, were there in their best array. Golf found a footing in this transformation.

The first impetus given to golf in the West was when Sir Henry Wood was appointed England's Commissioner General to the World's Fair. With him came a retinue of young college men who had all played golf at their universities, and who were clamoring for some outdoor sport. They talked golf incessantly wherever they went. Eventually they created an audience.

Then my friend, Hobart Chatfield-Taylor, knowing that I was a golf enthusiast, asked me if I wouldn't lay out a few holes on the estate of his father-in-law, Senator John B. Farwell, at Lake Forest, which I did in May or June, 1892. There were seven holes, not one of which was over 250 yards long and at least four not more than 50 to 75 yards long, running under the trees of the lawn and between flower beds. Of course, this was not real golf, any more than the course of the "Apple-tree Gang" at Yonkers. However, it gave Lake Forest an idea of what golf might be, and this eventually bore fruit in the formation of the Onwentsia Club.

After the Lake Forest venture I at once obtained a hearing in the Chicago Club. I passed around the hat, and some twenty or thirty of my friends contributed ten dollars each for me to spend in laying out nine holes on the stock farm of a Musselburgh man, A. Haddon Smith, at Belmont, some twenty-four miles west of Chicago on the Chicago, Burlington & Quincy Railroad. I was elated. There was no club house, not even a shed nor an apple-tree. We used a neighbor's barn to deposit our clubs and to take shelter in case of rain.

I had cabled to the Royal Liverpool Golf Club to send me out six sets of clubs. Never shall I forget my disappointment the Saturday afternoon when, after getting a promise from my contributors to accompany me to Belmont to be introduced to golf and after ordering an elaborate luncheon, only two of my party arrived, owing to the threatening nature of the weather. They were Edward S. Worthington and Harry Wilmerding.

Provided with clubs we sallied forth, small wagers were laid between them as to who would win. We played about five holes when it started to pour in torrents, and we had to take refuge in the barn nearby to wait until it was over. I had brought a pack of cards to divert their minds, and I am happy to say that between each hand they ran to the door to see if the rain was over, each being confident he would win the next hole. The result of all this was that golf won over two of the most enthusiastic men I have ever known, and throughout their lives they never ceased to be devoted to the game. From then on the Chicago Golf Club was established with an ever-increasing number of players.

In the spring of 1893 I increased the number of holes from nine to eighteen, and on the eighteenth day of July, 1893, the charter of the Chicago Golf Club was granted. The application for the charter was made by Charles B. Macdonald, J. Carolus Sterling, James B. Forgan, J. G. Watson, W. R. Farquhar, George A. H. Scott, and Urban H. Broughton. The directors the first year were myself, Sterling, Forgan, Broughton, Hobart Chatfield-Taylor, Farquhar, and Watson. We took out this charter regardless of the law that the petitioners must be United States citizens. Only two of these men were United States citizens at the time.

The Chicago Golf Club became so popular in 1894 we determined to buy a piece of property that we might construct an improved eighteen-hole golf course, comparable with the best inland courses abroad. In that year we bought the Patrick farm of 200 acres, a mile from the prosperous town of Wheaton, county seat of Du Page County, twenty-five miles from Chicago on the Chicago and Northwestern Railroad.

After the Chicago Golf Club abandoned their course at Belmont, Herbert J. Tweedie, late of the Royal Liverpool Golf Club, with a party of friends formed the Belmont Golf Club which has sometimes been confused with the original Chicago Golf Club. None of the members of the Chicago Golf Club were members of the Belmont Golf Club, and the clubs are not in the slightest degree identical. The charter of the Belmont Golf Club was not granted until 1899.

Concurrently with the development of the Chicago Golf Club from the seven holes I laid out on Senator Farwell's estate, grew the Lake Forest Golf Club. In 1894 they started the Lake Forest Golf Club with nine holes on the McCormick farm. There they played until 1896, when they bought the farm and residence of Henry Ives Cobb where they first had nine holes and then eighteen which H. J. Whigham laid out for them in 1898. The Club then took out its charter, and it was called the Onwentsia Club. In July, 1899, the United States Golf Association's amateur championship was held on this course.

With the inception of golf at Shinnecock Hills and Chicago, Bostonians awoke to the fascination of the game. In this instance a young lady

A LOST BALL BEYOND THE HOME HOLE AT THE
ORIGINAL CHICAGO GOLF COURSE, 1894.

from Pau, visiting the family of Arthur Hunnewell in the summer of 1893, brought with her a set of clubs and some golf balls. She demonstrated the way of playing golf. The Hunnewell place was at Wellesley, Mass. Arthur Hunnewell, R. G. Shaw, and Hollis Hunnewell owned adjacent estates, and all of them were ardent lovers of outdoor sports. They were quick to recognize the attraction of the new game, and they, with a few of their friends, eagerly adopted it. Lawrence Curtis writes about the introduction of golf over the Hunnewell grounds:

"During October and November several of Mr. Hunnewell's friends were invited to try it, and on his grounds about a dozen made their first acquaintance with the game. His course was not a bad one. It ran over undulating lawns and park, and consisted of seven holes of fair distances. The holes were sunken five-inch flower pots; the hazards consisted of avenues, dumps of trees, bushes, beds of rhododendrons and azaleas, an aviary, green-houses, and an occasional drawing room window pane; and many were the narrow escapes of ladies and children on the piazzas at the

THE AUTHOR IN 1895 AT THE TOP OF HIS SWING.

hands of the enthusiastic players who were totally ignorant of the force and 'carry' and range of a fairly hit golf ball."

Later the players became infatuated with the game, so Laurence Curtis wrote a letter to the executive committee of the Country Club and asked if golf could not be introduced on their property. The Country Club appointed Arthur Hunnewell, Laurence Curtis, and Robert Bacon a committee to lay out a course, the expense not to exceed fifty dollars. Nine holes were laid out in March, 1893.

Coincident with the development of golf in Boston was the introduction of golf in Newport, R. I. Lorillard Spencer and H. Mortimer Brooks were the instigators there in 1892. They engaged W. F. Davis, professional, to look over the available ground. He finally selected a place on Brenton's Point where, finally, nine holes were laid out.

The Club was organized on January 12, 1893. Mr. Theodore A. Havemeyer was elected president. Davis was engaged as club-maker and instructor. The Club was first limited to seventy-five members, and they at once adopted the Royal and Ancient rules of St. Andrews as the rules for the Newport Golf Club. The Club was incorporated the 4th of August, 1894, and in 1894 advertised an amateur tournament which the committee was pleased to call a championship tournament.

However, there was no organization of clubs justifying any club in calling its invitation tournament a championship. Likewise, the committee of the St. Andrews Golf Club advertised an amateur championship to take place at St. Andrews. Both these meetings gave zest and impetus to the popularity of the game. Neither had any championship authority except so far as it concerned its own club.

The five clubs whose history I have just narrated were the five clubs which formed the United States Golf Association established December 22, 1894.

Tuxedo and the Meadowbrook Hunt Club became golfing enthusiasts in 1893, and both had nine-hole golf courses. When I was visiting my friend Delancey Nicoll, then of Tuxedo, in July, 1893, immediately before my sailing for Europe, he spoke most scornfully to me when I insisted on spending the day on the Tuxedo links with Grenville Kane. Disdainfully he exclaimed, "I cannot understand how any one having manly instincts can fritter away his time rushing around a ten-acre lot after a small pill." I knew then I had fallen in his estimation many degrees. Imagine my surprise a year or two afterward when he came into my office in Chicago, and, after passing the pleasantries of meeting, exclaimed, "Charley, I want you to take me out to the Chicago Golf Club." I cried, "Why, Delancey! Why this change of heart?" He said: "I will tell you all about it. Tell me what time the train leaves, and on the way out I'll explain." So we took the noon train to Wheaton. Settling down, he began:

"When I found the men whom I looked upon as my best companions, whom I had finally regarded as the flower of mankind, gradually moving away from me, and when I found the reason was that they played golf, I made up my mind to find out about this game of golf. So I went where every man of intelligence must go—to the library—to get a line on what this game of golf was and meant. What did I find? This is what I found. I found that admirals who had sailed the seas all their lives, generals who had been on the battlefields of life in every part of the globe, lord chief justices of England, prime ministers, professors whose names were household words, and others of international fame spent their holidays playing golf, and when their life work was completed they went to St. Andrews to devote their declining years to the game. I then made up my mind that I was losing something in this life, so I was enticed to the golf links of Tuxedo and bought clubs and balls to play a round of golf. And here I am, Charley, coming out with you, wanting to see what I am told is the finest golf links in America. You see seated before you a golfer, one who understands the enchantment of the game which was once so meaningless. I, Delancey Nicoll, am seeking to improve my mind."

The reader may recall that when I first witnessed golf in Scotland it looked to me like a silly game for old men. I have just told you how one of the best and most intelligent sportsmen in New York had convinced himself that my first impression was true, only to be converted. Another friend to whom I am devoted, who loves everything worthwhile, from manly sports to horse-racing, and who knew all the men who first played golf in Chicago, was kindly contemptuous of the game. Nothing expresses his feelings so clearly and vividly as something he published in one of the "Dooley" articles. Looking on the game of golf as a weak, social amenity, here is how he expressed himself in 1896:

" 'Tis a good game to play in a hammick when ye're all tired out fr'm social duties or shovellin' coke. Out-iv-dure golf is played be th' followin' rules. If ye bring ye're wife f'r to see th' game, an' she has her name in th' paper, that counts ye wan. So th' first thing ye do is to find th' raypoorter, an' tell him ye're there. Thin ye ordher a bottle iv brown pop, an' have ye'er second fan ye with a towel. Afther this ye'd dhress, an' here ye've got to be dam particklar or ye'll be stuck f'r th' dhrinks. If ye'er necktie is not sthraight, that counts ye'er opponent wan. If both ye an' ye'er opponent have ye'er neckties on crooked, th' first man that sees it gets th' stakes. Thin ye ordher a carredge—'

" 'Order what?' demanded Mr. McKenna.

" 'A carredge.'

" 'What for?'

" 'F'r to take ye 'round th' links. Ye have a little boy followin' ye, carryin' ye'er clubs. Th' man that has th' smallest little boy it counts him two. If th' little boy has th' rickets, it counts th' man in th' carredge three—'

" 'Well whin ye dhrive up to th' tea grounds—'

" 'Th' what?' demanded Mr. Hennessy.

" 'Th' tea grounds, that's like th' home-plate in base-ball or ordherin' a piece iv chalk in a game iv spoil five. It's th' beginnin' iv ivrything. Whin ye get to th' tea grounds, ye step out, an' have ye'er hat irned by th' caddie. Thin ye'er man that ye'er going aginst comes up, an' he asks ye, 'Do you know Potther Pammer?' Well, if ye don't know Potther Pammer, it's all up with ye; ye lose two points. But ye come right back at him with an' upper cut; 'Do ye live on th' Lake Shore Dhrive?' If he doesn't, ye have him in th' nine hole. Ye needn't play with him anny more. But, if ye do play with him, he has to spot three balls. If he's a good man an' shifty on his feet, he'll counter be askin' ye where ye spent th' summer. Now ye can't tell him that ye spent th' summer with wan hook on th' free lunch an' another on th' ticker tape, an' so ye go back three. That needn't discourage ye at all, at all. Here's yer chance to mix up, an' ye ask him if he was iver in Scotland. If he wasn't, it counts ye five. Thin ye tell him that ye had an aunt wanst that heerd th' Jook iv Argyle talk in a phonograph; an' onless he comes back an' shoots it into ye that he was wanst run over by th' Prince iv Wales, ye have him groggy. I don't know whether th' Jook *iv Argyle or th' Prince iv Wales counts f'r most. They're like th' right an' left bower iv thrumps. Th' best players is called scratch-men.'*

" 'What's that f'r?' Mr. Hennessy asked.

" 'It's a Scotch game,' said Mr. Dooley, with a wave of his hand."

It was not long after—I think only one year later—that Finley Peter Dunne was enrolled in the membership of the Chicago Golf Club, an ardent devotee of the game. Coming to scoff he remained to pray like many others before him. While I am speaking of Peter, here is an episode that occurred on the tee at the time Robert T. Lincoln inveigled Marshall Field to take up the game.

Mr. Dunne was on the links at Wheaton one day with Marshall Field, the great merchant of his time. The financial positions of the two gentlemen were not exactly alike. Mr. Field was perhaps the richest man in America, and Mr. Dunne was—well, was not. The newspaper of which he was editor was struggling in a confused financial sea, a fact of which Mr. Field was well aware. Indeed, there was nothing about the financial affairs of his fellow man that escaped the eye of the millionaire.

A lady in the party bet Mr. Dunne that he couldn't drive the pond hole with a mashie. As he squared away for this feat Mr. Field called out from the crowd: "Make him put his money up first." Mr. Dunne promptly put the ball in the pond. A little later while we were all walking to the first tee, Mr. Field complained to Robert Lincoln with whom he was going to play, that he had "lost his drive." It was no great loss at most, but he never liked to lose anything, a shilling out of a million or a yard out of one hundred and thirty.

"But Mr. Field," piped up Peter still smarting from the gibe, "why don't you try putting a dollar on the ball?"

"Why?" the merchant asked. "What good would that do?"

"Because," said Mr. Dunne, "they say you can make a dollar go further than any one in the world."

He neglected to accept the suggestion, with the result that after making a mighty assault on the ball he propelled it a measured three and one-half feet from the tee.

Coming back to the two invitation tournaments in the East, Norman Fay, of Chicago and Newport, wired me to visit him at Newport and play in the tournament to be held the first week in September, 1894. I decided to go on from Niagara Falls where I had a country home. The tournament was two days of medal play, eighteen holes each day. The course was very crude, as it had only been laid out the year before, and we played over a pasture which had stone walls across the fairway. I failed to be the winner by one stroke, owing, as I remember it, to topping a ball under one of these stone walls.

The first day I made the lowest score for the eighteen holes, namely, 89. W. G. Lawrence, who learned his golf at Pau and won the golf cup there the year before, was 93 the first day. The second day I took 100 against Lawrence's 95; his total being 188 against my 189. In that tournament Herbert Leeds, Boston's crack player, was 217; and L. P. Stoddard, the St. Andrews crack golfer, was 102 for eighteen holes the first day, after which he withdrew.

I can recall that the tournament was extremely interesting, and the club's committee did everything to make the competitors happy.

The other eastern invitation tournament in which I played was the one at the St. Andrews Golf Club at Yonkers. It was held October 11th and 12th of the same year. There were thirty-two entries to be decided by eighteen holes (twice around nine holes) match play. In the semi-finals Archie Rogers played Stoddard, and my old antagonist at Newport, Lawrence, played me.

Returning to town after the first day's play, Stanford White gave me a dinner and supper party which lasted until five o'clock in the morning. I had an engagement to breakfast with Willie Lawrence at seven o'clock. Stanford drove me home to the Waldorf, and when I told him I did not believe I would be able to keep my engagement in the morning, he said to leave it to him and he would fix me. He did. When I got up in the morning I found a note from him and a few strychnine pellets with instructions as to how to take them. This I did, and, after breakfasting with Willie Lawrence, we took the train for Yonkers. In the morning round I won from Lawrence by two and one to play. I was fast fading away. Stanford White came out to luncheon with me. Again he insisted upon putting me together. He had evidently read Horace Hutchinson's article in "Badminton" on *Hints on Match and Medal Play*, in which he described "the man to back":

"If ever you see a man who has tied with another for a medal, toying in the luncheon interval with a biscuit and a lemon and soda, you may go out and bet your modest half-crown against that man with a light heart. But if you see him doctoring himself with a beef-steak and a bottle of beer, or, better still, a pint of champagne, you may go forth and back that man with as stout a heart as though you had yourself partaken of his luncheon. The golfer will not do good work unless he is fed. And it is real, good, hard work that he has to do—work that will need a stout heart to do it efficiently. For it is a game of hard rubs and annoyances, a game of which the exasperations no less than the fascinations were never better summarized than in these words of the grand old golfer: 'It's aye fechtin' against ye.' "

Never was more fallacious advice given the unsuspecting golfing community, and that from one of the best golfers and best men that ever played the game. This advice has ruined many a man's game.

Stanford insisted on a bottle of champagne and a steak. I do not wish the reader to think that Stoddard would not have beaten me anyway. That I do not know; but, in any event, I played wretched golf that afternoon. We were all square and one to play. I drove my ball from the tee at the last hole into some ploughed ground. Stoddard won the hole and the match. I had an able sympathetic caddy, J. C. Ten Eyck, a prominent member of the club, who was good enough to lug my clubs around.

As I look back through forty years, the growth of golf both in England and America seems incredible. It was not until 1890 that the English became inflamed with the contagion of golf. Then golf courses sprang up everywhere, both public and private. In 1891 there were only 395 golf clubs in the United Kingdom, and 34 of these were ladies clubs. There were really no golf courses in the United States worthy of the name in 1890. According to the present returns (1927) within the metropolitan district of New York there are about 400 golf clubs, and Chicago has nearly 200. All told there are 1,500 golf clubs in Great Britain and 4,000 in the United States.

Chapter VI

Beginning of U.S.G.A.—Bogey

After the invitation tournaments of the Newport Golf Club and the St. Andrews Golf Club there was much criticism by other clubs of their assuming to represent the golfing community in national championships. The Chicago Golf Club, having eighteen holes, held an invitation tournament, but made no such claim. The Shinnecock Hills Golf Club, which had the best nine golfing holes in the East, made no such claim. Other clubs probably did the same. Obviously, no championship could be held and designated national without a general concensus of opinion expressed by the leading clubs of the country; consequently an association had to be organized. H. O. Tallmadge instigated the movement to form such an association. He and Laurence Curtis sent out the invitations asking the Shinnecock Hills Golf Club, The Country Club of Brookline, Mass., and the Chicago Golf Club to join the St. Andrews Golf Club and the Newport Golf Club in forming a representative body to promote the interests of the game of golf, to decide on what links the amateur and open championships should be played, and to establish and enforce uniformity in the rules of the game.

H. O. Tallmadge gave a dinner at the Calumet Club on the 22d of December, 1894, and each of the above clubs was represented by two members. John Reid and H. O. Tallmadge represented the St. Andrews Club; Theodore A. Havemeyer and Winthrop Rutherford, the latter being unavoidably absent, represented the Newport Golf Club; General Barber and Samuel Parrish represented the Shinnecock Hills Golf Club; Laurence Curtis and P. Sears represented The Country Club; Arthur

Ryerson and myself represented the Chicago Golf Club. Theodore A. Havemeyer was elected president. At this meeting the following original agreement was adopted and signed:

"The undersigned Clubs, by their Presidents, and subject to ratification by their respective boards of management, do hereby agree to unite, and to invite other clubs to join them, as the

"Amateur Golf Association of the United States

"The purposes of this Association shall be to promote the interests of the game of golf, to promulgate a code of rules for the game, and to hold annual meetings at which competitions shall be conducted for the amateur and open championships in the United States.

"The times, places and conditions of such championship competitions shall be arranged at a meeting of the Association to be held in New York on the 22d day of December in the year 1894, at which meeting each club shall be represented by two members, and voting by proxy shall be allowed.

"Each club pledges itself to contribute, not exceeding fifty dollars, to a fund which shall provide for the expenses of formation of this Association, and for suitable trophies or prizes for the amateur and open championships.

*The St. Andrews Golf Club, of Yonkers-on-Hudson,
by John Reid, President.*

*The Shinnecock Hills Golf Club, of Southampton, L. I.,
by T. H. Barber, President.*

*The Country Club, of Brookline, Mass.,
by F. Murray Forbes, Chairman.*

*The Newport Golf Club, of Newport, R. I.,
by Theo. A. Havemeyer.*

*The Chicago Golf Club, of Chicago, Ill.,
By Charles M. Macdonald, Captain."*

```
The St. Andrews Golf Club       of Yonkers-on-Hudson
        by      John Reid, Prest.
The Shinnecock Hills Golf Club  of Southampton L. I.
        by      T. H. Barber Prest.
The Country Club                of Brookline, Mass.
        by      S. Murray Forbes, chairman
The Newport Golf Club           of Newport R. I.
        by      Theo. A. Havemeyer, Prest.
The Chicago Golf Club           of Chicago, Ill.
        by      Charles B. Macdonald, Captain
```

FACSIMILE OF THE SIGNATURES OF THE FOUNDERS OF THE AMATEUR GOLF ASSOCIATION OF THE UNITED STATES, LATER THE U.S.G.A.

You will note that it was first called the Amateur Golf Association. Later it was changed to the American Golf Association, but finally named the United States Golf Association when the constitution was adopted.

Mr. Reid, General Barber, and I were appointed a committee of three to draw up a constitution and by-laws, to report at the first annual meeting of the association, held on the 8th of February, 1895, and on this date the association convened and the constitution and by-laws were adopted as read. This constitution and these by-laws were not altered until 1901 except as to the amateur definition. This indicates how well the first seven meetings after the creation of the U.S.G.A. passed off. No serious disagreement marred the harmony with which we sought the betterment of the game.

At a meeting of the executive committee of the U.S.G.A., held at the Shinnecock Hills Golf Club, at Southampton, Long Island, July 18, 1896, it was voted: "That Mr. C. B. Macdonald and Mr. Laurence Curtis be appointed a special committee to interpret the rules of golf and to present their report for action at the annual meeting."

Naturally there was a great amount of work and investigation required. I corresponded with Horace Hutchinson, among others, seeking light. He wrote in an article in *Golf* of February, 1897, entitled "An Appeal from America," referring to my letter:

"The object of that letter is, as Mr. Macdonald puts it, to place American Golf in touch with golfing opinion in this country, for the special purpose of the better understanding and definition of certain of the rules which at present leave something to be wished in the way of intelligibility and definiteness. Mr. Macdonald and Mr. Curtis would be glad to place themselves in communication with the committee which the Royal and Ancient Club is endeavouring to form, to consider the very points about which the States are in difficulty....

"It is not the purpose of this article, however, to put forward my own or any other individual opinion, but simply to bring to the notice of golfers the desire of golfers in the States for a community of golfing opinion, and a uniformity of golfing rule.

"Mr. Macdonald also asks for an interpretation of that rule which has lately given rise to so much trouble here, the rule about replacing a ball which the opponent's ball has knocked away. He wants to know—we all want to know—when the replacement is to take effect, provided the owner of the ball elects to replace it. He also wants to know—and, again, we all want to know—'which side loses the hole when both balls are lost.'

"The one thing needful, which we want, and they want, and everyone wants, is something definite. We should not so much mind if the rules were cryingly unjust, if only they would weigh with equal and determined injustice on all alike. It is the indefiniteness of the rules that causes so much bother, and makes the necessity for some legislative body so obvious, although certain of the Scottish clubs demur to the constitution of the body that has been proposed. 'We find in America,' says Mr. Macdonald, 'that it is necessary to have rules more clearly defined, as people are inclined to play more by the letter than the spirit.'

"They have not got the guiding tradition which serves us, though none too well, when the 'letter' is found wanting. If the publication of this communication from the States shall evoke some useful expression of opinion as to the manner in which, failing the appointment of the committee by the Royal and Ancient, we may arrive at some satisfactory legislation, it will deserve the gratitude of golfers both here and in the States. If the committee proposed by the Royal and Ancient fails to take shape,

under stress of the opposition which is threatening it, we shall require a very strong expression of opinion to enable us to move the golfing legislation machinery out of the dead-lock into which it is likely to fall."

Our committee were unable to make the report until June 10, 1897, when the codification of rules and rulings was duly presented to the executive committee, and by them ratified and ordered to be promulgated and published as the law of the U.S.G.A. The report follows:

"The special committee have made no change in the words of the rules as they stand in the code of the Royal and Ancient Golf Club of St. Andrews, revised in 1891; but they have appended to said rules the rulings of the U.S.G.A., based upon the results of many decisions of committees or experts, or upon customs which have obtained in the best clubs in Scotland and England.

"They hereby acknowledge with thanks, assistance and advice received from the following authorities: The editor of "Golf" and Messrs. Horace G. Hutchinson, Harold H. Hilton, Leslie Balfour-Melville, W. T. Linskill, H. J. Whigham, and others.

" There will doubtless be found many points not covered in this work. Such are mostly those which should be made the subjects of local rules, or such as may be considered to belong to the etiquette of golf.

"Such would be questions as to:

"Dropping a ball at the edge of a hazard where it is impracticable to drop it behind the hazard. (Rule 19 and Medal Rule 8.)

"Outsiders looking for a lost ball. (Rule 37.)

"Unplayable balls (Rule 38), or mud adhering to a ball.

"Discontinuing play on account of sudden severe storms, or for taking refreshments. (Rule 11, Medal Play.)

"Lifting balls lying on putting greens other than the one played to.

"Casual water through the fair green.

"Boundaries, wall, fences, gates, rabbit holes, gopher holes, direction flags, etc.

"Strict definition of hazards on the course.

"Liability of players to suffer the full penalty when their caddies commit a breach of any rule.

"Restraint upon single players practicing on the course.

"Right of parties with caddies to pass parties without caddies, or a single to pass a foursome.

"Slow or inexperienced players blocking the course.

"Stringent rules for keeping scores in competitions.

"Charles Blair Macdonald.
Laurence Curtis."

The five charter clubs were unanimous on one point, and that was we should play the game of golf as it was played in Scotland, as evidenced by the rules adopted by the Royal and Ancient Golf Club of St. Andrews.

The only other matter of moment was the definition of amateur. In 1895 the game was so unimportant that no players thought of playing golf as amateurs for what money they could stealthily make out of it; consequently the amateur rule in the by-laws of 1895 was similar to the one adopted in Great Britain for their championships. However, we soon realized a rule for one community would not be effective in another community. We adopted the following rule:

"An amateur golfer shall be a golfer who has never received a money consideration for playing in a match or for giving lessons in or examples of his skill in the game, nor laid out nor taken charge of golf links for hire, who has never contended for a money prize in open competition, who has never personally made golf clubs, balls, or any other articles connected with the game for sale, and who, on and after January 1st, 1897, has never within the jurisdiction of this association played a match against a professional for a money bet or stake, nor played in a club competition for a money prize or sweepstake."

Not more than two years elapsed before the sporting-goods houses of the United States sent representatives to the championships, and in every way tried to commercialize and influence the conduct of the game. Further than that, in many places where club competitions were held it was thought good sportsmanship to induce men who played the game well to join a certain club by offering them remuneration, either in the way of free club dues or paying their expenses when they went from place to place in club or amateur championships. College sports at that time carried such a system to an unsportsmanlike length. In view of this, in 1898 the amateur rule was changed, and in 1899 the rule was again altered, becoming more strict and specifically stating that no person may be eligible to compete for the amateur championship who "has received compensation for services performed in any athletic organization, or who plays the game or who frequents golf courses, for the purpose of exploiting his business; nor shall any one be eligible to compete who hereafter shall enter any golfing competition under an assumed name." In 1901, the rules were made still more drastic by listing as ineligible any one: "Who receives a money consideration, either directly or indirectly, by reason of his connection with, or skill displayed in playing the game of golf; who is classified as a professional in any athletic sport; who sells or pledges any prize or token obtained through connection with the game of golf; who, with the intention of promoting any business, receives transportation or board, or any reduction or equivalent thereof, as a consideration of his playing golf or exhibiting his skill as a player; who has club dues or charges paid by another person, as an inducement to become a member of a club."

By this time the game, as every one knows, has spread like wildfire throughout the country. North, east, west, and south there were golf clubs galore. This naturally brought about many disputes. It is curious to note that the first meetings of the U.S.G.A. occupied only fifty-five pages in the minute book.

Unhappily, one of these meetings was a special one, held May 26, 1897, a meeting of condolence on the loss of our distinguished president, Theodore A. Havemeyer. It is difficult to speak dispassionately of T. A. Havemeyer. In all his official relations he exhibited a broad and liberal spirit, meeting every one with that courtesy of manner for which he was so distinguished. His administrative ability was combined with the most lovable characteristics of a gentleman sportsman, and the Association was extraordinarily fortunate in the selection of its first president. His death was an irreparable loss particularly to all who were nurturing the infancy of our favorite pastime. He was much beloved and mourned.

The meeting held in 1901 occupied *59 pages* of minutes—four more than the first seven meetings combined—and that of 1902, *66 pages*. The troubles of the U.S.G.A. began right here. R. H. Robertson was elected president in 1901. He had an attractive personality, was serious-minded, kindly, and generous, with a host of friends; and I am happy to recall I was one of them. His address to the delegates in the meeting was excellent

THEODORE A. HAVEMEYER, DONOR OF THE U.S.G.A. CHAMPIONSHIP CUP.

as a whole, but it was fraught with expressions which presaged trouble. Here are extracts from his maiden address: "I am fully in accord, as far as I understand it, with the management and policy of your committee in the past....We should see to it that the line of professional golf and that the line of amateur golf be so clearly defined, so clearly marked, and so thoroughly appreciated and recognized, that those two lines can never converge....I do not know which of the two hybrids is the most undesirable—a professional amateur, or an amateur professional....I am convinced that we should be on our guard and keep our association up to very high standards of membership....Let us play the game as we have always played it—like gentlemen."

But now comes the "rift in the lute." "I know," he said, "that we are all grateful for what England and Scotland have done for us in exporting this game for our delectation and amusement; but I think we should guard against being too much restricted and *held down by precedent and tradition. I fear that is the fault of the game on the other side. Do not let us be afraid of innovations simply because they are innovations. Nothing can come to America and stay very long without being Americanized in character; and I hope this game will be no exception to this rule. I should like to see American golf.*" How about the Church of Rome and the Church of England? Traditions surrounding golf are relatively as absorbing and powerful. Why Americanize Golf?

Just before President Robertson and Travis left for a golfing pilgrimage to Scotland and England in July, 1901, Casper Whitney caused a tremendous stir in golfing circles by an article in his magazine, *Outing*, in which he declared Walter J. Travis and A. G. Lockwood professionals:

"So the fine sentiments and the sportsmanlike assurances of Mr. Robertson, at his inauguration as President of the United States Golf Association, were only 'talk'! What a pity, too! because he had such an opportunity of dealing a mortal blow to the evil which at present menaces the game most seriously....Frankly the President and the Executive Committee of the U.S.G.A. have been false to their duty and their promises to keep golf clean of this semi-professionalism....

"Herewith I challenge the right of entry to all amateur golf tournaments of Mr. W. J. Travis and Mr. A. G. Lockwood. The conduct of Messrs. Travis and Lockwood in receiving hotel board and railroad

transportation this spring, during a Florida golfing campaign, makes them obviously ineligible to rank as amateurs. By the rules of every amateur game, including golf, they are professionals, for, if they did not receive money for their services as touring hotel billboards, they did receive its equivalent in several hundred dollars worth of board and lodging and railroad fare."

The president of the U.S.G.A. replied to this attack in a letter to the editor of *The Sun*:

"Sir,—Referring to a reprint in the Sun of yesterday of a protest, unsigned, which, I understand, appeared in the June issue of Outing, challenging the amateur standing of Messrs. Travis and Lockwood and their right to enter any amateur tournament, I can only say that in my opinion no formal recognition can be taken of it, in its present indefinite form by the committee of the U.S.G.A....The officers and the committee of this association...have in the past, and will in the future, earnestly and impartially consider any complaints, protests or criticisms when properly presented to them, with facts given, sustaining or bearing upon the grievance....

"I am yours very truly,
R. H. Robertson, President, U.S.G.A."

Stringent as the 1901 definition of amateur was, many thought it did not appear to contain any specific clause which directly covered the practice which *Outing* condemned, but the former Executive Committee intended it should.

We all knew that President Robertson had not been imbued with the ancient and honorable traditions of the game in his youth any more than Travis had been, but we thought after their spending three months together in Scotland and England during the summer they would have absorbed some reverence for these same ancient and honorable traditions. We were doomed to be disappointed. As Rider Haggard said: "Golf, like Art, is a Goddess whom we woo in early youth if we would win her."

On his return Robertson proposed many changes which were contrary to past policies, false to the traditions. He said: "You will perhaps admit we have outgrown our Constitution." He advocated the revision of the constitution and the by-laws. He pointed out that the Executive Committee could revise the by-laws, but could not revise the constitution without a meeting of all the clubs. He advocated representation of member clubs by eliminating the distinction in class. He also suggested that the Association might have a sectional subdivision. He advocated a change in the constitution regarding proxies. He stated that "there are many modifications necessary in the letter and spirit of the rules of golf as they now exist." Beside all this he advocated a change in the method of playing the championships.

To many of us much of this was treason. Fortunately most of these proposed changes were turned down at later special meetings. However, in 1902 the Executive Committee altered the by-laws changing the amateur rule and also the method of playing the amateur competitions. The amateur rule was made to read as follows:

"Sec. 7. No person shall be considered an amateur golfer or shall be eligible to compete in the amateur championships of this Association, who receives a money consideration, either directly or indirectly, by reason of connection with or skill displayed in playing the game of golf, or other branches of athletics.

"Protests against an individual concerning any violation of the letter or spirit of this Section, must be made by a member of a club belonging to the Association, and must be submitted in writing to the Secretary of the Association, properly certified to by an officer of his club."

This rule proved so flexible one could drive a coach and four through it. The golfing community deplored its leniency, and altered it after the Robertson regime expired, and made another rule as stringent as the one of 1901.

Politics had now entered into the conduct of many of the golf clubs throughout the country, and subsequently entered into the conduct of the U.S.G.A. From then until recently it has been with the utmost difficulty that the U.S.G.A. has been able to protect itself against this insidious influence. Lawyers kept us up all night arguing technical points that had little or nothing to do with the conduct and real welfare of the game. Fortunately the Association rode the storm well.

It was a wise provision by which the founders of the U.S.G.A. set up originally two classes of members, for at that time little was known of golf and the community had to be educated. Article IV read:

"Section 1. Other clubs eligible to be admitted to membership in the Association, as associated clubs, shall be any club, in an accessible part of the United States, where the links, accommodations, constitution and by-laws of the club are such as to make it representative, and such clubs may be admitted on a four-fifths vote of the Executive Committee of the Association.

"Section 2. Any regularly organized Golf club in the United States may at any time, be admitted as an allied club by a two-thirds vote of the Executive Committee, upon subscribing to and fulfilling the conditions of the Association Constitution and By-laws."

How Robertson could reconcile his advocating "the elimination of all distinction of class" with his statement in his maiden address in 1901 that "expansion should consist of quality and not quantity," I cannot comprehend. Quality and not quantity the Association had consistently advocated and maintained.

If any association of men having a six, nine, or even an eighteen-hole golf course in nothing but name, a golf course laid out in any old place, inaccessible, unrepresentative, a hotel course, perhaps, could have had the same voting power as the leading clubs in the country where clean sportsmanship reigned supreme, we should to-day have as many varieties of golfing rules as we have clubs! I violently opposed this change in the constitution at the great fight in 1905 and happily it did not occur until 1927—a quarter of a century later when it was assumed men had become familiar with the game and understood it. I still doubt the wisdom of the change.

Aside from the question of adopting the Royal and Ancient rules, on which the golfers of the United States are now almost unanimous, the only other question of vast importance for the U.S.G.A. to determine was the definition of "amateur golfer." You cannot make a rule and then make exceptions for individuals. The rule must be made regardless of individuals. I think the amateur definition is now excellent.

Many of my friends in the West informed me at this time that the one serious criticism of the U.S.G.A. was that it was "an autocratic body run by the East." For my part, I firmly believe the ruling of any sport by an intelligent autocratic body is infinitely preferable to mob rule, which always lowers the morale of games. The West was always represented on the U.S.G.A. board, though in the early days few of its delegates attended the meetings. Criticism arose nevertheless, and soon the Western refractory contingent had their press hammering the U.S.G.A. As we all know, there is nothing the sporting reporters love more than a row. It makes copy. For twenty years they have kept it up—thank heaven to no purpose.

As I was Western representative of the U.S.G.A. from 1894 to 1899, and probably had more than any other individual to do with framing the rules, and the constitution and by-laws of the U.S.G.A. during that period, I may say that I never saw the slightest evidence of the East trying to be autocratic. On the contrary, it always leaned backwards in placing the competitions where they would do the most good. The Association has only one point in view and one object to attain, and that is to keep the game of golf clean, and to play golf and not a modification of it.

Colonel Bogey was created in England in the nineties, and the various English clubs, especially the Manchester Golf Club, made their own rules. The Royal and Ancient absolutely refused to take cognizance of the genial Colonel, who is a mythical golfer who never makes a grievous error, never gets into bunkers, can always reach the putting green in reasonable length of strokes and then (always putts down in two strokes) never takes more than two putts.

It is interesting to record the origin of Colonel Bogey, and the following is an excerpt from the London *Daily Mail*:

> *"Two officers of the British Military Service created the redoubtable star of the Links, which is none other than Colonel Bogey.*
>
> *"The score, now known the world over as the 'bogey score,' was until 1890 known as the 'ground score' and represented the figures that would be made by a very good player. Once established this would remain as the ground score on that particular links. Doctor Thomas Browne, Royal Navy, and Major Charles Wellman, of the Army, in 1890 were playing on the links at Great Yarmouth, each seeing whether he could do better than his 'ground score.'*

"About that time a very popular song in the London music halls dealt with the bogey man and the liability of his catching you if you didn't look out, somewhat after the fashion of James Whitcomb Riley's 'The gobelins'll get ye if you don't watch out.' Major Wellman was so often worse than this ground score that he finally exclaimed: 'Why, this ground score is like a bogey man; it's always catching me.' Doctor Browne was so taken with the phrase that he had his club call the ground score the 'bogey' for the links.

"Some days later Doctor Browne went to play at the links of the United Service Club at Alverstoke, in Hampshire, and to one of the members, Captain Seely Vidal, Royal Engineers, he presented as a joke his phantom friend, the bogey man. They worked out a score for the links according to the new idea and started out to play against this hastily improvised bogey.

"As they teed up Captain Vidal exclaimed: 'Stay! We must proceed in a proper service way. Every member of this Club has a proper service rank. Our new invisible member who never made a mistake ought surely to be a commanding officer. He must be a colonel,' and then, with a desire to carry the joke to the end, gravely saluting the phantom visitor, he added: 'Colonel Bogey, we are delighted to find you on the links, sir, I could not well say 'see you.' "

Colonel Bogey became quite popular by 1900 in the United States and the United States Golf Association was prevailed upon to make rules for bogey competitions. They decided the competitions should be played under special rules for stroke competitions with two or three exceptions.

It was not until 1912 that St. Andrews succumbed to the universal demand throughout the golfing world and issued rules for bogey play. They adopted the same rules as those which prevailed in the United States.

There was considerable objection to stroke conditions by the English clubs, *Golf Illustrated* violently protested, claiming match play rules should govern the competitions. However, to date the rules have not been altered.

Chapter VII

Personal Golf, 1894-1906

Without doubt the creation of the U.S.G.A. gave fresh impetus to the formation of golf clubs throughout the country. Whereas there were only five charter members at the beginning of 1895, by the end of the year the association had enrolled ten associate members and thirteen allied members. To-day, 1927, there are 943 members.

The Chicago Golf Club took possession of their 200-acre farm in 1895 and by the first of May were playing over eighteen well-laid-out holes, the length of which more or less corresponded with the length of holes in St. Andrews, Scotland, totaling about 6,200 yards. But here the resemblance ceased, for the Wheaton Farm was rich black loam and after a long drought the fairway would crack. However, the red-top grass grew luxuriantly so the fairway was usually good. On the putting greens we had the finest bent grasses. Water was piped to all the putting greens guaranteeing at all times an excellent putting surface. I think the Chicago Golf Club was the first club in America, if not in the golfing world, to water their eighteen greens with water piped from a central plant.

The first important tournament in 1895 was known as the International Championship Tournament, between Canada and the United States, and was held the first week of September at Niagara-on-the-Lake situated on Lake Ontario at the mouth of the Niagara River.

I had a country home in Lundy's Lane, Niagara Falls, close to the battleground. It was there my mother was born. I was born there also. My mother's forebear, Sir William Johnson, who died in 1773, owned the entire Mohawk Valley and he divided about 120,000 acres of land among his eleven children by Mollie Brant. His son, Sir John Johnson, stood firmly as a loyalist and influenced the Five Nations against the Colonials. After the war the provisional government confiscated the Mohawk Valley property and the children of Sir William Johnson migrated. My mother's grandmother married John Lefferty, a surgeon in the British army, and he bought property and a home in Lundy's Lane. I can remember well my grandmother telling me how, when a child, she swung on the gate waiting for her father to return from the battle-ground half a mile away. This was in 1814. The homestead plot, some 40 acres, I bought in 1883 and planted it entirely in grapes and peaches. Until a few years ago, I maintained it, but after a time sentiment died out and I parted with it, being unable to use it.

I asked some of my Chicago golfing friends to stop with me in Lundy's Lane and play in the tournament. They were Mr. and Mrs. George S. Willets, Mr. and Mrs. Hobart Chatfield-Taylor, James Deering, Edward S. Worthington, and G. Wilmerding. Among the other players in the tournament were E. S. Knapp, of the Westbrook Club; A. L. Livermore, Captain of the St. Andrews Club; A. W. Smith, the recognized leader of golf in Canada; J. P. Upham, of St. Andrews; R. B. Kerr and H. O. Tallmadge.

The first competition was an open handicap won by George Willets with a handicap of 18. I was second with a scratch score of 87, which established a record for the course. The last day there was a consolation handicap which was won by James Deering. In the ladies' championship Miss Gertie Gale, of the home club, proved the winner, and Mrs. Chatfield-Taylor was the runner-up.

The chief feature of the meeting was, of course, the International Championship decided by eighteen-hole match play elimination. A. W. Smith, of the Toronto Golf Club, won from Livermore by one up, and Smith and I reached the finals. Smith was a very good Scotch player and, I think, quite my equal in playing the game. We were all square at the seventeenth hole. The eighteenth hole was a dog-leg hole, an orchard which was out of bounds butted into the fairway. To carry the trees made the hole an easy four. Smith attempted a long and difficult lofting shot for a four, but he pulled his ball badly and it went over the cliff. Failing to get it back on the fairway he picked his ball up, giving me the hole and the match. I shall never forget my caddy, who was Edward S. Worthington, lying over my ball to see that no one tampered with it, as the feeling was running very high.

A regrettable but amusing incident occurred in our match. As the golf course was quite rough, with bogs full of long grass in many places, we decided to have a fore-caddy. At one of the holes, Smith drove and almost hit the fore-caddy and then I drove. I noticed the fore-caddy going at once to where my ball lay. Coming up, we were looking for Smith's ball. We asked the fore-caddy where it was. He denied having any knowledge of it whatever. We told him we saw he had to dodge for fear it would hit him, but he was adamant. Finding Smith's ball all right, we went on. Late in the evening, after due celebration of our victory of the day, one of my party confessed to me that he had given the boy five dollars to be sure and always stand by my ball.

I also won the long driving competition with a carry of 179 yards, one foot and six inches. The result of this meeting was that my house-guests and myself walked up to the table where the prizes were exhibited and carried off everything with the exception of the first prize for women golfers.

The second week in September the Chicago Golf Club held their fall tournament and there I won both the scratch medal and the handicap cup at scratch. I was then playing better than I had since 1884 at Hoylake and was in good form to enter the first annual amateur championship under the auspices of the U.S.G.A. to be held at Newport the first three days in October. There was no qualifying round in the first championship. It was decided by eighteen-hole matches with the final match thirty-six holes. There was only one entry who had played golf abroad, namely, L. B. Stoddard, who beat me on the St. Andrews' course by one up the year before. He was put out the third round by Winthrop Rutherford. All my matches I won easily, 7 and 6; 8 and 6; 5 and 3; 8 and 7; and, finally, the one from C. E. Sands, 12 and 11. This made me the first American champion. I entered this championship in excellent form and was well taken care of, stopping with Mr. and Mrs. Henry Clews. My rounds in the Newport tournament averaged 43 to 44 for each nine holes.

There was an unusual incident in the Newport championship. Richard Peters put a billiard cue in his golf bag and insisted on putting out with it. Of course, the cue was disbarred by the Executive Committee. This is the first decision the U.S.G.A. made on the "form and make of golf clubs," which some fifteen years later became a burning question with the Royal and Ancient when the Schenectady putter dispute arose and disrupted unification.

After the Newport championship, I visited Boston and played on the Country Club course. I am a little hazy about the game there, but I think I played with Willie Campbell, the professional. Campbell had been one of the finest players in Great Britain and had a most beautiful style. Undoubtedly I lost, but cannot recall the match. I can remember one incident only. I had a distinguished caddy. My friend, Robert Bacon, carried my clubs.

In the fall of 1895 H. J. Whigham, a late graduate from Oxford, came on a lecture tour in America, bringing a letter to Franklin McVeagh, who asked Wm. Farquhar to take him out and introduce him at the Chicago Golf Club, and this is where we first met. We played some golf together in the autumn and in 1896 very considerable golf. Hobart Chatfield-Taylor induced him to join the Onwentsia Club. So he played under their name. It was always "nip and tuck" between Whigham and myself on the golf course. In our matches we always broke about even.

The second amateur championship was held in 1896 at the Shinnecock Hills Golf Club in the middle of July. The method of holding the championship had been altered by the U.S.G.A. There was now a thirty-six hole qualifying round, the best sixteen scores to play-off eighteen-hole matches until the final thirty-six holes. President Havemeyer, Laurence Curtis, and myself stopped with General Barber, the president of the club. During my practice rounds before the tournament I was scoring very regularly slightly below 80. The day before the qualifying round, at luncheon or dinner, I had some seafood, which gave me ptomaine poisoning, and I was very limp starting my round next morning. I will never forget the agony of climbing the hill at the last hole in the first qualifying round. The best I could do was to turn in an 88. I immediately went to bed in the club house.

Doctor George A. Dixon was sent for, and attended me for ptomaine poisoning. Doctor Dixon advised me not to play, but remain in bed, to which I replied: "I must play this afternoon. It's not etiquette to default if one is alive." He still protesting said: "If you do you will be a wreck for the next four or five days."

THE FIRST AMERICAN CHAMPIONSHIP CUP, WON BY
CHARLES B. MACDONALD IN NEWPORT 1895.

I was paired to play with J. R. Chadwick. I sent him word I would default as I could not be on the tee at the appointed hour. However, Chadwick kindly insisted on waiting for me and was willing to play at any time it was possible for me to be on the tee. I made the supreme effort and went out with him about four o'clock. This time I made a 90, a total of 178 strokes, fifteen more than Whigham, who won the qualifying medal. This illness shattered my nerves and I was not able to pull myself together for several days. I met J. G. Thorp in the first round and lost by 3 and 2. Whigham's only hard match was with L. P. Bayard, Jr., who was a very promising young player, Whigham winning by two up. Thorp went into the finals to meet Whigham, losing by 8 and 7. After the tournament the following Sunday, Jim Whigham and I spent the day at the Meadowbrook Hunt Club and played an eighteen-hole match. In that match I beat Whigham, if I remember correctly, by 2 and 1 to play.

The Chicago Golf Club Invitation Tournament was held the second week in September, 1896. Whigham and I were in the finals. I lost by one hole, so Whigham won the scratch medal for that year. The following week in the invitation tournament of the Onwentsia Club for the Onwentsia Cup thirty-six-hole medal play I won, having the low score 185, against Tweedie's, Forgan's, and Whigham's tied score of 197. In the 1898 tournament I won the Chicago Cup at the Chicago Golf Club.

The Third Amateur Championship was held at the Chicago Golf Club September 14 to 16, 1897. In the thirty-six-hole qualifying round I won the cup for the low score, 174, Whigham 177, Fenn 178, Emmet 181, Douglas 182, Harriman 183. I first beat John Reid by one up. Whigham beat Stillman 4 and 3. Playing Stuart, of the Prestwick Golf Club, who was a very fine player, I won by finishing 2 up. Whigham beat Coats one up, then beat Douglas 6 and 5 in the semi-finals. Rossiter Betts won from me at the thirty-seventh hole in the semi-finals. Whigham won the championship by beating Betts 8 and 6.

In Chicago there was a tendency to inject college ethics into club matches. This I deplored as foreign to the game. Golf and companionship were synonymous terms with me outside of an individual competition or match, so while some clubs wanted their team matches fashioned after the Yale, Harvard, and Princeton football games, I was entirely opposed to it. Wanting to give evidence of my sincerity I arranged a team match between the Chicago Golf Club and the Country Club of Cleveland. Harvey Brown, Ben Crowell, Coburn Haskell, and Roy York were the moving spirits in Cleveland. I gathered together ten men in the club known particular for their comradeship and I asked Ben Crowell to do the same thing in Cleveland. We chartered a car and arrived at Cleveland at seven o'clock in the morning. We found at the last moment we had only nine men so I drafted Commander Baker, of the United States Navy, who had never swung a golf club and wired Ben Crowell to that effect asking him to match him. I never will forget how the Cleveland contingent met us in a body at the station at 7 a.m. and we all filed up in coaches funereally to the Union Club in Cleveland where we had a wonderful breakfast, after which we went out to the Country Club and played a preliminary nine holes before luncheon. The luncheon was of a character not calculated to improve a person's golf. I remember I was matched against their crack player, T. S. Beckwith. By some happy accident I managed to halve the match with him. The most amusing incident of the entire competition happened as follows:

At the fifth hole there was a brook running through a grove across the fairway. In this grove a table was set out with attractive libations, presided over by an excellent negro waiter. Beckwith and I followed Ben Crowell and Arthur Clark. As we putted out we saw them at the libation table. Discovering us, both got up and walked over the brook and went on. We could not understand it, as we hadn't seen them drive off. The explanation came afterwards. It seems that when they saw we were pressing them they sent their caddies up to the tee and asked them to drive their balls off and then they took their own balls wherever they were and went on, afterward calling the match halved. Now this is what I call real companionship, possibly not real golf, but great fun. It reminds me of the refrain of the old song, "It matters not whether we win or lose, but how we play the game."

The next amateur championship of the U.S.G.A. was held at the Morris County Golf Club the middle of September, 1898. This was Findlay Douglas's year. J. H. Choate, Jr., of Stockbridge, a member of the Harvard team, won the cup for the lowest score in the qualifying round with a brilliant 175. He was the first home-bred golfer to capture this honor. W. B. Smith, Robert Crowell, and I tied for second place with 178 strokes. Winning my matches from O. G. Hubbard, John Reid, and A. M. Coats, I met Walter B. Smith, champion cupholder of Yale, in the semi-finals, and was beaten by 2 and 1. Douglas, by defeating Smith 5 up and 3 to play, won his first amateur championship.

In this year was instituted an international match of ten players on a side between Canada and the United States. It was decided at Toronto by thirty-six holes match play. We won from the Canadians by 27 points against their 7. Whigham won by 3 points from A. W. Smith and I won by 2 points from George S. Lyon, who later was for several years the Canadian champion. The men who played and their scores are as follows:

H. J. Whigham	5	0	3	A. W. Smith	0	2	0
C. B. Macdonald	2	0	2	G. S. Lyon	0	0	0
A. M. Coats	4	0	0	W. A. H. Kerr	0	6	2
H. M. Harriman	0	0	0	J. Patison	1	2	3
G. D. Fowle	3	2	5	J. Gillespie	0	0	0
F. Keene	0	6	5	G. T. Brown	0	0	0
J. F. Curtis	2	3	5	V. Brown	0	0	0
O. G. Hubbard	0	6	0	J. Taylor	8	0	2
J. Lynch	1	2	3	F. C. Hood	0	0	0
D. K. Forgan	3	1	4	D. H. Blake	0	0	0
			27				7

The fifth amateur championship of the U.S.G.A. was held on July 3 to 8, 1899, at the Onwentsia Club, Lake Forest. In the qualifying round I had the lowest score, winning the cup for that event. The scores were: Macdonald 168, John Reid 170, Travis and Douglas each 173, Harriman 174, Hubbard 178, and Thorpe 179. In the final thirty-six holes Harriman won from Douglas by 3 and 2. In the morning round Harriman was 7 up. In the last eighteen holes Douglas struck his stride and played brilliant golf, while Harriman's golf was indifferent and it looked at one time as if Douglas would overtake him, but Douglas's overdriving the short sixteenth hole into the woods lost him the match and the championship.

The second international tournament, Canada versus United States, was held at the Morris County Golf Club on October 17, 1899. The U.S.G.A. team beat the Canadians by 93 to 1. *The Spirit of the Times*, in commenting upon this match, stated the following: "In beating Vere Brown, C. B. Macdonald completed a unique record, for Brown was the fifth amateur champion of Canada that the Western player has defeated.

TRAVIS, MACDONALD, DOUGLAS, AND HARRIMAN
AT ONWENTSIA IN 1899.

Five years ago Macdonald beat A. W. Smith at Niagara, and in succession he has beaten J. S. Gillespie, Archie Kerr, and G. S. Lyon." My score against Brown was 3 up and 4 up. A. W. Smith beat Harriman 1 up in the afternoon, Harriman having beaten him 3 up in the morning.

In this year Colonel George Harvey, our late ambassador to the Court of St. James, being interested in Harper Brothers, which firm published "American Golf" (edited by Van Tassel Sutphen), sponsored J. H. Taylor, the open champion of Great Britain, in his visit to the States. Taylor is one of the finest exponents of professional golf that I have known since the days of young Tom Morris. George Harvey's course was at Deal, N. J. My friend, Robert T. Lincoln, the son of our martyred President, invited me to spend a week-end with him there. There it was I first met the Honorable Morgan J. O'Brien, who to-day is one of my most beloved friends. We played a foursome, J. H. Taylor partnered by Judge O'Brien and Robert T. Lincoln partnered by myself. Coming to the tee of the last hole we were all even. Robert Lincoln had been driving badly from the tee. The last hole was a short one, I should say less than 300 yards. I cautioned my partner to take an iron, with which he was extremely good, and not his driver, with which he had been playing erratically. Nothing daunted, he exclaimed, "I shall take my driver," with a determination, so far as I could see, of reaching the green off the tee. Taking a mighty swipe at the ball, he sliced badly to the right on to a tennis court. Judge O'Brien, with his judicial, careful manner of doing everything, gave the ball a gentle tap down through the centre of the fairway, leaving Taylor an easy shot for the green. Robert Lincoln was most depressed. I found our ball directly under the net of the tennis court. It was a desperate situation, so desperate that I took every chance, and most fortunately with an iron drove our ball 150 yards from under the net within four or five yards of the hole—a very lucky shot. Halving the hole thereby, we halved the match. That did not pacify Robert Lincoln. He turned to his caddy and said: "Caddy, take these clubs and throw them into the lake, and if you don't do that I will make you a present of them." So home we went.

At dinner that night Robert Lincoln scarcely opened his head. Mrs. Lincoln and his daughter could not understand his apparent gloominess. There was a pipe organ in the house, and after dinner Robert Lincoln played the organ for nearly an hour. Suddenly he wheeled about on his stool and called out: "Charley, you don't have to go up to town tomorrow." "Why not?" I asked. "I want you to stay another day. I'll get Judge O'Brien and Taylor and we'll have that match over again." Such is the power of music to soothe the ruffled feelings of fine sportsmen. Unfortunately, I did have to go to town and this ended the episode.

In 1900 I left Chicago and took up my residence in New York. That same year I returned to witness the open championship meeting on October 4th and 5th at the Chicago Golf Club. Besides our own home players there were the two great players of Great Britain, Harry Vardon and J. H. Taylor. Vardon won the championship in 313 strokes. J. H. Taylor was second, with 315. There were a number of amateurs entered, and I had the lowest score among them, 354. Hugo R. Johnston was 355, W. H. Holabird 361; the others had somewhat higher scores. It is interesting to note that these scores of Vardon's and Taylor's averaged only slightly below 80 and did not equal young Tom Morris's scores at Prestwick when he won the championship belt in 1868, 1869, and 1870. Tom Morris averaged 76 and a fraction, while Vardon's score was not as low as that. This supports my contention that young Tom has never been excelled in golf.

I played considerable golf in 1901. The first tournament I entered was at Lakewood in April. After qualifying, Travis beat me 5 and 4, and in the finals Douglas beat Travis by 1 up. The Shinnecock Hills Golf Club held a tournament the first week in August. I reached the finals and then I was beaten by Robert C. Watson. In the middle of August I was invited by Edward S. Isham, who was president of the Ekwanok Country Club, Manchester, Vermont, to stop with him and play. Besides the president's cup, which was for the low score, Mr. Isham presented a golf medal for the winner of the tournament. *The Spirit of the Times* gives the following account of the tournament:

"C. B. Macdonald played in championship form. With 169 in the medal round he tied with Mortimer M. Singer, of Fox Hills, for low score and winning all his intervening matches, had to play the final against H. R. Sweeney (Albany Country Club) and won it by 4 up and 2 to play. His most brilliant work was that in the second round against C. B. Cleghorn (Ekwanok Country Club) whom he beat by 4 up and 3 to play going around in 78, which is very fine work on a course 6012 yards long. His hardest fight was with C. B. Cory (Oakly Country Club), the Bostonian being only beaten on the last green. His putt for a par four hanging on the rim of the cup."

In the play-off with Singer I won the cup for the qualifying round and the medal as the winner of the tournament.

In an invitation tournament at Tuxedo, September 18, 1901, I qualified, but was put out by Douglas by 4 and 3.

The U.S.G.A. Amateur Championship was held at Atlantic City, September 9th to 14th. Travis had the low score, 157, and my score was 174. I won my first match 1 up, but meeting Travis in the second round I was beaten by 5 and 3. The semi-finals were most interesting, as they were between Travis and Douglas. Travis played with the Haskell and Douglas with the gutta. Travis won from Douglas at the thirty-eighth hole. My opinion is that it was the Haskell ball that won this tournament from Douglas. The magazine *Golf,* in reporting the semi-finals, said it was "more a case of ball against ball than player against player. There was a general impression that it was mainly to the use of the rubber-cored ball that Travis owed his victory. Douglas was playing a superb long game, the champion (Travis) would have been out-driven if he had stuck to the gutta, and he was generally out-driven as it was. It was the fine action of the rubber-cored ball in the case of the irons which saved Travis. Practically the stroke that won the match at the thirty-eighth hole was with a mid-iron. It is doubtful if he could have reached the green on his second with the gutta." I share this view. In the finals Travis won from Walter Egan. This made him champion for the second time. It is interesting to note there were 124 players in the tournament, and twenty out of this number used the rubber-cored ball. I believe this was the last meeting in which players used the gutta.

I also played in the Metropolitan Golf Association's Amateur Championship held at the Apawamis Golf Club in May. I won my first three matches and then was beaten by Douglas, who eventually won the championship. I also played in the Metropolitan Golf Association's Championship in 1902 at Tuxedo Golf Club, and in 1904 at the Garden City Golf Club.

The years 1901 and 1902 proved memorable ones in my golfing life, for the events which occurred in the golfing world at that time awoke me from a lethargic sense of existence, and in 1902 I determined that my solace lay in giving up the struggle to become the game's master, but should rather become its servant. I concluded that was far better than upbraiding myself with the waste of time trying to compete in a supremacy my muscles would not respond to as the years slyly stole vigor from my limbs. This was my renunciation.

Secondly, the events of 1901 and 1902 fortunately gave me a happy thought, convincing me as they did that I could be of some service to the game of golf in America if by endeavor I could successfully implant into the player's mind and heart the character of the game as I knew it as a boy in Scotland, ennobling and endearing as it always has been to me. President Robertson, advocating Americanized golf, advocating changing the constitution of the U.S.G.A., speaking slightingly of tradition, determined me to fight for real golf with all its traditions and high sportsmanship. For twenty-five years I have faithfully worked to this end, and, I believe, with some degree of success.

Thirdly, inspired by the "best hole" controversy, which London *Golf Illustrated* put up to the leading amateurs and professionals of the United Kingdom, I conceived the idea of building the National Golf Links, constructing a course ideally built on classical grounds, trusting and hoping to be sufficiently successful so that it might lead to a better understanding of the merits of the game. Finally, in 1901 the Haskell ball became firmly established in the States and to a lesser degree in Scotland and England in 1902. These four influences reconciled me to be placed as a golfer in the "also-ran" class, and I was contented when after 1906 I was usually referred to in the reports of scratch golf events as among others "in the gallery."

After my renunciation there were only two victories that I can recall that gave me a slight thrill. In both instances I beat a better golfer. The first happened at Lakewood and I quote here from *Golf*:

"Travis did a very fine medal round, playing the eighteen holes in 77, which was seven strokes lower than his nearest competitors, Messrs. Macdonald and Douglas, who tied at 84. The match play was notable for a fine game between Messrs. Travis and Macdonald in the semi-finals, which resulted in the defeat of the former. They were all even at the eighteenth hole and had to play two extra holes to decide the match. Macdonald and Douglas were left in for the final, the younger player, Douglas, having a comparatively easy victory by 3 up and 2 to play. All through the tournament Douglas demonstrated conclusively that he has no equal in the amateur ranks at the long game. It has always been on the green that he has come to grief so badly. Various are the tools he has tried to improve his putting and at Lakewood he adopted what is known as the hammer-headed putter, a club somewhat recently invented, which has the handle somewhat towards the middle of the blade, as in a croquet mallet, instead of at the end. Incidentally, the Lakewood Tournament was not encouraging to the admirers of the rubber-cored balls, for Douglas was faithful to the gutty."

The other event was again beating Travis in the fall of 1903 for the Garden City Golf Club's championship medal. This I won by beating Travis one up. Eight months later Travis won the amateur championship of Great Britain at the Royal St. George's Golf Club, Sandwich, England.

The vision of a classical golf course for America having possessed me, I went abroad in 1902 to ponder over the possibility of its accomplishment. I concluded it was feasible if I could only find a property adapted to it and then find a backing to carry it out. I determined to try it, and for the next four or five years I worked to that end, but this is another story which will be told in a coming chapter. I returned home in the autumn in time to enter the Lakewood Fall Tournament.

The Oxford and Cambridge Golfing Society, on the invitation of the U.S.G.A., arrived in Boston August 10, 1903, captained by John L. Low. They were a noteworthy gathering, representing the flower of Great Britain's youth in learning and in sportsmanship, reflecting the best feeling of the Empire. Other than the captain, there were Norman F. Hunter and his brother, Mansfield Hunter, G. A. Bramston, H. G. B. Ellis, and others—eleven in all. Bramston was a remarkable driver and putter. Throughout all his matches he played with the gutta, whereas the others played with the rubber-cored ball, and yet Bramston was equal with any of them in driving and superior in putting. Norman Hunter was erratic, but remarkably brilliant at times. He made a 71 at the Chicago Golf Club, which was the record of the links, and stood so for many years. Seventy-one was five strokes better than either Vardon or Taylor made in the open championship in 1900. They played first at Myopia, then at the Essex County Golf Club, then at the Chicago Golf Club, Wheaton, Shinnecock Hills Golf Club, Garden City, and finally in the all-American team match at the Nassau County Golf Club. Out of all these matches they only lost one, and that was at the Nassau County Golf Club. Most of the matches were foursomes in the morning and singles in the afternoon. Only one defeat was scored against them throughout the tour, this being by a picked team of nine American golfers drawn from all parts of the country. The Americans won by a single point, which was largely due to the fact that G. A. Bramston and D. F. Ransom were unable to go for any long distance in their best form. Bramston, who was not a very strong man, was so exhausted he could not sustain his game. He was 5 up in the morning. I played in two of these matches, one at Garden City and the other at the Shinnecock Hills Golf Club. I scored one for the Americans at Garden City, when I won from Ellis in the singles. This visit of the university golfers won the admiration of the leading golfing enthusiasts in America. I do not believe there was one instance where there was any

CHARLES B. MACDONALD, JAMES BLACKWELL (TED'S BROTHER),
AND WILLIAM T. LINSKILL, TAKEN IN 1906 AT ST. ANDREWS.
A reunion of the golfing friends of 1873.

question as to rules. They played in the spirit of comradeship, having perfect faith that no player would take advantage of them, and they certainly had no thought of taking advantage of any one else. The fine spirit of their game enlightened the golfing community of America, developing an appreciation of its many-sided features, and did much to bring the various warring factions in the States together, inspiring them in some measure to live up to the traditional golf of Scotland.

One English player, J. A. T. Bramston, of the Oxford and Cambridge Golfing Society, expressing his opinion in an article referring to American golf as compared with English golf, wrote that the Americans played golf as they did almost everything else, as if it were a business. He said, probably, neither the Americans nor the English take the same joy out of golf that the Scotch do, for while the English play golf "with pleasure that is almost pain," the Americans play golf "with pain that is almost pleasure." Americans always wish to establish firmly who is the finest player, as America is interested in the tallest building, the richest man, the longest street, the fastest train, etc., etc. I think, probably, there was something in this in the past, but not so much now.

My golfing since 1905 onwards must be taken more or less as a joy ride, loving the game, loving the comradeship, and all the charming associations which attached me to it. I entered a number of tournaments and championships, knowing I had little or no chance of eventually winning, but seemed to take a fiendish delight in occasionally putting out a better man. But, all in all, my efforts proved insignificant.

In one respect, 1904 was a memorable year for American golf, for Walter J. Travis won the amateur championship of Great Britain, held at the Royal St. George's Golf Club, at Sandwich, England, working his way through a very strong field. He also entered the open championship, and although it was held over the same course on which he won the amateur championship, he failed to qualify among the first fifty-four. He failed by three strokes, his score was 171 against Vardon's low score of 149. The gruelling fight he had at Sandwich in the amateur championship evidently had tired him out. It is interesting to record that Travis first used the Schenectady putter at Sandwich, which was given to him the day before by a member of the Apawamis Club—I think by Simeon Ford.

I entered the amateur championship at Baltusrol in 1904, but did not qualify. I entered the amateur championship held at the Chicago Golf

Club in 1905, where I did qualify and carried the champion, H. C. Egan, in my match with him to the eighteenth hole, losing by 2 up. I played in the Olympic Cup Team meeting held at the Chicago Golf Club, and cut a very sorry figure for the New York team. I did not enter the championship at Englewood in 1906. *The Sun* remarked: "H. J. Whigham and Charles B. Macdonald were in the crowd." Looking back on this remark, it looks to me like a prophecy, because Jim Whigham and myself have been in the gallery ever since. I entered the championship held in Cleveland at the Euclid Golf Club. Five of us tied for thirty-second place. In playing off the tie I "plunked" my second into a bunker guarding the green and walked back into the gallery. I played in two of the Lesley Cup matches, one in 1905 and the other in 1906, and I also played in a great many small competitive tournaments too numerous to mention, all minor events and not worth recording.

In 1906 I spent several months abroad. The primary object of my visit was to study the great golfing holes of Great Britain to fulfil my dream of building a national golfing links for America. While in England I took a cottage at Hoylake and entered the amateur championship of Great Britain. Horace Hutchinson stopped with me, and from him I received much valuable advice as to the National layout. I won my first match, but meeting C. C. Lingen I was defeated by 4 and 3. Lingen was defeated in the finals by James Robb, who became the amateur champion for that year. I spent a week at St. Andrews, playing with H. S. C. Everhard, Alec Macfie, and other fine golfers. They and others at St. Andrews took a very friendly interest in my project of building the National, and I gathered many useful notes. While in St. Andrews my old friends of the early 70s were both in Scotland, W. T. Linskill and J. H. Blackwell. After a round of golf, recalling our boyhood days we went to a photographer's and had our picture taken, which is herewith shown.

Chapter VIII

Activities of U.S.G.A., 1902-1912
I Return to the U.S.G.A.

At the special meeting of the U.S.G.A., November 18, 1902, President Robertson was authorized to appoint a committee of three to revise as they thought necessary the rules of golf and interpret them and make a report at the next annual meeting. The president appointed Charles B. Macdonald, G. Herbert Windeler, and Walter J. Travis. At the next annual meeting, February 17, 1903, the committee on rules reported as follows:

"To the President of the United States Golf Association,
"Dear Sir:—

"In accordance with the Resolution passed at the last meeting of the U.S.G.A., we, the undersigned, beg to report that we have given the matter of the new rules our most earnest consideration and are unanimously of the opinion that it is inadvisable to make any changes solely in order that the game in this country may be played under exactly the same rules as are operative in Great Britain.
"Nevertheless, we cannot refrain from expressing the opinion that the following changes, at least, might advantageously have been made:—
"A. A penalty of one stroke for playing outside the limits of the teeing ground, in stroke competition, the stroke is to be replayed inside the

proper limits—instead of the present penalty of disqualification (Rule V for stroke competitions) which is far too stringent.

"B. *Where a player on a putting green is stymied by casual water, or his ball lies therein, he should be allowed to place it as near as possible on either side, but not nearer the hole, without penalty, instead of having to place it by hand behind the water without penalty, in accordance with Section 3 of Rule XIV.*

"*We think this rule should operate in both match and medal play—certainly in the latter. If, in match play, the object is to preserve the relative positions of the balls in the case of a stymie, then we may be permitted to suggest that the rule should be more explicit on this point. As it is, it merely says the ball may be placed 'behind' the water, which may be construed to mean anywhere so long as it is behind the water, and not necessarily to mean in a line with the spot it was lifted from.*

"C. *In the case of casual water through the green, Section 2 of Rule XIV, preferably should read, 'But if a ball lie or be lost (1) in casual water through the green, a ball may be dropped, without penalty, either directly behind, or, if that be impossible, as near as possible at the side of the casual water nearest to which it lies, but not nearer the hole.'*

"*The option permitted of dropping at the side might, under certain conceivable circumstances, be taken advantage of to allow the player to avoid negotiating a hazard directly in front of the casual water but practically non-existent at the side, particularly as no limitation of distance is specified 'at the side,' the only condition in this respect being that the ball must be dropped 'not nearer the hole.'*

"D. *Rule XXVIII might be amplified by the words 'as a result of the first stroke' after the words 'while the ball is moving.'*

"*In the interest of unanimity, however, it is not deemed expedient to make any alteration whatever in the above as embodied in The New Rules, as already stated. We have therefore merely confined ourselves to the work of interpreting the Rules as they have been laid down. We have deemed it advisable to retain the 'Etiquette of Golf' and also to make one or two additions thereto. We offer the suggestion, however, that in any future consideration of the Rules of Golf Committee of the Royal and Ancient Golf Club of St. Andrews, looking to any changes therein, your*

Association be permitted to make such recommendations as they may see fit, in the best interest of the game.

"*Respectfully submitted,
(S'd) Charles B. Macdonald, Chairman.
(") G. Herbert Windeler,
(") Walter J. Travis."*

After discussion the report was unanimously adopted. The same meeting passed a motion to extend a "dignified and courteous invitation" to the Oxford and Cambridge University team to visit America.

At the next annual meeting of the U.S.G.A., held in New York, February 11, 1904, a petition was read requesting "The constitution and by-laws of the Association be so amended as to eliminate the distinction between allied and associate members, and that thereafter there be only one class of membership." This petition was signed by fourteen western clubs, all of them in Chicago or vicinity (Chicago being the hot-bed of recalcitrants).

A resolution was adopted that the president appoint a committee of seven representing all sections of the country and both associate and allied clubs, which committee shall carefully consider the present status of associate and allied members, and shall at the coming annual meeting of the association present their report, including any amendments to the constitution recommended by the unanimous vote of the committee, the president of the association to act as *ex-officio chairman* of this committee.

At the annual meeting, held in February, 1905, I made my first battle to keep the game clean in America and prevent it being controlled by a mob. Following is an extract from my address to the meeting:

"*Mr. President and Gentlemen: In view of the importance of the question to be considered here tonight in reference to altering the constitution of the United States Golf Association, I would like to say a few words.*

"*After mature deliberation the organizers of the association determined that it was necessary to have a property and educational qualifica-*

tion to merit golfers having a voice in its affairs, thereby making the legislation of the selected committee intelligent.

"The question arose how such educational and property qualification should be determined, and it was unanimously decided that the method of discrimination by which we should decide should be the quality of the course over which the members played. It not only requires intelligence, but it also takes money to build a good golf course.

"Consequently we finally determined to have two classes of members. Any representative club where the links, accommodations and by-laws were such as to make it representative should be eligible as an associate member. All other clubs could ally themselves with the association by paying a small fee.

"Well I remember how bitterly it was contended that certain clubs should be rejected as allied members of the association, owing to their courses having been laid out near hotels or for the purpose of real estate speculation.

"The committee found it almost impossible to draw the line as to the allied clubs, until finally the executive committee at that time concluded so long as we kept the associate clubs free from all contamination of schemes, and professionalism, we might let in any organization called a 'club' for the purpose of playing golf, no matter what the motive behind the formation of the club was, even if it was a nine-hole course laid out in a cow pasture, as an allied member. The only point where the committee tried to draw the line rigidly was on the question of professionalism, and here the amateur rule applied.

"Now, Mr. President and Gentlemen, these allied clubs, regardless of their qualifications, ask to have an equal voice in the association affairs. Why these gentlemen should ask to have a voice in the association's affairs, when the way is open to them by having a properly constituted golf course and paying a small advanced fee for membership, I do not appreciate.

"Let us take the first paragraph of the petition of the fourteen clubs presented at the last annual meeting of this association in February 1904, I quote:

" 'We, the undersigned, on behalf of each of our respective clubs, hereby respectfully request that the constitution and by-laws of the association be so amended as to eliminate the distinction between associate and allied members, and that there be but one class of membership; that each of our respective clubs be permitted to have a voice in the affairs of the association, and that all clubs pay dues and be entitled to vote according to their membership and standing.'

"What does that paragraph mean? We must take it for granted that it means what it says—that the gentlemen who signed it, and those who were in favor of it, recommend that the delegates attending these annual meetings be increased from 31, the present number of associate clubs, to 288, the total number of associate and allied clubs at the present time, with one stroke of the pen. In such a move I see a menace to the life of the association and to the best interests of golf.

"Is it not clear to you that with any such change in the methods and management it would cease to be what it has always been, a deliberative and conservative body?

"And now I would like to ask right here, where does this demand for these radical changes come from? Do you know of any number of golfers with enterprise and public spirit enough to organize a club and to make application for allied membership in this association that has been refused without the very best of reasons?

"Does it occur to you that, with clubs organized in thirty-five states of the union, this organization has been growing and expanding about as satisfactorily as its best friends could wish?

"Do you know of any private club that has been on the whole more successfully or conservatively managed? Do you consider that it has been a failure, when the committee's report tonight shows you that we have a total of 388 clubs in the association and $10,000 in the treasury?

"Now consider the recommendations of the committee of seven. They do not afford any relief to the gentlemen who are in favor of these radical changes, and in my opinion will serve only as an entering wedge for future legislation on these lines; and I believe it is for the best interests of this association, its permanency and its future welfare, to vote down each and every recommendation that has been made referring to the make-up of the committee and the management of the association.

"My personal opinion is that should this not be done, we will soon be playing some other game besides golf in this country, and professionalism will certainly creep in, for the reason that the moment politics enters *into any sport, that moment there are other motives besides the good of the game which move man to action."*

The petition of the fourteen clubs was decisively turned down, and it was not until 1927, twenty-two years later, that the constitution was altered, making only one class of members.

Peace and harmony the coming two years reigned supreme in the councils of the U.S.G.A. Much time was spent in the annual meetings contending as to what should be the manner of conducting the amateur championships. First, if they should be all match play as in Great Britain; second, if there should be an eliminating qualifying round reducing the field to 16, 32, or 64. They tried three different methods in three consecutive years, namely, 1902, 1903, and 1904, but finally in 1905, went back to the old method of 36 hole qualifying round, 32 low scores to carry on at match play. There is little doubt in golfers' minds that match play is the true game of golf, and most people contend that 36 hole match is better than 18 hole match play. To my mind this is true, but it would take an unconscionable time to play-off a big field at 36 hole match play, and the game would become one of endurance. Consequently, a qualifying round had to be adopted unless they played off their fields by 18 holes of match play as they do in Great Britain. The objection to medal play is that competitors frequently have to play under vastly varying conditions; rain, sunshine, or wind may at various times during the day put certain competitors under a marked disadvantage, but when all is said and done, it seems as if the present way of playing the amateur championship cannot be improved upon.

It was not until the summer of 1907 that the storm broke in a wave of indignation, demanding a revision of the St. Andrews rules. I must say that I had much sympathy with this movement. The rules of golf as applied to St. Andrews worked out well enough with golfers born and bred there who intuitively absorbed the spirit and traditions of the game, although they might know really little about the letter of the law. Custom made the law and so St. Andrews has ever been a law unto itself in golf. When the myriad of golf clubs sprang up throughout the world, with every variety of golf course, some laid out in the Garden of the Gods in Colorado, others on the torrid lands about Aden, in Arabia, by the rocks, rills, ravines, and woods of Ardsley-on-the-Hudson, or in the cotton

CHICAGO, 1909.
The players are, reading from left to right: Messrs. Macdonald, Herbert Jacques, Fellowes Morgan, Joe Clark, Bob Watson, and George Watson.

fields or amidst the piny woods of Georgia, with their clay and sand putting greens, and elsewhere, the custom at St. Andrews did not satisfy, nor could it meet the emergencies arising from the new conditions. Then again, in America every person was comparatively a beginner in golf.

St. Andrews had to consent to a revision; otherwise America would certainly have written her own golfing laws.

Happily this was averted, for fortunately that fine sportsman and stalwart, Daniel Chauncey, was president of the association, and he handled the whole matter in a masterly manner. In July the association addressed a letter to Captain Burn, Chairman of the Royal and Ancient Rules of Golf Committee, stating in part that it wished to "present for the consideration of your honorable committee a matter which, in our opinion, is of the greatest importance. The U.S.G.A. has always been a loyal supporter and follower of the ancient game of golf as handed down by your ancestors to you, and, in turn, by you to us, and we earnestly hope that this support and allegiance will exist as long as the game is known and played. It is this strong sense of loyalty on the part of our executive committee that impels us to send you this communication, because in this country there is growing up a wide-spread feeling of dissatisfaction with the existing rules of the game which has already gone so far as to call into prominence a demand for an American code of rules without regard to those laid down by your honorable committee."

The letter went on asking the opinion of the Royal and Ancient as to what course of action the U.S.G.A. should take, saying it did not believe in any drastic or radical legislation. It stated the belief that the time had come for a revision of the rules and implied in the letter that they would like to confer in such a revision with the Royal and Ancient. To this letter Captain Burn replied in a most conciliatory tone, and at the Royal and Ancient's September meeting a revision of the rules was decided upon, when Horace Hutchinson introduced the resolution that the golf committee on rules be authorized to invite the U.S.G.A. to appoint a representative member of the Rules of Golf Committee. The resolution was adopted, and being a member of the Royal and Ancient, I was appointed on the committee and confirmed by the U.S.G.A., and through me the U.S.G.A. voiced their wishes.

Much serious work was done by the U.S.G.A. committee the coming year; working hard, they mulled over the rules from beginning to end, eventually printing their suggestions and sending the same to St. Andrews. There was nothing radical in any of the changes, but the rules were made clearer so a child should know what they meant. Of course, not all of the American suggestions were adopted, but in the main they were, and harmony prevailed for some time to come.

For the first time there was embodied in the rules of golf, a clause on form and make of golf-clubs, which read as follows:

"The Rules of Golf Committee intimates that it will not sanction any substantial departure from the traditional and accepted form and make of golf clubs which, in its opinion, consist of a plain shaft and a head which does not contain any mechanical contrivance, such as springs."

How any person reading the above clause could apply it to centre-shafted clubs which had been played with for fifty years, I fail to comprehend, and so did the American golfing community, and this standardization was the rock on which the U.S.G.A. and the Royal and Ancient were eventually going to break. It is much to be regretted that the two bodies, when they were in conference, did not make a strict definition at the time of what was a traditional golf cub. Why this rule was not made more definite it is now difficult to conceive.

Centre-shafted clubs had been known for more than fifty years and had been played with in various parts of the United Kingdom. Travis was presented with a Schenectady putter at Sandwich immediately before the amateur championship by an Apawamis member, Simeon Ford, I think, and Travis played with it through that championship which he won. It became generally played with in America. There never was an objection made to the Schenectady putter that I know of, but suddenly the Royal and Ancient was called upon to pass upon two inquiries in 1909 and 1910 as to the application of the clause.

It did not occur to me that the clause on make and form of golf clubs could be interpreted so as to make a croquet mallet and a Schenectady putter similar implements of the game and come under the same head; consequently I thought nothing of the ruling. The gravity of this situation I think justifies the following lengthy explanation. Here is the statement I made to the secretary of the U.S.G.A., January 5, 1911:

"Robert C. Watson, Esq., Secretary.
United States Golf Association,
51 East 44th St., N. Y. City.

"Dear Sir:

"Referring to your letter of December 1st in which you ask me to send you a 'history of the facts leading to the recent ruling of the Royal and Ancient Golf Club regarding form and make of golf club,' so that there may be no misconception at the meeting of the United States Golf Association to be held in Chicago in January next, where the question will arise of adopting the clause:

" 'The Rules of Golf Committee intimates that it will not sanction any substantial departure from the traditional and accepted form and make of golf clubs, which, in its opinion, consist of a plain shaft and a head which does not contain any mechanical contrivance, such as springs; it regards as illegal the use of such clubs as those of the mallet-headed type, or such clubs as have the neck so bent as to produce a similar effect,' "

together with the Note:

" 'The Rules of Golf Committee intimates that the following general considerations will guide it in interpreting this Rule:
" ' *"(1) The head of a golf club shall be so constructed that the length of the head from the back of the heel to the toe shall be greater than the breadth from the face to the back of the head.*
" ' *"(2) The shaft shall be fixed at the heel, or to a neck, socket or hose which terminates at the heel.*
" ' *"(3) The lower part of the shaft shall, if produced, meet the heel of the club, or (as for example in the case of the Park and Fairlie Clubs) a point opposite the heel, either to right or left, when the club is soled in the ordinary position for play,'* "

which I am now informed is part of the Rules. I beg to state that the history of the facts is as follows:

"Until the adoption of the last Code of the Rules of Golf in September 1908, in which the United States Golf Association took an active part, there has never been in the Rules of Golf any clause referring to the form and make of golf clubs. A player has always been left to play with any kind of club he desired, no matter how great a freak. The first restriction that I have any memory of was back in 1895, when a player in our National Championship attempted to putt with a billiard cue. The matter was referred to the U.S.G.A., and they ruled against the billiard cue. The next ruling came in 1908 when the new Code was adopted and included a clause on form and make of golf clubs, as follows:

" *'The Rules of Golf Committee intimates that it will not sanction any substantial departure from the traditional and accepted form and make of golf clubs, which, in its opinion, consist of a plain shaft and a head which does not contain any mechanical contrivance such as springs.'* "

"However, trouble did not commence brewing until 1909 when the Nga Motu Golf Club asked the question:

" '*With regard to form and make of golf club, is it permissible to use a small croquet mallet to putt with?*' "

The reply to this question, Decision No. 47, was as follows:

" 'A small croquet mallet is not a golf club and is inadmissible.' This caused much comment in golfing circles abroad, especially in England, and there was considerable pressure brought to bear on the Rules of Golf Committee to define more particularly the form and make of golf club which was permissible. On the 8th of April 1910, the Rules of Golf Committee sent to each member of the Committee the following communication:

" 'In reply to the Pickering Golf Club, No. 71, The Committee has undertaken to submit to the General Meeting the question of mallet-headed clubs. The following motion has been drafted by the Sub-Committee to meet the case. The motion requires to be given notice by the 17th court.'

Motion by the Rules of Golf Committee Referred to

" 'That the Rules of Golf Committee be empowered to add to the clause on form and make of golf clubs words which shall declare all clubs with heads of the mallet type to be a substantial departure from the traditional and accepted form and make of golf clubs.' "

" 'Under date of the 18th of April 1910, the Royal and Ancient Golf Club notified its members that at the meeting to be held on Tuesday, the 3rd of May 1910, they would under Note of Business No. 12, put the motion of the Rules of Golf Committee as above stated. The following is an excerpt from the Minute of the General Meeting held 4th of May 1910:

"Captain Burn submitted the following motion on behalf of the Rules of Golf Committee, viz.: That the Rules of Golf Committee be empowered to add to the clause on Form and Make of Golf Club words which shall declare that all clubs with heads of the mallet type are a 'substantial departure from the traditional and accepted form and make of golf clubs,' " and this was seconded by Mr. Edward Blackwell.

"Mr. J. B. Pease moved to exclude the Schenectady putter from the proposed embargo, and this was seconded by Mr. M. R. C. Kavanagh. On a division Mr. Pease's amendment found no support."

"You will note by this that the question of the Schenectady came up particularly, and was barred as a lawful golf club.

"Personally I am sorry to see that it was necessary to standardize the golf club, but to be consistent, if you don't allow a man to play with a billiard cue or a croquet mallet, a golf club should be defined. Knowing how many players in this country were wedded to the Schenectady, and disliking to see standardization enter into golf, I corresponded with the Rules of Golf Committee expressing my objections, stating the light in which I feared the American golfing world would view the situation. To these letters I received from both Captain Burn and the Rules of Golf Committee replies expressing regret that the Royal and Ancient Golf Club did not meet with the approval of the American golfers generally, and the Rules of Golf Committee state in their letter:

" 'The Committee deeply regrets that American golfers are not in sympathy with the views of the Royal and Ancient Golf Club on this subject.'

"Captain Burn expressed the same regret. It seems that in Scotland and England there is a strong feeling against centre-shafted clubs. At the Autumn meeting of the Royal and Ancient Golf Club held on the 27th of September, 1910, the following motion was adopted:

"That the first paragraph of Rule one (1) be altered so as to read as follows, viz.: 'That the game of golf is played by two sides, each playing its own ball, with clubs made in conformity with the directions laid down in the clause on Form and Make of Golf Clubs.'

"Those are the directions as adopted by the Rules of Golf Committee as I have stated in the forepart of this letter.

"Now, to come to the situation in this country. Since the formation of the United States Golf Association in 1894, the strongest sentiment has animated the Association to play the same game of golf as is played in the home of its birth, and not to have two different games. The varied and widespread interests of golf under conditions in this country only emphasize the importance of our adhering to a standard and avoiding the adoption or permission of anything that would seem to place one competitor at a disadvantage with his adversary. There has always been a By-Law of the United States Golf Association stating:

" 'Competitions shall be played in accordance with the Rules of Golf as adopted by the Royal and Ancient Golf Club of St. Andrews with the rulings and interpretations as adopted by the United States Golf Association.'

"In view of the present situation all of us in this country must decide whether we will play the game as it is played in Scotland or whether we shall break away and play the game according to various whims and fancies, which certainly must mean that there would be a different game of golf in nearly every section of the United States before long.

"There is another way out—one of compromise. The United States Golf Association can adopt the St. Andrews rules and interpret a mallet-headed type of club so as not to bar the Schenectady. I have a letter from Captain Burn, Chairman of the Rules Committee, as follows:

"The enclosed is a copy of the clause on Form and Make of Golf Clubs as added to by the Rules Committee under the mandate of the General Meeting of the Club in May. The wording is not what the Committee would have selected had it not been for the views expressed in your letter of June 10th to the Committee, who have endeavored by inserting the Note, to leave to the United States Golf Association an opportunity to interpret the clause on form and make of golf club to its own satisfaction without nominally refusing to adopt the Rules of Golf as passed by the R. & A. Club,"

"which, I think, clearly shows that in this instance, as in every instance to my knowledge, the Rules of Golf Committee have tried to do everything in their power to meet the wishes and desires of the United States Golf Association and American Golfers.

"Yours faithfully,
Charles B. Macdonald. July 1910"

However, as soon as I realized what was meant by "mallet-type" I sent the following letter to the Committee at St. Andrews, hoping to divert so sweeping an interpretation:

"Rules of Golf Committee,
Royal and Ancient Golf Club,
St. Andrews, Scotland.

"Dear Sir:

"I received the notice of the Spring Meeting of the Royal and Ancient Golf Club at St. Andrews, and particularly noted the motion by the Rules of Golf Committee, No. 12:—
" 'That the Rules of Golf Committee be empowered to add to the clause on form and make of golf clubs, words which will declare that all clubs with heads of the mallet type, are "a substantial departure from the traditional and accepted form and make of golf clubs." ' "

Later I have had notice that the motion was carried practically unanimously as stated.
"Upon receiving the notice of the Spring Meeting I naturally concluded that this motion was brought before the Royal and Ancient Golf Club on account of the comments regarding Decision No. 47 of the Nga Motu Golf Club, New Zealand, which asked the question: 'With regard to form and make of golf clubs, is it permissible to use a small croquet mallet to putt with?' The answer to this was: 'A croquet mallet is not a golf club and is inadmissible.'
"From the data and information at hand which I received as a member of the Committee, it never occurred to me that this motion covered anything but that of clubs which are generally known as 'mallets'. By that I mean the kind of a mallet a carpenter uses, a croquet mallet, etc., etc.,—that is, where there is a right-angled centered shaft with two heads to strike with. Further, the motion itself states that the mallet type are 'a substantial departure from the accepted form and make of golf clubs'. Now, Schenectady putters and wry-neck clubs have been an accepted form and make of golf club for over ten years. Much as golfers of the old school felt that they were an innovation, they were generally accepted. I believe fifty per cent of the golfers in the United States play with a Schenectady. As for the United States Golf Association, the carrying of this motion, conveying with it the interpretation made by Captain Burn by cable that Schenectady and wry-neck clubs were included under the 'mal-

let-headed type', caused a great sensation, even to a point of the parting of the ways. Had action immediately been taken by the United States Golf Association, I fear they would have repudiated their allegiance to the Royal and Ancient Golf Club. However, Section 10 of their by-laws reads as follows:

"'The competition shall be played in accordance with the Rules of Golf, as adopted by the Royal and Ancient Golf Club of St. Andrews, Scotland, with the rulings and interpretations as adopted by the United States Golf Association, together with such local rules as are in force and published on the Green over which the Competition takes place.'

"Being consulted, I pointed out to members of the Committee that when they met they could embody the new rule as passed by the Royal and Ancient Golf Club and interpret it so as not to bar the Schenectady putter, taking the definition of a mallet as universally understood and interpreted in this country. This will, I think, obviate a distinct breach.

"If Captain Burn is to be sustained in his interpretation of the mallet type of club it occurs to me that the Rules of Golf Committee must make a ruling as a body on that subject. For my part, I do not think that the Schenectady is a mallet. Neither is a wry-neck putter. Neither of these clubs really makes the slightest difference in a man's play. It is only his character of mind. There are a few people in this country stupid enough to think, owing to Travis's uncalled for and undignified criticism of his treatment at Sandwich, that this is in the line of retaliation. That can be dismissed without thought. Travis is now putting with a Braid aluminum, and, if anything, putting better than ever.

"The Royal and Ancient Golf Club maintains an allegiance throughout the world in golf that no other sport has anything like or comparable with it. A regime so honorably and effectively administered in a game that encircles the world, appealing to all classes, should to my mind be conserved with the utmost care and delicacy, and it would be a source of the deepest regret should that allegiance be jeopardized by so small and unnecessary a matter as the interpretation of the word 'mallet,' which means nothing to the game itself.

"*Believe me,*
Yours faithfully,
Charles B. Macdonald."

The above letter was sent to all the members of the St. Andrews Rules Committee, but it accomplished little, for the Royal and Ancient Golf Club at their September Meeting confirmed the earlier ruling of the Rules Committee with a slight alteration in the wording of the clause. and there were but few dissenting voices.

The barring of the Schenectady putter created a storm in America and the ruling was none too popular in England. While Johnny Ball, J. L. Low, Robert Maxwell, J. H. Taylor, Jack White, and others, supported the Royal and Ancient, Harold Hilton, Eric Hambro, S. H. Fry, Vardon, Herd, Duncan, A. Mitchell, and others criticized it.

The assertion that the barring of the Schenectady was in retaliation of Travis's win in 1904 will not stand the light of reason. It was not until 1909 that the mallet controversy arose, and then only because a club in New Zealand asked a question; and it was only in 1910 that the Schenectady was mentioned, and then only because it was impossible to define a mallet in such a way as not to include a Schenectady. Obviously the victory of Travis had nothing to do with the case.

In an editorial by Gardner Smith, Editor of London *Golf Illustrated*, he stated that the barring of the Schenectady was "uncalled for," and he also stated in an article that "a mallet is no more a menace to golf than a Jew's harp is to music."

My personal opinion has always been that the Royal and Ancient made a grievous error in barring the Schenectady. Once there was this parting of the ways, the recalcitrants in this country used it as a leverage in their endeavors to force the U.S.G.A. to finally break with St. Andrews.

The U.S.G.A. Committee were unanimous in their wish to have St. Andrews maintain her position as the universal law giver, but it was impossible to stem the tide. That this standardized club which had been played with for many years and was generally used in the United States, should be declared illegal without some good reason seemed illogical.

In 1908 Henry B. Wood placed on exhibition a collection of golfing curios in the North Manchester Golf Club. In this collection there was a centre-shafted mid-iron patented by Anderson, of Edinburgh, about 1870. In 1904 and 1905 a centre-shafted club, known as the simplex, was widely advertised, as well as Mills aluminum putters. When Andra Kirkcaldy was shown a simplex, he remarked: "I wad suner play with a tay spune."

Wood writes, July 3, 1908:

"The mid-iron appears to be multum in parvo and may still be used more or less successfully for driving, approaching, running up, and putting. The club enjoyed a certain amount of popularity in its day. In fact, one of the old-time professionals at North Prestwick frequently played with a club of this description 'against the field' (of clubs) and usually won. Sir Walter Dalrymple played with a centre-shafted club in 1892."

Captain Burn was aware of all this history of centre-shafted clubs, for he wrote me in December, 1910, as follows:

"The Schenectady is a putter which was first made by Mr. Hodge (a member of the Royal and Ancient and a medal winner) in the seventies and again made by Mr. A. F. Macfie some twenty years ago, but with wooden heads,"

and expresses himself in the same letter:

"My private opinion is that had the croquet mallet and the implements that were forged in iron to attain the same balance never been used, no objection would ever have come to us about the Schenectady. It fell under the ban because the only definition which would meet the case of all the others, included it. To be logical, we had no other course. We certainly could not have permitted mallets in view of the very strong feeling among the best British golfers against them."

The announcement of the U.S.G.A.'s annual meeting was always a red flag to the West, and they fairly boiled over with indignation. The announcement was fraught with much bitterness to the Westerners, and the press clans called the U.S.G.A. unpleasant names—alien, an aristocratic body, un-American, unrepresentative, (taxation without representation), crying for more rules, threatening secession. All this made copy for the scribes, but little impression on the intelligence of the best Western golfers, and none whatever upon the Eastern players except possibly a few lawyers who desired advertising.

At Chicago on January 14, 1911, occurred the momentous annual meeting of the U.S.G.A. It was in the enemy's camp that the decision of the vexed question, the Schenectady putter, was to be decided. The Royal and Ancient had added a note to the clause on the "Form and Make of Golf Clubs."

In accordance with the mandate of the General Meeting of the Club, held on 2nd May, the clause on Form and Make of Golf Clubs now reads as follows:

"The Rules of Golf Committee intimates that it will not sanction any substantial departure from the traditional and accepted form and make of golf clubs, which, in its opinion, consists of a plain shaft and a head which does not contain any mechanical contrivance, such as springs; it also regards as illegal the use of such clubs as those of the mallet-headed type, or such clubs as have the neck so bent as to produce a similar effect.

"Note.—The Rules of Golf Committee intimates that the following general considerations will guide it in interpreting this Rule:

"(1) The head of a Golf Club shall be so constructed that the length of the head from the back of the heel to the toe shall be greater than the breadth from the face to the back of the head.

"(2) The shaft shall be fixed to the heel, or to a neck, socket, or hose which terminates at the heel.

"(3) The lower part of the shaft shall, if produced, meet the heel of the club, or (as for example in the case of the Park and Fairlie Clubs) a point opposite the heel, either to right or left, when the club is soled in the ordinary position for play."

At this meeting I pleaded for unification and made the following address:

"Mr. President:

"The only reason I have come here tonight is to speak for unity in Golf. Breaking away from St. Andrews, while important in itself, is even less than the fact that should we do so in America, it would be but a short time when every association in this country would have its own rules, and then there would be chaos—no such thing as a common standard.

Scotland's Gift: Golf

"There would be the Western Golf Association with their inland courses; the Southern Golf Association with their sand greens; the Atlantic Golf Association with seaside courses; and the Pacific Golf Association with their dry and rainy season. We all know the American temperament, always influenced by the particular environment. Golfers seem to be quite of one mind in this country in believing that the Royal and Ancient Golf Club has been misguided in adopting the recent ruling on the Form and Make of Golf Clubs, particularly in the note interpreting the clause wherein the Schenectady putter is barred. It is not my purpose to enter into the wisdom of that action. I can see many reasons for and against it. Personally, I am inclined to think that such sweeping action, with more deliberation, might have been averted. However, the act, so far as they are concerned, is an accomplished one. At the meeting of May 3rd, the clause was adopted by a two-thirds majority of the Royal and Ancient Golf Club, and at the meeting in September, the clause was enlarged upon and carried practically unanimously.

"Golf is a world encircling game. One of its charms is that no matter where you go, whether America, Asia, Africa, Australia, Europe, or Scotland, the game is the same, with only such local rules as are necessary to govern the local situation. To my mind, for the United States Golf Association to break away from St. Andrews would be as great a calamity as schism from any great church. We have played the game of golf for some twenty years, and if I may be permitted to state this without offense, I do not think the golfers in this country are imbued with the highest spirit of the game as yet. In a nation of the magnitude of the United States, it is impossible that the highest significance of the game could be imbued in so short a time; much as the United States Golf Association has done to accomplish that end. I believe breaking away from St. Andrews would serve no useful purpose, nor lead to the desired goal.

"I can remember perfectly well when in 1897 I went from Chicago to New York to play in a small tournament, meeting one of the then crack golfers at Knowlwood. At the tee the first question asked was: 'Macdonald, are we going to play technicalities?' Nothing is more natural in adopting a game unfamiliar to one than that we should run to the rules, and from the rules to a dictionary, and there the never-ending debate starts.

"When I first played the game in 1872 at St. Andrews I doubt if any one ever read the rules. You put a ball on a tee and played for a hole. You were never allowed to touch that ball without a penalty. There was no difference between water and casual water, it was just water. Lift your ball and lose a stroke. It was the invasion of the English in the 80's into the Scotch game of golf that forced the rules to be changed, so now you can lift your ball without penalty under three different rules. In the olden days this would have been sacrilegious.

"Now, Gentlemen, what we want is to get together on the best and most feasible basis with St. Andrews and let the note of this meeting be 'Unification.' I believe it will be best accomplished if you will adopt their clause and then take the matter up with the Royal and Ancient Golf Club. You will never regret it. I am perfectly confident they will meet any suggestions made by the United States Golf Association with deliberate consideration and courtesy. Therefore, Gentlemen, if I am right why change anything? Section 10 of the U.S.G.A. covers it all. The U.S.G.A. to my knowledge has never retrograded, never done a foolish thing, and for my part I am perfectly willing to let the matter rest in their hands."

In the aftermath I received from Captain Burn a letter, dated the 20th of February, 1911, commenting upon the U.S.G.A.'s action in not adopting completely the decision of the Royal and Ancient. He writes:

"The Rules Committee has been blamed in the press on many occasions for not 'saying so sooner.' I have sympathy with these critics, but the Rules Committee is not a police force, and cannot act until some Club raises a point for decision. The real cause for regret is that the question of mallets was not raised previous to the date of the present Rules, when full details would have been discussed by St. Andrews and America before anything was drafted. The only local effect of barring the Schenectady putter was that W. E. Farlie putted most remarkably well with another club, and won the Medal."

He here gives vent to the point which I have already expressed—that the question should have been decided when the 1908 rules were drafted in convention.

St. Andrews states her position as follows:

Scotland's Gift: Golf

"For centuries we have played the game in Scotland called golf which our forebears have handed down to us, and we have been taught it along with our education and manners from childhood. It has pleased us that England, and later America, adopted the game with enthusiasm, and that to-day, in almost every part of the world there is a golf course.

"However, it is not our desire to dictate to any one. When asked, we are happy to tell those in other countries who are interested, what the rules of golf are as played here in St. Andrews."

To-day, here in America, no one worries about the Schenectady putter, no one worries about centre-shafted clubs, and it does appear that the ruling bodies in golf have been making a mountain out of a mole hill. Although the Western Golf Association repeatedly pounded at the doors of the U.S.G.A. Committee to change the rules in golf, and their constitution, thanks to able leadership in the U.S.G.A. through their presidents, golf to-day is played practically in the same way as it is in Scotland.

One reason why I am writing this so fully is that I do hope I shall carry the doctrine—unification—into every man's club and have them take it to heart. My readers probably will recall in my first chapter at the time I was leaving St. Andrews, I made the note, "Would that I could hand on unimpaired the great game as it was my good fortune to know it."

Chapter IX

Inception of Ideal Golf Course

Living in Chicago, I wrote an article, published in December, 1897, saying, in part:

"The ideal first-class golf links has yet to be selected and the course laid out in America. No course can be called first-class with less than eighteen holes. A sandy soil sufficiently rich to make turf is the best. Long Island is a natural links. A first-class course can only be made in time. It must develop. The proper distance between the holes, the shrewd placing of bunkers and other hazards, the perfecting of putting greens, all must be evolved by a process of growth and it requires study and patience."

Little did I dream I should live in New York and carry out this prophecy. Coming to New York in 1900 this idea assumed tangible form in 1901. Inspired by the controversy started in the London *Golf Illustrated* and known as the "Best Hole Discussion," the following question was put to the leading golfers in Great Britain:

"Which do you consider the most testing holes on any course in the United Kingdom, having special regard to these salient features: (1) length, (2) accidents of hazard? This question should be answered in respect to the three great classes of holes; namely, those which require one, two, and three shots each to reach the putting green."

Some twenty or thirty in all responded. Among the amateurs were John H. Low, Horace Hutchinson, Lester Balfour Melville, Herbert Fowler, Harold Hilton, S. Muir Ferguson. Among the more prominent

HORACE HUTCHINSON
From the drawing by Sargent.

professionals were Harry Vardon, J. H. Taylor, Braid, Park, Jr., Herd and Jack White.

In the statements and opinions expressed there was, of course, much variation, which is not surprising in selecting special holes from some hundreds of courses. For a one-shot hole the Eden, or Eleventh, St. Andrews, was mentioned most favorably. The Redan, or Fifteenth, at North Berwick was a good second. For a two-shot hole the Alps, or Seventeenth, at Prestwick was the greatest favorite.

There was much diversity of opinion regarding three-shot holes, and well there might be as they are the most difficult to make interesting. The Road Hole, or Seventeenth, at St. Andrews seemed the favorite. Many did not mention three-shotters, but the fourteenth at St. Andrews stood second.

I was intensely interested, and it was from this discussion I was urged to carry out the idea of building a classical golf course in America, one which would eventually compare favorably with the championship links abroad and serve as an incentive to the elevation of the game in America. I believe this was the first effort at establishing golfing architecture—at least there is no record I can find preceding it.

In 1902 I went abroad to gather material, ventilating my original idea with various old golfing friends and from many of them I received much encouragement. Finally I concluded my conception was feasible.

I labored four years to that end. In 1904 I again made a study of foreign courses, reflecting on the "whys" and "wherefores." In 1906, after four months in Europe, I completed my research studies and brought home with me surveyors' maps of the more famous holes; the Alps, Redan, Eden, and the Road Hole, also some twenty or thirty sketches, personally drawn, of holes embodying distinctive features, which in themselves seemed misplaced, but could be utilized to harmonize with a certain character of undulating ground and lay the foundation for an ideal hole.

While abroad in 1906 I started a newspaper controversy regarding an ideal golf links and the copying of the great holes in Great Britain. Looking back these past twenty years, it is most interesting to note the comments. For instance, one writer said that America was a country of new ideas and marvelled that we should entertain new ideas regarding the game of golf which they thought was perfect as exemplified by their own courses. It never seemed to occur to them that although they had eighteen holes in golf on each course, there never were more than four or five holes that a player who was devoted to the game in its best expression might regard as a shrine to which he might kneel. Now why should not one try to absorb the sanctified tradition of each particular hole by copying its best features in another climate where in time tradition might sanctify its existence. The flowers of transplanted plants in time shed a perfume comparable to that of their indigenous home.

Here is another comment:

"A strange land of composite people is nothing if not revolutionary in its breaking away from sanctified tradition.

"Of course, any person with refinement of feeling must know perfectly well that in constructing classical bunkers they could not carry with them the undefinable network or associations known as the 'genius of locality,' any more than they could take with them the memories of Holyrood or the Tower of London, assuming that they could transfer these monuments bodily and put them down in Chicago or Manhattan Island. Sentiment in tradition and history counts for much even in golf, and whether in the future the form of the ideal links is to loom across the golfing horizon from America, it is quite certain that playing upon them will neither induce the same amount of interest nor the same exhilaration of spirit as may still be gathered when treading one's crowded way to the first hole across the Swilcan."

All very true when it was written, but how about tomorrow? The birth of a nation creates a new soul. As we gaze back we will reverence the past, but it is to the future we must look.

There were many articles in the London *Times*, most of which called my dream "visionary," many of which referred to it humorously. I assured the humorous critics that they need not sit up nights fearing there was any danger of my carrying away the Maiden, Cardinal, Swilcan burn, or the "genius of locality."

In 1904 I drew up the following agreement, which in time was subscribed to by seventy friends interested in golf:

"Any golfer conversant with the golf courses abroad and the best we have in America, which are generally conceded to be Garden City, Myo-

pia, and the Chicago Golf Club, knows that in America as yet we have no first-class golf course comparable with the classic golf courses in Great Britain and Ireland.

"There is no reason why this should be so, and it is the object of this association to build such a course, making it as near national as possible, and further, with the object of promoting the best interests of the game of golf in the United States.

"With this end in view it is proposed to buy two hundred or more acres of ground on Long Island, where the soil is best suited for the purpose of laying out a golf course, and which, at the same time, is most accessible to the larger body of golfers in this country. The idea is to ask sixty men to subscribe $1000 each for this purpose. (Later increased to seventy.) The ground should cost between forty and fifty thousand dollars. The remainder of the money will be spent in building the course.

"The sixty subscribers—in order to designate them—we will call the Founders.

"While the $1000 subscription, it is trusted, will be made in a spirit of advancing the sport in this country and not as an investment, at the same time it is proposed to give something for the $1000.

"As to the building of the golf course, it is well known that certain holes on certain links abroad are famous as being the best, considering their various lengths. It is the object of this association to model each of the eighteen holes after the most famous holes abroad, so that each hole would be representative and classic in itself.

"Mr. Charles B. Macdonald will take charge of this matter and associate with himself two qualified golfers in America, making a committee of three capable of carrying out this general scheme. In the meantime you are asked to subscribe and leave the matter entirely in his hands."

The National Golf Links of America was incorporated the 11th day of March, 1908. The incorporators were:

James A. Stillman, New York	Charles B. Macdonald, New York
William D. Sloane, New York	John M. Bowers, New York
Washington B. Thomas, Boston	James Deering, Florida
Daniel Chauncey, New York	Robert T. Lincoln Washington
Henry M. Atkinson, Atlanta	

Charles Blair Macdonald

The seventy original founders of the National Golf Links of America:

H. M. Atkinson	Daniel Chauncey
Daniel Bacon	Stephen C. Clark
Robert Bacon	T. Jefferson Coolidge, Jr.
George W. Baxter	Charles Deering
Watson F. Blair	James Deering
John M. Bowers	Findlay S. Douglas
Urban H. Broughton	F. P. Dunne
E. M. Byers	Devereaux Emmet
Henry C. Frick	Howard Page
Elbert H. Gary	J. C. Parrish
Hugh J. Grant	W. A. Putnam
Joseph P. Grace	Roy A. Rainey
John P. Grier	Norman B. Ream
J. Horace Harding	Winthrop Rutherford
Herbert M. Harriman	Arthur Ryerson
J. Borden Harriman	Edward L. Ryerson
H. B. Hollins	S. L. Schoonmaker
Jarvis Hunt	Quincy A. Shaw
Leigh Hunt	W. D. Sloane
William V. Kelley	Charles D. Stickney
Robert Bage Kerr	James A. Stillman
Joseph P. Knapp	James L. Taylor
F. S. Layng	R. H. Thomas
J. Bowers Lee	Washington B. Thomas
Robert T. Lincoln	Robert M. Thompson
Charles B. Macdonald	T. Toscani
Clarence H. Mackay	H. McK. Twombly
Samuel McRoberts	William K. Vanderbilt
J. J. Manning	C. F. Watson
James Hobart Moore	Robert C. Watson
William H. Moore	H. J. Whigham
J. L. B. Mott	Harry Payne Whitney
DeLancey Nicoll	R. H. Williams
Alfred L. Norris	B. F. Yoakum
Morgan J. O'Brien	Richard N. Young

We determined to call the course the "National Golf Course of America." Therefore, I was extremely desirous of having founders from the different sections of the country. I succeeded in having the South represented, a large number of subscribers from Chicago, a number from Boston, but, of course, the majority from New York. Most of these subscribers gave the $1,000 in the same spirit that they would subscribe to a hospital. I can remember full well asking Robert T. Lincoln to subscribe, and with alacrity he signed for $1,000 and made this statement: "Of course I'll give you $1,000. The golf that you have taught me has saved me that much a year in doctors' bills, and I am perfectly confident it will add years to my life"—which it did.

As I stated in my agreement to associate with me two qualified golfers in America, making a committee of three to carry out this general scheme, I asked Jim Whigham and Walter Travis as associates. Eventually I dropped Travis, and Jim Whigham and myself, with the kindly interest taken by Joseph P. Knapp, James A. Stillman, Devereaux Emmet, Charles A. Sabin, and others, forged ahead with the construction from the surveyors' maps and the thirty or forty drawings which I had made myself abroad of different holes which I thought were worth while. These drawings were not necessarily copies of the particular hole from tee to the putting green, but in most instances were of the outstanding features which I thought made the hole interesting and which might be adapted to a hole of different length. Two or three of such features might be put in a hole which would make it more or less composite in its nature.

Feeling I should address myself to the founders and express as clearly as I could the goal which I was trying to attain, I penned the following article for *Outing* on my return home in 1906:

During the past few months I have listened to many heated and intelligent discussions as to the merits pro and con of the various great golfing greens, as well as to the merits of particular holes.

It seems to me the disputants were not so far apart as the heat of the argument might imply. The differences were more apparent than real. The basic principles they were together on. It was only when they came to 'Splitting hairs' that the fun began—a certain pot bunker or a certain hummock was alleged to be in the wrong place, or this or that hole was a few yards too short or too long, otherwise the hole was perfect. Further, it appeared to me that the combatants always pleaded for the hole they were most familiar with. Finally, I became convinced that any hole warranting warm or acrimonious discussion over a term of years must be 'worth while,' otherwise it would have been consigned to oblivion with less comment.

So far as I have been able to determine, no one course has the consensus of opinion as being preeminently the best. All agree generically on seaside courses. Undoubtedly St. Andrews has the greater number of advocates as being the Queen of Golf Links, though that greatest of golfers of the past decade, Vardon, decries St. Andrews as unfair; but then, Vardon has never been successful there.

Mr. J. L. Low somewhere says that most courses are too physical and mathematical, while only the best introduces as well the philosophical and strategical element. Doubtless there are many professionals who do not appreciate the subtle aspect of golf and do not care for that which is temperamental in the game.

After St. Andrews, I think that Prestwick ran for second place, the chief criticism of Prestwick being the lack of length and number of blind holes.

After the above two courses opinion seemed to be pretty evenly divided between North Berwick, Machrinhanish, Westward Ho, Deal, Hoylake, Littleston, Brancaster and Sandwich. Each had its champions. I found it very popular to abuse Sandwich—surely there is no better soil or turf or more attractive undulations on any green—the fundamentals of a good golf course. True, the holes are too short, especially the first nine, the putting greens much too large, with no variety of hazard calling for accurate approaching; and besides all this, the majority of the holes are blind—a sad fault. I was told that the Royal St. George's Greens Committee were at loggerheads; it is to be hoped that they will soon agree and make Sandwich what it has all the possibility of being, second to no course.

Hoylake was a disappointment to me. Twenty to thirty years ago I think the course, though shorter, was much better. The greens were infinitely finer, and the bent rushes and side hazards prevented playing 'all over the lot.' To-day the course is mediocre from the point of view of being a championship green—nothing exceptionally fine, nothing brilliant, nothing very bad; fair length of hole, fair putting greens, reasonable hazards, and the green generally appeared to me to be verging more toward an inland than a seaside course. I think Formby has the possibilities of becoming a better course.

In discussing and comparing the merits of the various courses, one is struck immediately with the futility of argument unless some basis of excellence is agreed upon, premises on which to anchor. In view of this, I have tried to enumerate all the essential features of a perfect golf course in accordance with the enlightened criticism of to-day, and to give each of these essential characteristics a value, the sum total of which would be 100, or perfection. Following is the result:

Essential Characteristics		Merit
1. Course		
(a) Nature of the soil	23	
(b) Perfection in undulation and hillocks	22	
	—	45
2. Putting Greens		
(a) Quality of turf	10	
(b) Nature of undulation well placed	5	
(c) Variety	3	
	—	18
3. Bunkers and other hazards		
(a) Nature, size and variety	4	
(b) Proper placing	9	
	—	13
4. Length of hole		
(a) Best length of holes	8	
(b) Variety and arrangement of length	5	
	—	13
5. Quality of turf of fair green		6
6. Width of fair green of the course 45 to 60 yards		3
7. Nature of teeing grounds and proximity to putting greens		2
		100

"(1) Studying the above qualities in detail, there can be but one opinion as to the nature of the soil the course should be built upon, as well as the contour of the surface of the fairway green—running as this should in more or less gentle undulations as at St. Andrews, breaking in hillocks in a few places, more or less bold in certain parts as at Sandwich and North Berwick.

The three courses above mentioned fulfill the ideal in this respect. There can be no really first class golf course without such material to work upon. Securing such a course is really more than half the battle, though I have credited this phase of the question with only 45 points, the other 5 points to make the half blending themselves with the other features. Having the material in hand to work upon, the completion of an ideal course becomes a matter of experience, gardening and mathematics. The courses in Great Britain abound in classic and notable holes, and one has only to study them and adopt their best and boldest features. Yet, in most of the best holes there is always some little room for improvement.

(2) Regarding quality, nothing induces more to the charm of the game than perfect putting greens. Some should be large, but the majority should be of moderate size, some flat, some hillocky, one or two at an angle; but the great majority should have natural undulations, some more and others less undulating. *It is absolutely essential that the turf should be very fine so the ball will run perfectly true.*

(3) When one comes to the quality of the bunkers and other hazards we pass into the realm of much dispute and argument. Primarily bunkers should be sand-bunkers purely, not composed of gravel, stones or dirt. Whether this or that bunker is well placed, has caused more intensely heated arguments outside of the realms of religion, than has ever been my lot to listen to. However, one may rest assured when a controversy between 'cracks' is hotly contested throughout years as to whether this or that hazard is fair or properly placed, that it is the kind of hazard you want and that it has real merit. When there is a unanimous opinion that such and such a hazard is perfect, one usually finds it commonplace. Fortunately, I know of no classic hole that has not its decriers.

The Eleventh hole at St. Andrews which four out of five golfers—a greater concensus of opinion than I have found regarding any other hole—concede to be if not the best, second to no short hole in existence, is berated vigorously by some able exponents of the game. At the last championship meeting at Hoylake, Mr. H. H. Hilton told me it would be a good hole if a cross bunker was put in and Strath closed. Heaven forbid!

To my mind, an ideal course should have at least six bold bunkers like the Alps at Prestwick, the Ninth at Brancaster, Sahara or Maiden (I only approve of the Maiden as to bunkering, not a hole) at Sandwich, and the Sixteenth at Littleton. Such bold bunkers should be at the end of a two-shot hole or a very long carry from the tee.

Further, I believe the course would be improved by opening the fair green to one side or the other, giving short or timid players an opportunity to play around the hazard if so desired, but, of course, properly penalized by loss of distance for so playing.

Other than these bold bunkers I should have no hazards stretching directly across the course.

Let the hazard be in the center or to either side or graduated in distance from the hole across the course. A very great number should be pot bunkers, particularly to the side; bunkers in which one can take a full shot with a wooden club are a travesty—some such bunkers as they have at Sunningdale.[1]

A burn or brook is a most excellent hazard and is utilized to the greatest advantage at Prestwick and Leven.

As to side hazards other than bunkers, no doubt bent rushes and whins are the best. Long grass entails too much searching for balls. However, in the case of long grass from the fair green proper to the full growth of the grass the cutting should be graduated, being shorter nearer the line to the hole.

(4) Treating length of hole, we must again, as in the placing of hazards, revert to the experience history has taught us in the past to guide us in our judgment. Speaking roughly, the generally accepted best total length of a golf course is somewhat over 6,000 yards. I have before me cards giving the distances to twenty of the first courses in the United Kingdom. The average distance of holes sum up as follows:

200 yards and under	2 7-10
300 " " "	2 7-10
400 " " "	8
499 " " "	4
500 " " "	6-10

---

[1] 1906

I don't believe one can go far wrong if he takes the above as an approximate guide.

True, nearly all these courses were laid out before the advent of the Haskell ball, adding as it does about twenty yards to wood and iron. Now, while the Haskell ball has marred many excellent holes, it has made just as many indifferent holes excellent. The majority of greens committees have failed to realize this and have expended their energy in devising means to lengthen every hole. It would be much better if they would shorten some, lengthen some and leave the others alone.

The large majority of old golfers—notably Mr. Low, Mr. Horace Hutchinson and the Messrs. Whigham (men all brought up in different schools)—declare that bad as too short a course may be, too long a course is infinitely worse. What a golfer most desires is variety in the one, two, and three shot holes, calling for accuracy in placing the ball, not alone in the approach, but from the tee. Let the first shot be played in relation to the second shot in accordance with the run of the ground and the wind. Holes so designed that the player can, if he so wish, take risks commensurate to the gravity of the situation—playing, as it were, 'to the score.'

Let the two-shot holes over 380 yards call for long driving less accurate than others where less length calls for greater accuracy. The more accurate the drive in placing the ball, the better the approach.

Without generalizing further on the question of the best holes, following are eighteen holes which occur to me as being about right. Of course, the reader must assume that the run of the ground and the hazards are correct:

1. 370 yards. Similar to the bottle hole at Sunningdale, placing deep graduated bunkers in place of ditch and bunker the green properly.
2. 340 yards. Composite first shot of the 14th or Perfection at North Berwick, with green and bunker guards like 15th Muirfield.
3. 320 yards. Similar to 3rd St. Andrews.
4. 187 yards. Resembling Redan, North Berwick.

5.	510 yards.	Suggested by 16th Littlestone, a dog-leg hole. Direct length, 410 yards. Latter route could be made excessively dangerous by calling for long and accurate play.[2]
6.	400 yards.	Similar to 4th Sandwich.
7.	130 yards.	Similar 5th Brancaster with tee raised so player can see where pin enters hole.
8.	420 yards.	Similar to 9th Leven.
9.	350 yards.	Similar to 9th Brancaster.
10.	240 yards.	Similar to 3rd, or Sahara, Sandwich, making carry full 175 yards direct, then a fair run to green with alternative to play around.
11.	450 yards.	Similar to 17th St. Andrews, making very bad hazard where the dike calls for out of bounds, and while keeping the green same size as at present would alter face of plateau approaching.
12.	160 yards.	Resembling the 11th St. Andrews.
13.	400 yards.	Similar to 3rd Prestwick.
14.	490 yards.	Like the 14th St. Andrews, making green larger and making run up less fluky.
15.	210 yards.	Suggested by the 12th Biarritz, making sharp hog back in middle of course. Stop 80 yards from hole bunkered to the right of green and good low ground to the left of plateau green.
16.	300 yards.	Suggested by 7th Leven, which is only 240 yards, with burn running at a bias, and green guarded by sharp hillocks.
17.	380 yards.	Resembling 17th, or Alps, Prestwick.
18.	360 yards.	Resembling 8th New St. Andrews, which is now too long for the bunkering.

A grand total of 6,017 yards.

---

[2] Exemplified by 4th at Lido.

These distances are measured from middle of teeing ground to middle of putting green. With proper teeing space and putting greens each hole could be lengthened at will from 20 to 30 *yards*.

I have notes of many holes equally as good as a number of the above, but this list will convey to the mind of the reader a fair idea of what I have gleaned during the last few months as constituting a perfect length of hole consistent with variety.

(5) For quality of turf throughout fair green there is no excuse for its not being good enough, so I have allowed only eight marks for it.

(6) The tendency to widen courses is much to be lamented. Forty-five to sixty yards is plenty wide enough. This is wider than St. Andrews used to be thirty years ago, when the course was better than it is now. I note that Mr. Deally, Mr. Lucas and Mr. Charles Hutchins in laying out the new course (that last word in golf) at Sandwich have kept a width of rather under than over fifty yards.

(7) I would give the proper width three marks, as well as two marks for good tees in close proximity to the putting green. Walking fifty to one hundred and fifty yards to the tee mars the course and delays the game. Between hole and teeing ground people sometimes forget and commence playing some other game.

Before closing I wish to enumerate a few defects which unavoidably exist on some really good courses:

'More than three blind holes are a defect and they should be at the end of a fine long shot only. Excessive climbing is a detriment. Mountain climbing is a sport in itself and has no place on a golf course. Trees in the course are a serious defect, and even when in close proximity prove a detriment. Out of bounds should be avoided if possible. Cops are an abomination. Glaring artificiality of any kind detracts from the fascination of the game.'

Chapter X

History of National Golf Links of America

Having the stage all set and definitely knowing what I wanted to accomplish, with maps, sketches, and descriptions of all the more famous holes in Great Britain, and having the $60,000—which later was increased to $70,000—subscribed, I continued my search to find the property on which it was possible to build the classic golf course.

Cape Cod was very alluring, but it was too remote to attract enough men to join the club to bring in sufficient income to preserve it.

The land between Amagansett and Montauk was ideal, and it would have been easy to purchase for a reasonable sum, but then, there was no soil on which grass would grow. It would be necessary to top dress at least sixty acres of land. To do that with six inches of top soil would cost over $5,000 an acre. This was prohibitive.

Shinnecock Hills also was very attractive, but I preferred not getting too close to the Shinnecock Hills Golf Course. The Shinnecock Hills property, some 2,000 acres, had been owned by a London syndicate and was sold at about $50 an acre to a Brooklyn company a few weeks before I determined that we should build a course there if we could secure the land. I offered the Shinnecock Hills and Peconic Bay Realty Company $200 per acre for some 120 acres near the canal connecting Shinnecock Bay with the Great Peconic Bay, but the owners refused it.

However, there happened to be some 450 acres of land on Sebonac Neck, having a mile frontage on Peconic Bay and lying between Cold Spring Harbor and Bull's Head Bay. This property was little known and had never been surveyed. Every one thought it more or less worthless. It abounded in bogs and swamps and was covered with an entanglement of bayberry, huckleberry, blackberry, and other bushes and was infested by insects. The only way one could get over the ground was on ponies. So Jim Whigham and myself spent two or three days riding over it, studying the contours of the ground. Finally we determined it was what we wanted, providing we could get it reasonably. It adjoined the Shinnecock Hills Golf Course. The company agreed to sell us 205 acres, and we were permitted to locate it as best to serve our purpose. Again we studied the contours earnestly; selecting those that would fit in naturally with the various classical holes I had in mind, after which we staked out the land we wanted.

We found an Alps; we found an ideal Redan; then we discovered a place where we could put the Eden hole which would not permit a topped ball to run up on the green. Then we found a wonderful waterhole, now the Cape. We had a little over a quarter of a mile frontage on Peconic Bay, and we skirted Bull's Head Bay for about a mile. The property was more or less remote, three miles from Southampton, where thoroughfares and railroads would never bother us—a much-desired situation.

When playing golf you want to be alone with Nature.

We obtained an option on the land in November, 1906, and took title to the property in the spring of 1907. Immediately we commenced development. In many places the land was impoverished. These had to be top dressed. Roughly speaking, I think we have probably put some 10,000 loads of good soil, including manure, on the property. We did not have enough money to consider building a club house at once, so our intention was to have the first hole close to the Shinnecock Inn, which had recently been built by the Realty Company. The old saying, "Ill blows the wind that profits nobody," is quite apropos here, for the Inn burned down in 1909, which drove us to building a club house.

We abandoned the site near the old Shinnecock Inn and determined to build it on the high ground overlooking Peconic Bay; so our first hole now is what was intended to be the tenth, and our eighteenth hole is what was intended to be the ninth. This proved most fortunate, for to-day we have an unexcelled site. There are no more beautiful golfing vistas in the world than those from the National Golf Club, unless it be those from the Mid-Ocean Club in Bermuda.

Scotland's Gift: Golf

APPROACHING THE FOURTH, REDAN, AT THE NATIONAL GOLF LINKS.

I first placed the golf holes which were almost unanimously considered the finest of their character in Great Britain. We found a setting for the Alps hole which the Whighams, fine golfers, who were brought up in Prestwick, considered to be superior to the original type. Strange as it may seem, we had but to look back and find a perfect Redan which was absolutely natural. Ben Sayers, well-known professional at North Berwick, told me he thought it superior to the original.

Although the Eden was voted to be the best one-shot hole in Great Britain, it had many detractors for the reason that a player could top his ball on the tee and it was possible to reach the green without fear of punishment. So while I built the green identically with that at St. Andrews, I had the tee shot played over some seventy-five yards of water and meadow-grass, which, of course, satisfied the justified criticism.

The Sahara of the Royal St. George's at Sandwich I found in our second hole. In one sense it is not a replica, but it is a mental picture of that fine hole, embodying the underlying principle—a golfer's reward is granted to him who can negotiate the carry he is capable of accomplishing. The real carry on the line of the hole is over an immense bunker calling for 210 to 220 yards. The ball then can run to the putting green. Less powerful players must satisfy themselves with placing their ball from the tee advantageously to reach the green in two. I am confident that it is a much better hole than the original Sahara.

The seventeenth or Road hole at St. Andrews was, of course, easy to duplicate, but I determined that the station-master's garden should not be out of bounds as that is a forced situation, so I made it a great expanse of bunkers and mounds, so that one who played into it would find difficulty in getting out with one shot capable of making any distance. When it came to building the green, the size and bunkering were identical duplications with two exceptions. The sharp juttings on the bank running up to the green I made less unfair by smoothing the juttings off somewhat. I had read many criticisms of this flukey approach and agreed with them. Where the road with its mud, ditches, and walk are on the right of the green at St. Andrews, I built a formidable sand-bunker running the entire length of the green with a five to six foot face; therefore giving a player, unfortunate enough to get in, an honest golfing shot.

All the other holes at the National are more or less composite, but some are absolutely original. The bunkering we have been doing in the past twenty years has been done after the most studious thought and painstaking care. I think a number of the holes of the composite type are among the best on the course. Horace Hutchinson thought so and wrote to that effect. By the way, when Horace Hutchinson visited America on Lord Brassey's yacht in 1910 he spent a week with me at Roslyn and three or four days at Southampton. Together we made a study of the National, and I received much valuable advice. I listened attentively to everything he suggested—where the bunkers should be placed, where undulations should be created on the putting greens, etc., etc. I know he impressed on me that the human mind could not devise undulations superior to those of nature, saying that if I wished to make undulations on the greens to take a number of pebbles in my hand and drop them on a miniature space representing a putting green on a small scale, releasing them, and as they dropped on the diagram, place the undulations according to their fall. This I did for some of the National greens where I had no copies of the original undulations which nature had made on the great greens of the world.

During the last twenty years I have studied the course from every angle and listened with an attentive ear; consequently very few of the holes have not been altered, although most of the changes have been slight. Only this last year I have distinctly altered the fourteenth and seventeenth, making these holes, which were both rather short drive and pitch holes, some thirty yards longer and bunkering them more closely. On many of the holes I have, at different times, built entirely new putting greens, lengthening some and shortening others. I am not confident the course is perfect and beyond criticism to-day.

The only thing that I do now is to endeavor to make the hazards as natural as possible. I try not to make the course any harder, but to make it more interesting, never forgetting that 80 per cent of the members of any golf-club cannot on an average drive more than 175 yards, so I always study to give them their way out, permitting them without having to negotiate unsurmountable difficulties to reach the green, by taking a course much as a yachtsman does against an adverse wind, by tacking. To my mind this is a fundamental in golf-course construction.

Any one in this world who attempts to accomplish anything worth while for the good of his fellow beings without emolument, no matter how pure his intention, is always sure to find numbers who will decry his efforts, while from others he finds praise. Detractors of any purpose, honestly conceived, usually spur one on to accomplishment, while praise gives him heart. I profited by this.

There were many who thought my idea a pipe dream, and even some of my best friends felt I was throwing away my time and my friends' affections and money by trying to build an ideal golf course. I remember well when in the autumn of 1907 with little or nothing to show but a weary waste of land with a beautiful sunset and stretches of water and meadow I was enthusiastically declaiming to a few friends whom I had asked for luncheon at the Shinnecock Hills Golf Club the possibility of the future classical course, an intimate friend of mine, Urban H. Broughton, left the table. Later he confided to John Grier that he feared, because of his affection for me and believing that I would be so much disappointed, he would drop a tear.

In 1909, when we first played over the course tentatively, from the regular tees, it was, roughly speaking, 6,100 yards in length, identical with the old course at St. Andrews in the seventies of the last century. To-day, from the middle of the championship tees to the middle of the putting green, the course is approximately 6,650 yards long. The extra 550 yards has been well distributed, the long holes are little, if any, longer, while the three drive and pitch holes are from twenty to thirty-five yards longer. The remaining 400 yards are distributed about equally on the nine two-shot holes. Nearly everybody plays from what we call the regular tees, which course is some 300 yards shorter than from the championship tees.

It was not until 1909 that some twenty friends played over the course in an improvised competition, our club house a tent. The course was very rough and, as I have said, distinctly shorter than it is now, but John M. Ward made a 74. The holes that are now the first holes he did in 2-2-4-2; the second hole was some thirty yards shorter than it is now, but the other three were practically the same as they are now from what we call the regular tees.

In playing off the match play rounds Fred Herreshoff beat Ward, but Herreshoff was finally beaten by W. T. Tuckerman who won the first prize of the first eight, while I won the first prize of the second eight by beating Robert Watson one up. From that time on we had enlightened criticism.

In 1910 Horace Hutchinson wrote an article in the *Metropolitan Magazine* in which he describes the National as it then was:

"This National Golf Course of which the world on both sides of the Atlantic has heard a good deal, and of which my friend, Mr. C. B. Macdonald, is the architect. What has been said and written of that course is that its intent was to make itself a replica and compendium of the best eighteen holes to be found in the whole world of golf. That heroic counsel and Titanic idea may have animated Mr. Macdonald at one time; and in point of fact, several of the best and most victorious holes on the other side are here seen reproduced with a faithfulness which is a testimony to the scientific care, the labor and the money which have been lavished on it. There is a Redan Hole, an Alps Hole, a Sahara—all really very reminiscent of the various holes that have these names at North Berwick, at Prestwick, and at Sandwich respectively. There are also two holes representing, respectively, the eleventh and the seventeenth at St. Andrews. But the larger number, and possibly the best in character, have been planned out of the designer's brain with such suggestions as his experience, gathered in Europe, and the natural trend of the ground he had to deal with, supplied to it.

"This is a course that is well up to date in all its ideas. It has its bunkers guarding the green all carefully placed, sometimes with a view to giving reward to accurate playing of the previous shots. It has its lengths very carefully considered; variety has been introduced; the diagonal principle in the placing of the bunkers through the green has been regarded;

FIRST GREEN AT THE NATIONAL GOLF LINKS.
Charles Sabin and Monk Jones of the Guaranty Trust, Jim Stillman of the National City, New York, and David Forgan of the First National, Chicago.

the 'blind' shots have been reduced to a minimum. The undulating ground has given opportunity for the introduction of much variety. At one moment we are playing up to a green set on a rather perilous terrace; at the next you are driving from a height down toward the plain and the shore of the beautiful Peconic Bay, and that 'Shelter Island' where, as some say, the English made their first landing. 'Terrace,' by the way, is a bad word in the context, because it suggests an idea of artificiality; and all this course is natural in its aspects, though there is a great deal of art concealing art about it. There will be no trouble at all about the turf. It is good already both on putting greens and through the green.

"My own opinion of the qualities of this course is so high that I am almost afraid of stating it too strongly. As I write, I am perhaps suffering from the reaction from a previous apprehension. Knowing what the enthusiasm of a creator is, and how apt it is to mislead him, I had a fear that Mr. Macdonald might be seeing a swan in what was really not a more glorious bird than a goose when he gave me descriptions of his course in the making. The practical trial, several rounds over the course and a critical examination of it, has removed that base suspicion altogether. It may be, as I say, that in the reaction my judgment may be tottering, but however unbalanced it may be, I can rely on it enough to be sure of this, that when the National Links is opened next year it will be far and away the best in the United States. It will be long, it will be of varied interest, its turf will be good, and its bunkering severe but fair. It has no weak point."

Here is an amusing story: After playing over the Shinnecock Hills Golf Course I asked Horace what he thought of it. He said:

"Very nice, extremely nice. It is very, very lady-like. It is so lady-like that when I make a bad shot I haven't the heart to give vent to my feelings, fearing I would offend some one and break the third commandment."

The well-known golf professional of North Berwick, Ben Sayers, visited America in 1913, and in the course of an article in the July *Golf Monthly*, lavished high praise on the National Golf Links. Sayers expressed himself as follows:

"Having travelled and visited all the leading courses on this side of the Atlantic, I have stood and sworn by old St. Andrews as the finest course I have played on, but after visiting the National course, the links designed by Mr. Macdonald, with touches of St. Andrews, Prestwick, and other British links in it, the famous course of the premier club, in my estimation, must take second place. What a place! and you have got to play the right stuff to get around in a respectable score. The National, in my opinion, is the course in the world. That sounds high praise for a professional who has lived practically all his life at North Berwick and played so often at St. Andrews, but I am saying just what I think."

After our third invitation tournament at the National another tribute was paid the course in the London *Times*, of September 30, 1913, from which I would like to quote, in part. I think it was written by my friend Bernard Darwin:

"Every one has heard of the National Golf Links of America, that monument more enduring than brass which Mr. C. B. Macdonald has raised for himself by Shinnecock Hills on Long Island, so that it is with a perceptible thrill that one catches one's first glimpse of the course—

something of the same feeling with which for the first time one peered out of the railway carriage window between Leuchars and St. Andrews in search of the corner of the Dyke and the station-master's garden. It was my good fortune to arrive at the course at just the hour when the spirit of romance most palpably brooded over it. The sun was setting, and as we drove along the sandy road, winding between the huckleberry bushes that were to punish our errors on the morrow, the green strips of fairway dotted here and there with bunker, the water of Bull's Head Bay, and the low woods that crown the further shore were one and all bathed in a fading and fantastic light. Towards Peconic Bay the horizon was one broad strip of flame, while between the sky and the water a jet black line marked the hills on the further side of the bay. The twilight dies quickly in America, and when but a short time afterward we left the club house the moon was shining brightly and the night breeze with the blessed scent of the sea in it was so fresh and so cold and so different from New York that we were glad to snuggle under rugs and great coats....How good a course it is I hardly dare trust myself to say on a short acquaintance; there is too much to learn about it and the temptation to frantic enthusiasm is so great, but this much I can say: Those who think that it is the greatest golf course in the world may be right or wrong, but are certainly not to be accused of any intemperateness of judgment."*

Then follows a description of some of the holes which I will omit, and he concludes:

"Finally there is, I think, the finest eighteenth hole in all the world. The tee shot must first be hit straight and long between a vast bunker on the left which whispers 'slice' in the player's ear, and a wilderness on the right which induces a hurried hook. Then if the drive has been far and sure there is a grand slashing second to be hit over a big cross-bunker, and at last comes a little running shot at once pretty and terrifying on to a green of subtle undulations backed by a sheer drop into unspeakable perdition.

"If there is one feature of the course that strikes one more than another it is the constant strain to which the player is subjected; he is perpetually on the rack, always having to play for the flag itself, never able to say to himself that 'anywhere over the bunker will do.' He is mercilessly *harried all the way round from the first tee to the eighteenth hole, and there is not one single hole that can be called dull; one may not think equally highly of all of them, but there are assuredly no obvious lapses from a high level such as the eighth and ninth and tenth holes at St. Andrews. Now and then one fancies that an easygoing hole would be rather a relief, just as in an unworthy moment one might like the curtain down and a band playing the 'Mikado' between the acts of, let us say, Mr. Galsworthy—but this is an unmanly weakness. The National Links is a truly great course; even as I write I feel my allegiance to Westward Ho! to Hoylake, to St. Andrews tottering to its fall."*

Now as far as the National is concerned, I think this can reasonably finish my story, although I would like to copy the best part of an article, again by Bernard Darwin, which was printed in the *Times*, August 26, 1922:

"It was generous and thoughtful of the American authorities to make the National Links the battlefield for the International match (Walker Cup), for it is a course which makes British players feel at home. There are fresh sea breezes, fast kittle putting greens, and an occasional opportunity of playing a running shot, in place of the continual high-stopping pitch. In the British sense, it is not a seaside course, though the view over Peconic Bay is one of the loveliest in the world. The turf is inland turf and the rough is inland rough; nevertheless, Mr. C. B. Macdonald, who as an architect is a true artist, has been able to breathe into his creation something of the real seaside feeling. He is a passionate admirer of St. Andrews, and, though the ground here is far hillier than in Fife, yet there is a likeness.

"I do not mean merely that there are two scrupulously exact copies of the eleventh and seventeenth holes, because each course has atmosphere of its own which cannot be explained. There is likeness in the fact that on both courses one is always learning; let the wind shift but a point or two, and every shot is changed. Men who have known the course for years will argue learnedly, with no hope of agreeing, on the best line to a particular hole, with a particular wind. There is absolutely nothing cut and dried about it, and the more you play the course the more humble you become, and the more you realize how little you know about it. Apart from the

two St. Andrews holes there are others modelled on those at home; the Sahara from Sandwich, the Alps from Prestwick, the Redan from North Berwick, all are good, but better still I think are holes which owe nothing to any model but spring from the unfettered genius of Mr. Macdonald.

"As compared with most American courses, the ground is hard and fast, and the ball has to be soothed toward the hole rather than bludgeoned. It is not extraordinarily long, but it is long enough for any one; and save for one or two home-coming holes with the wind behind, there is no respite and breathing space. Every shot keeps you on tenterhooks and must be played properly, and the number of bunkers it is possible to get into without losing your self-respect as regards your driving is amazing. In fact, it is a course that is always fascinating you, and always fighting against you."

Incidentally at the National we have an excellent yachting basin with all accessories presided over by H. H. Rogers and J. A. Stillman. We also have fine bathing houses immediately below the eighteenth green. Dan Pomeroy presides there.

The National has now fulfilled its mission, having caused the reconstruction of all the best known golf courses existing in the first decade of this century in the United States, and, further, has caused the study of golf architecture resulting in the building of numerous meritorious courses of great interest throughout the country.

After the National had gained more or less of an international reputation I was approached and importuned by various friends in different parts of the country to make plans for constructing golf courses for them, they little dreaming the time and work this involved. This labor did not pall on me at first, for I was flattered and happy to feel I was attaining the much dreamed of objective, architecturally constructing classical golfing holes that would challenge criticism throughout the golfing world. I was contented with the knowledge that I was really contributing something to American Golf and at the same time had the pleasing sense of gratifying my more intimate friends.

In accomplishing this end it was imperative I secure an associate, one well-educated with wide engineering capabilities, including surveying, companionable, with a fine sense of humor, but above all, earnest and ideally honorable. Such a man I found in Seth J. Raynor.

Charles Blair Macdonald

THE SIXTH, TWELFTH, AND THIRTEENTH GREENS AT
THE NATIONAL GOLF LINKS.

Seth Raynor was born in Suffolk County in 1878 and settled in Southampton as a surveyor. Employing him to survey our Sebonac Neck property, I was so much impressed with his dependability and seriousness I had him make a contour map and later gave him my surveyor's maps which I had brought from Scotland and England, telling him that I wanted those holes laid out faithfully to those maps. For three to four years he worked by my side. He scarcely knew a golf ball from a tennis ball when we first met, and although he never became much of an expert in playing golf, yet the facility with which he absorbed the feeling which animates old and enthusiastic golfers to the manner born was truly amazing, eventually qualifying him to discriminate between a really fine hole and an indifferent one.

When it came to accurate surveying, contours, plastic relief models of the land, draining, piping water in quantity over the entire course, wells and pumps, and in many instances clearing land of forests, eradicating the stones, finally resulting in preparing the course for seeding, he had no peer.

In 1911 Roger Winthrop, Frank Crocker, Clarence Mackay, and other Locust Valley friends wished me to build the Piping Rock Golf Club course. I found they wanted a hunt club as well as a golf-club. Some of the leading promoters thought golf ephemeral and hunting eternal. Consequently, I had my troubles. The first nine holes were sacrificed to a racetrack and polo fields. However, all's well that ends well, for to-day golf is King and Queen in Locust Valley. I employed Raynor on this job. It would have been difficult to accomplish it without him. There was too much work and too much interference.

Next, James A. Stillman's friends lassoed me to lay out a golf course in Sleepy Hollow. It seemed an almost impossible task to carry through; because we were told that William Rockefeller would not consent to any trees being cut down or removed. I was almost inclined to throw up the task. However, at a meeting which Cooper Hewitt, Jim Whigham, and I had with William Rockefeller and Frank Vanderlip, I was given a free hand. This was a hard task for Raynor in appalling summer heat.

Next came the St. Louis Country Club, then the White Sulphur Springs layout, and then finally came the colossal task of the Lido at Long Beach. By this time Raynor had become a post-graduate in golfing architecture, and since 1917 built or reconstructed some 100 to 150 courses, which I have never seen. The Mid-Ocean Club, the Yale Golf Club, the Links Golf Course, the Gibson Island Golf Course, the Deepdale, and the Creek Club were the only ones I gave any personal attention to after 1917.

Raynor built courses in every climate, in Puerto Rico, the Sandwich Islands, three or four in Florida, two in California, and numberless elsewhere. He was a world builder. I had given him all my plans and only occasionally was I asked for advice.

Sad to relate he died ere his prime at Palm Beach in 1925 while building a course there for Paris Singer. Raynor was a great loss to the community, but a still greater loss to me. I admired him from every point of view.

Chapter XI

Tournaments, 1911-1924

Nineteen hundred eleven was a memorable year in golf not only for Harold Hilton but for the National Golf Links of America, for in that year the National Club house was formally opened and the first invitation tournament was held.

Harold Hilton's visit to this country was after he had won the amateur championship in Great Britain, and his trip to America was known in the English journals as "Childe Harold's Pilgrimage." He not only won the amateur championship of the United States, but he won the first tournament at the National.

Harold Hilton's golfing record is phenomenal. In 1892 he won the British open championship—the first time any amateur ever won it—and in 1897 he won it again. He did not win the amateur championship until 1900, then he won it in 1901. Having a come-back in 1911 he not only won the amateur championship of Great Britain but also in the United States. He was runner up in the British amateur championship in 1891 and 1892. Later he won the amateur championship of Great Britain in 1913.

At that time no amateur in the world of golf had any such record with the exception, possibly, of Johnny Ball, of whom it is recorded he won eight amateur championships though only one open championship.

The U.S.G.A. championship was held at Apawamis. I entered this championship, tying with nine others for four places with an 84. I failed to make good. That year my handicap was 6, which I think was more or less complimentary.

HAROLD HILTON DRIVING
Old Tom Morris and Johnny Low in the background.

Hilton won the qualifying round in 150 strokes. In the match play rounds he won more or less easily all his matches and finally played Fred Herreshoff for the title. Hilton was 4 up and 7 to play. Fred Herreshoff played brilliantly and Hilton sloppily these seven holes, so that they were all even at the thirty-sixth hole and had to play an extra hole. Following the match as I remember it, both made good drives, Hilton playing the odd well to the right of the green hit the bank and the ball bounced at an angle on to the green. He always had a way of pulling his ball, and I was under the impression that he did it purposely, but he took great chances. There was much contention as to what happened to the ball. Many thought it a lucky stroke and hit a rock from which it bounded to the green. Findlay Douglas says he was sitting just above where the ball struck and thought it a well conceived shot, but Hilton himself admits it was not a good stroke.

Hilton got his 4 and Herreshoff his 5, and Hilton thereby became champion, the only Britisher who has ever won the U.S.G.A. championship.

The National extended an invitation to all the leading golf players, and some of them came over in Ledyard Blair's yacht, the *Diana*. The scores were as follows:

> Fred Herreshoff, Ekwanok..................84
> A. Seckel, Riverside......................85
> H. H. Hilton, Royal Liverpool.............86
> W. C. Fownes, Jr., Oakmont................87
> Max Behr, Morris County...................89
> E. P. Rogers, Shinnecock..................89
> Charles Evans, Jr., Edgewater.............90
> W. R. Simons, Garden City.................91
> J. P. Knapp, Garden City..................92
> T. M. Robertson, Shinnecock...............93
> J. M. Ward, Garden City...................93
> F. S. Wheeler, Apawamis...................93
> W. Watson, Baltusrol......................94
> C. B. Macdonald, National.................96
> Philip Carter, Nassau.....................97

You will note that Fred Herreshoff won the Gold Medal for the lowest score. Hilton beat me in the second round, 4 up and 3 to go—easy mark—and he won from Fownes 1 up in nineteen holes. The finals were between Hilton and "Chick" Evans, whom Hilton beat by 3 up and 2 to go. Howard Whitney won the cup for the second sixteen and Grant B. Schley won the cup for the third sixteen.

Writing to the New York *Herald* at this time, Hilton said in September, 1911:

"Now, to the National course and its affairs. I had heard so many varied accounts of these links, situated at Shinnecock, that I really did not know what to believe. Some had told me that I would find it merely an

unfinished dream of 'Charlie' Macdonald's. Others were loud in its praise and its possibilities. The only thing they seemed agreed upon was the fact that I would still find it in a very rough condition, and so much was this opinion impressed upon me that I anticipated nothing but iron play through the green. Well, I played there for four days and only once did I get a lie on the fairway of the course, to which I did not think it advisable to take a wooden club if such a club was required. I must acknowledge to a little habit of taking wooden clubs to shots to which other players prefer to use an iron club. But admitting this little penchant of mine, I seldom came across a lie in which an average good wooden club player could not take wood if he wanted to.

"The course itself and the condition it was in were both a revelation to me. I am not going to say that it is laid out as perfectly as a course can be laid out, as no course can arrive at a state of perfect golf architecture until it has been in existence for many years. Failings in their planning only become evident after much play upon them. But I have seldom come across a course in which greater ingenuity has been exhibited in arranging the holes so that one has an infinite variety of strokes to play.

"There are no two holes on the course in any way alike, and to Charles Blair Macdonald and to those who have helped him in the great task I take off my hat. You have accomplished wonders and will eventually have a course in every way worthy of American golf, and just about as good as any in the world.

"In particular I am in love with the short holes. Looking at the fourth I can see in my mind's eyes the 'Redan' at North Berwick. This hole at Shinnecock is every bit as good a hole as the famous 'one-shotter' in Scotland. Again the thirteenth is a splendid reproduction of the 'Eden' hole at St. Andrews, and one can have nothing but praise for the short sixth hole. It is an ideal hole for its length, and in the matter of short holes the National course is in a happier position than any course I can call to mind.

"The seventh is a very colorable imitation of the 'Road' hole at St. Andrews. Being familiar with the seventeenth hole on the classic green, this hole with the bunker right in front of the green does not strike me as in any way strange, but I can quite understand any one not familiar with the idiosyncrasies of the classic green feeling a little dumbfounded by the devilish ingenuity of the man who planned the hole. But I can assure *them they will become quite accustomed to it in time. It is a great course, this National course, and should do much for American golf."*

Hilton never liked the Road hole at St. Andrews (the seventh at the National), and for very good reason. The road bunker in this green nearly lost him the amateur championship of Great Britain in 1913. Referring to it he wrote once: "No hole in existence has been the innocent cause of so many opprobrious epithets and language of so lurid hue as the Road hole."

At the time of the 1913 championships in the fifth round he played the American champion of Massachusetts, Heinrich Schmidt, about whom no one had heard much. They were all square going to the seventeenth hole. Hilton made two fine shots close to the green, while Schmidt had played his fourth within six feet of the hole. Hilton took his putter and struck one of the juttings of the green and went off at right angles to the line into the Road bunker. It looked to the gallery as if it were all up with Hilton. However, he made a remarkable recovery from a very dangerous bunker. Placing his ball within 6 ½ feet of the hole he missed and took a 6. Schmidt missed his six-foot putt, getting a 6; so the hole was halved, and the eighteenth hole was halved in four. Hilton won the nineteenth hole.

Another time it put out an aspirant for the British championship when it looked as if he had the match he was playing with Johnny Ball in his pocket going to the seventeenth at St. Andrews. Douglas was 1 up and 2 to play, and it looked a sure thing for him as Ball drove out of bounds and his second was in a road. Ball took 5 to reach the green. Douglas played what he thought a safe third, but trickled into the Road bunker which has ruined so many good players. He took 3 to get out and 8 for the hole, and lost to Johnny Ball who made a 7. Ball won the eighteenth hole and the match.

In 1912 Harold Hilton again visited America to defend his title as amateur golf champion of the United States. The championship was held at the Chicago Golf Club early in September. The heat was intense and Hilton and Norman Hunter, the only two entries from Great Britain, insisted on playing in their coats, which must have been a trying ordeal. However, Hilton tied with "Chick" Evans in the qualifying round, 152 strokes, Hilton eventually winning out in the play-off. I entered but did

JERRY TRAVERS

not qualify as my score was 171. Neither did Fred Herreshoff who was the runner-up with Hilton at Apawamis, Fred having tied for the last qualifying place with Heinrich Schmidt and Howard Perrin. Schmidt was successful. Hilton meeting C. C. Waldo, Jr., of Brookline, in the first round was defeated by 2 and 1. Jerry Travers finally won the championship in the finals against "Chick" Evans by 7 and 6.

After this Hilton's golf seemed to suffer a relapse. 1912 proved an off year, but in 1913 he came back and won the British amateur. My own opinion is that as a man grows older one who has been accustomed to a certain amount of stimulants cannot brace himself on tea, and Harold Hilton, although he took much rest simply consumed quantities of strong tea which in time only weakened his nerves.

After the championship he stopped with me at Southampton, entering the second invitation tournament of the National Golf Links in 1912. His initial rounds were up to their general excellence but he gradually faded away, and when in the semi-finals he met E. M. Barnes he seemed to be all in. He was so nervous he could not play. At the eighteenth hole Barnes and Hilton were all even, Hilton taking three putts where he was almost expected to go down in one putt. He told me after the match was over he was so nervous he could hardly hold his club. At the nineteenth hole Barnes took a par 4 and Hilton a 5. Without reflecting upon Barnes' play one must wonder how a player of Hilton's superiority could fall from his usual round of 74 into the eighties, but such was the case. Fred Herreshoff won easily from Barnes in the finals.

In 1912 Hilton again gave his impression of the National, stating:

"Some day the show course in America will undoubtedly be the National course at Shinnecock. It is a true seaside course and has advantage over a great many of our seaside courses in the matter of contour in the surface of the ground. There are several very commendable imitations of well-known holes on British courses—the Sahara, or third hole, at Sandwich; the Alps, or seventeenth, at Prestwick; the Redan at North Berwick; the Road hole, or seventeenth, at St. Andrews, and the Eden, or eleventh, at St. Andrews.

"The copies of the Redan and Eden holes are both excellent and readily recognized at first sight from the tee. In the case of others the copy is probably not quite so good; still in every case it is very recognizable. But

every hole in this National course has character. In the West the courses are not up to the class of those of the East, but I must acknowledge that I found the latter much better than I ever expected."

At the Garden City U.S.G.A. championship in September, 1913, Schmidt tied for the last place, and in the play-off failed to qualify. It is rather interesting to note that both Travers and Schmidt tied with twelve others for the last place. Schmidt failing, Travers qualifying, he finally won the championship.

I remember well playing with Travers in a four-ball match a day or two before the qualifying rounds at Garden City. He was playing badly. I have always noted that in championships the man who is at the top of his game and makes the low score in the initial rounds rarely sustains his game, whereas the man who has the quality and power keeps coming on until finally he gets to the top of his game in the finals. Of course, Bobby Jones is a law unto himself, and no rule holds good for him.

The open championship of the U.S.G.A. was held in September, 1913, at the Country Club, Brookline. I went to Boston to witness the play, having backed Vardon and Ray against the field. Ouimet's victory was the most dramatic event I have ever known in sports and it was the biggest win to my mind in golfing history. His finish was amazing.

The day he tied Vardon and Ray was rainy and the course was more or less swampy. He took 45 to go out and 5 to the short tenth hole, which was a par 3. Eventually he was made to realize he had to do the last six holes in 22 to tie. At the thirteenth hole he holed out a mashie shot for a birdie 3; at the fourteenth he had a par 5; at the fifteenth he was very fortunate in getting a 4, as his second was to the right of the green, but he pitched to the edge of the hole and had nothing to do but tap his ball for a par 4; at the short sixteenth he made a 3, but it was by a narrow margin, as he over-played the hole.

The seventeenth was the sensation of this round. It is a dog-leg hole and it took two fine shots to reach the green. The ball was some twelve yards or more to the right of the hole and Ouimet was left, a very ticklish putt. As it was downhill he might easily run two or more yards beyond, but in hitting the ball truly he found the bottom of the cup for a birdie 3. Now all he had to do to tie was to make the last hole in par 4. He made a fine drive. His second was over the racetrack hitting the bank, it bounced

Scotland's Gift: Golf

FRANCIS OUIMET ABOUT TO HOLE FINAL PUTT IN PLAY-OFF WITH VARDON AND RAY IN THE OPEN CHAMPIONSHIP, SEPTEMBER 20, 1913, AT THE COUNTRY CLUB, BROOKLINE, MASS.
Final scores: Ouimet, 72; Vardon, 77; Ray, 78.

up just short of the putting green. Again he had a downhill putt, and he putted short within four feet of the hole, sinking the ball to the bottom of the cup with great confidence. Doing so he tied with the two greatest professionals of their time, Ray and Vardon, in 304 strokes.

I felt as if it were all over, and with the wager I had I might as well hurry to New York and spend, ten and fifteen to one being wagered against Ouimet winning. But the miraculous occurred! Ouimet played faultless golf the following day, making a 72, five strokes better than Vardon and six strokes better than Ray. Golf truly is unfathomable!

After 1912 I cannot recall any tournament of international interest until 1922.

An incident I think worth recording occurred at the invitation tournament of the National Golf Links in 1914. The Metropolitan and New Jersey champion, Oswald Kirkby, was badly off his game and only qualified in the third sixteen. He was quite perturbed over this and approached Bob Watson, President of the U.S.G.A., and myself as to whether he should not withdraw as he did not think it would be right for him to play, with the certainty that he would walk away with the cup for the third sixteen. I told him to play, asking if it had occurred to him that there might be some other first-class golfer in that sixteen who had been badly off his game. So Kirkby was drawn to play at eight o'clock in the morning with McKim Hollins, who was very erratic but a very fine player at times. When I came down in the morning about seven o'clock I found Hollins sleeping on the lounge in evening clothes. He had been out with Percy Pyne and a number of their mutual friends and had only been there about an hour and a half. Awaking him I told him he had to be on the tee at eight o'clock He asked me what he should do, as he had no golfing clothes. They were at Reggie Brook's, with whom he was stopping, and it was too late to go for them. So Percy Pyne, who was stopping with me, lent him some golfing clothes, but golfing shoes there were none he could hold on his feet. Forthwith we sent the chauffeur to Reggie Brook's for his shoes, and in the meantime he was on the tee in his pumps, starting out with Kirkby in them. He played the first five holes in his pumps or stocking feet as best suited him, and he was 4 up at the fourth hole when his shoes arrived. Putting them on, he held his lead throughout the match and beat Kirkby 4 and 3.

Although the United States did not enter the World War until 1917, it would seem that during the entire war period no one had any heart to play games, and there were, of course, no tournaments in America in 1917 and 1918.

Things simmered along as far as the National was concerned until the Walker International Cup was played for in 1922. George Herbert Walker was President of the U.S.G.A. in 1920, and retiring from the presidency he presented the Walker Cup to be played for between teams of Great Britain and the United States. Back in 1913 I had offered to put up an international cup to be played for by teams of four from any country. The Royal and Ancient authorities discussed the idea for some time, but the war intervening, all else was forgotten. However, Bert Walker presented a very handsome cup through the U.S.G.A. and asked the Royal and Ancient to make the terms.

It was decided that the first match should be played over the National Golf Links of America and afterward over the links at St. Andrews. Bert Walker's idea was that all the matches should be played over the National in this country and over St. Andrews in Great Britain, but the U.S.G.A.

THE TEAMS OF THE WALKER TOURNAMENT HELD AT
THE NATIONAL GOLF LINKS, 1922.

pointed out that Southampton was not a centrally located place and was not easily reached, and concluded, quite rightfully, that the matches should be played where a larger number of the people in the United States could witness them. They have been held besides at the National at Garden City in 1924 and this coming year, 1928, if held, will be over the Chicago Golf Course at Chicago.

Much as the golf enthusiasts on the other side desired to compete for the Walker Cup, they were up against a problem that the United States players were not, namely, that of expense. The U.S.G.A. could father the players in America, but there was no such association in England. It had to be done by private subscription or by the members of the team bearing their own expenses. It certainly looked at one time as if the competition would fall to the ground, but the U.S.G.A. leading the way, contrary to the finest spirit of the game, started to make a spectacle of golf competitions and demand entrance money. This could be accomplished only where the competition was played over private courses. At St. Andrews it would be difficult because the course is controlled jointly by the town and the Royal and Ancient. However, the golfers of Great Britain followed the example of the U.S.G.A. and began charging admission fees to witness golf competitions at Muirfield in 1926, so that to-day they are receiving sufficient funds to finance their teams visiting this country.

I cannot say I like the idea of charging admissions, but it seems there is no other way out. The team matches are certainly a great incentive to the game and they have to be financed. Who should do it but the golfing public?

It is interesting to note that after the play at the National the Walker teams entered the amateur championship at the Country Club, Brookline. The British entry was not particularly successful. The day before the finals Roger Wethered and Cyril Tolley, being out of the running, came to me and asked if they might go to my place and spend a couple of days golfing at the National, which they considered the finest golfing they had ever experienced. Needless to say, I opened my house to them, although I could not be present.

The International Matches for the Walker Cup were played at St. Andrews in 1923, resulting in a win for the American team.

In September, 1924, the International Matches for the Walker Cup, it was decided, should be played at Garden City on the 12th and 13th of September. The British team were as follows: Cyril J. H. Tolley, Eustace A. Storey, William L. Hope, Dennis Kyle, T. A. Torrance, Major Charles O. Hezlet, A. C. Bristowe, William A. Murray, Hon. Michael Scott, and Robert Scott, Jr. Henry Gullen, Secretary of the Royal and Ancient, accompanied them as manager of the team.

The invitation tournament at the National was the week preceding the Garden City matches, and the National Golf Links of America invited them to be the guests of the club and enter our invitation tournament. Tolley won the medal in the qualifying round with a 76, but he was beaten in the second round by T. A. Torrance. The Britons made a clean sweep of the tournament, the four semi-finalists being W. L. Hope, who defeated Major C. O. Hezlet 2 and 1, and W. A. Murray, who defeated T. A. Torrance 2 and 1. In the finals Murray beat Hope by one hole.

ROBERT GARDNER AND CYRIL TOLLEY.

BOBBY JONES AND ROGER WETHERED.

Chapter XII

Lido—Yale—Bermuda

I first went to Bermuda in 1904, and every few years afterward visited the island again. There was no golf course in Bermuda worthy of the name in 1919. When the eighteenth amendment was passed and the nineteenth hole abolished, I discussed with a number of friends the propriety of having a golf course in Bermuda. Many friends thought it was better to go to Cuba, but I felt confident Bermuda was the place.

It happened about this time that the Furness, Withy Steamship Company thought of taking an interest in developing Bermuda, and among other things they desired a golf course. Sir Frederick Lewis diverted one of his steamships, the *Moorish Prince*, for a trip to Bermuda, and invited me to join them. I also asked the noted architect, Charles D. Wetmore, at Sir Frederick's request, to join us, as they thought they would be interested in a hotel. Charlie Wetmore was aware of the desire of a number of our friends to buy some property in Bermuda and build a golf course. He and I travelled over the island, and finally we found desirable property at Tucker's Town, of which we were told 500 acres could be bought for $550,000 to $200,000. Tucker's Town district was inhabited mostly by the native negroes, being half way between St. George's and Hamilton. I at once asked Mr. S. S. Spurling, the leading administrator on the islands, to obtain options on the property. This he did on a large acreage. My intention was to have ten or fifteen men put up $15,000 or $20,000 apiece in New York, and then in time develop our purchase for a playground. The beauty of the situation is unsurpassed. Charlie Wetmore said he could not go along with me in the purchase unless Sir Frederick

THE FIFTH HOLE AT THE MID-OCEAN CLUB, BERMUDA.

Lewis would consent to his doing so, as he was there in a professional capacity. Sir Frederick proposed that his partner, H. C. Blackiston, Charlie, and myself should buy the property together. The purchase of the property was left in Furness, Withy's hands owing to their having agents in Bermuda.

Practically every one of the owners who had given an option on his property went back on his contract, and I think everybody in Bermuda connected with the situation lay awake nights wondering how they could get something out of it. Well, it's a long story, but finally it resulted in securing about 600 acres of property at a cost of about $600,000.

It was only through the valleys that there was any soil. In these valleys the principal products were onions, potatoes, and Easter lilies. Below the six inches of soil there was coral rock. We pursued the same course making contour and relief maps as we had in building other courses. One great difficulty was to build the course so that there wouldn't be too much mountain climbing. After much study we succeeded in doing this, so that to-day there is only one real climb, that is, at the sixteenth hole.

After the completion of the course on December 15, 1921, I wrote Mr. Blackiston the following letter, every word of which I can indorse to-day:

"*My Dear Mr. Blackiston:*

"*Regarding the Mid-Ocean Golf Club in Bermuda, the following is a description which I think will convey to the Golfers of the United States and Canada, the beauty, charm and excellence of the Links.*

"*To begin with, I doubt if there is an eighteen-hole golf course which will equal, certainly not surpass from a Golfer's standpoint, this Links in any semi-tropical clime, nor at any health resort in any zone, for the following reasons:*

"*The contours of the property are unsurpassed, delightful valleys, one hundred to two hundred yards in width, winding through coral hills from twenty to seventy-five feet in height, along the line of play; well wooded with cedars, oleanders, bougainvilleas and hibiscus, lending the most fascinating color scheme to the whole. The contours are inviting to the golf architect to construct unique and scientific putting greens consistent with the length of hole demanded.*

"*I may say here that championship golf courses are to-day architecturally built, not laid out. Previous to 1905, let us say, no one thought of building putting greens. All the great courses in the United Kingdom were natural—St. Andrew's, Prestwick, Machrehanish, Carnoustie, North Berwick, Sandwich, Hoylake and Westward-Ho. To-day, both here and abroad, putting greens are usually constructed after some well-known green which has stood the test of criticism for ages.*

"*Mr. Seth J. Raynor, who for some fourteen years has been associated with me and who has all my models and data, was employed to carry out the practical work in Bermuda. Mr. Raynor is most competent, having now to his credit some hundred and fifty golf links.*

"*Bermuda was a hard task, owing to climatic conditions, but all difficulties have been surmounted, and I am confident the course will stand in golfing circles as an achievement in a semi-tropical climate as great as the National Golf Links of America has been in the temperate zone.*

"*The glory of this semi-tropical course, other than its picturesque side, will be the lies in the fairway. St. Augustine grass, so abominable in the temperate zone, grows so thick and luxuriantly that every ball sits up in the fairway and it is doubtful if a brassy will be necessary in one's bag. The bunkering has been cunningly devised so that a golfer, to make a low*

THE EIGHTEENTH HOLE FROM THE TEE AT THE MID-OCEAN CLUB.
The club house is on the left.

score is compelled to drive to a particular spot, thereby placing his ball for an advantageous second. All badly topped shots will be well punished.

"Again I can assure my golfing friends, a more fascinating, more picturesque course than the Mid-Ocean, when completed, will not be found in a pilgrimage around the world. There is nothing commonplace about it.

"This reminds me of the remark made by a Prestwick habitue about the Prestwick Links:

" 'A bull nickit, hog backit, bandy leggit chiel, and shapes fine for a gowfer.'

"I remain,
Yours faithfully,
(Signed) Charles B. Macdonald."

There is no semi-tropical golf course of merit as easy of access from New York that I am aware of. One leaving New York about noon Saturday in the dead of winter can by ten o'clock Monday morning be teeing off in a summer climate and play over this wonderful, unexcelled golf course.

There is a somewhat amusing story connected with the first ball which I ever drove at the Mid-Ocean Club. The Governor General Sir James Wilcox and Admiral Packenham wished to look over the Mid-

Holes	NAME	Championship	Regular	Par	Short	Self	Partner	Opp.	Opp.	Holes	NAME	Championship	Regular	Par	Short	Self	Partner	Opp.	Opp.
1	ATLANTIC	400	380	4	347					10	MERCER HILL	405	369	4	320				
2	LONG	440	404	5	375					11	TROTTS	435	380	5	313				
3	EDEN	160	132	3	125					12	HILLSIDE	410	383	4	344				
4	MANGROVE	336	310	4	242					13	BIARRITZ	225	213	3	178				
5	CAPE	400	363	4	310					14	LEVEN	340	277	4	221				
6	BROW	337	293	4	243					15	PUNCHBOWL	420	385	4	364				
7	SHORT	130	125	3	90					16	LOOKOUT	386	333	4	291				
8	VALLEY	332	314	4	281					17	REDAN	190	166	3	136				
9	SOUND	360	327	4	297					18	HOME	415	387	5	360				
OUT		2895	2648	35	2310					IN		3226	2893	36	2527				
										OUT		2895	2648	35	2310				
										TOTAL		6121	5541	71	4837				

SCORE-CARD OF THE MID-OCEAN CLUB.

Ocean development. So they luncheoned with me at the temporary club house. After luncheon going over the course we came to the fifth hole, looking over Mangrove Lake. The Admiral doubted if any one could drive over the water. I explained to him that it was very easy if you did not try to carry too much of the water. He said he would like to see it done; golf balls and clubs were procured and I teed a ball. He asked me where I was going to drive to. There were two dogs about 160 to 170 yards from the tee, one running ahead of the other. I told him I was going to drive where the dogs were. He asked, "Which one?" and I said, "The second one," and, strange to say, I did and hit the second dog on the rump. I think the Admiral is still telling that story—of what a wonderful golfer I was.

To-day the club has some 120 members. The initiation is $1,000; dues $100 per annum. Some twenty to thirty residences and bungalows have been built, and the Mid-Ocean to-day is a charming, delightful colony of fine sportsmen.

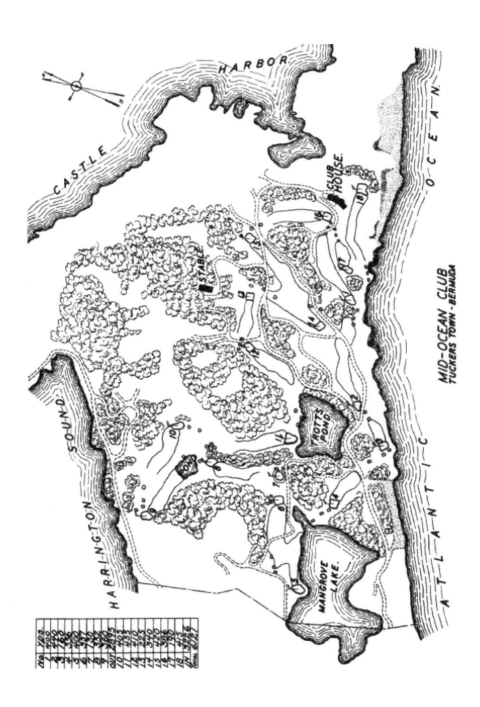

Probably the most daring experiment that has ever been conceived in creating a golf course was that undertaken by a part of New York men in 1913. The men who were principally identified with this undertaking were Otto Kahn, Paul D. Cravath, T. De Witt Cuyler, Cornelius Vanderbilt, Robert Goelet, and James A. Stillman.

LIDO

It was Roger Winthrop, President of the Piping Rock Golf Club, which course I had planned, who asked me if I would undertake laying it out and direct the building of it. When he told me that it was to be built over 115 acres of marsh land and swamps, with a lake of considerable size in the middle, I refused to have anything to do with it, saying that a first-class golf course could not be laid over a filled in marsh and could not be constructed without water hazards and with a variety of undulations resembling the real thing.

In trying to persuade me he assured me I could do anything I wanted in constructing holes, as in making the fill hills, hollows, mounds and lakes could be created at will and they would pump them up or out according to any contour map I might submit. He said he knew I had in mind a number of wonderful holes I had seen on the other side, but for which I had never found any fitting place, exclaiming: "Here is an opportunity for you, Charlie, to build anything you want to build." To me it seemed a dream. The more I thought it over the more it fascinated me. It really made me feel like a creator.

Finally I consented to have the plans drawn up, securing the services of Seth Raynor and others to carry out this ambitious scheme. Raynor was the engineer of construction.

I knew that no improvement could be made over the great holes which I had reproduced at the National, such as the Alps, the Redan, the Eden, and one or two others, but there was one hole I had always been crazy to build. That one was similar to the sixteenth at Littlestone in England.

I realized that it was not wise to have all the holes on this wonderful layout duplicates of holes which I had on my other courses. So when Bernard Darwin visited America in 1914 I discussed the Lido with him and asked if he would be willing to start a competition for a first, second, and third prize of 15, 10, and 5 guineas, respectively, for the best design of a two-shot hole in *Country Life* in England. It was designated that the two-shot hole should be one of 360 to 460 yards in length. He very kindly undertook to do this and asked Mr. Horace Hutchinson and Mr. G. Herbert Fowler to be associate judges with him.

There were some eighty-one competitors. The committee decided that there were not more than sixteen of the eighty-one designs worth considering.

It is interesting to note that out of the eighty-one plans over fifty of them were dog-leg holes. *Country Life* only sent me some sixteen, and they were very similar. What was most interesting was the way they designed the putting greens, and this was of real value to me.

I adopted as the eighteenth hole Dr. Mackenzie's plan, which had been awarded the first prize, but I altered it because it took up too much room. He was making a separate fairway for men who could only drive 120 yards and then a fairway for men who could drive 160 yards and then for the men who could carry 180 yards on a direct line. This made three distinct fairways, which in breadth was something like 200-odd yards. Of course it was quite easy to do away with the fairway for the 120-yard men simply by building a short tee, which I did.

I did not adopt any of the other holes in their entirety, but I certainly did incorporate certain excellent features from some of them.

It was a pity that toward the end of the fill the company did not carry out exactly the contours of our original map. So the course was not exactly what it might have been.

The total expenditure by the Lido Corporation was about $1,430,000, of which from $750,000 to $800,000, including the cost of the land, was attributable to the golf course. The lease between the corporation and the club, which was prepared but never signed, fixed the rent on the basis of the golf course expenditure, including the cost of the land, being $750,000, and gave the club an option on the course at this figure.

The total area purchased from the Estates of Long Beach contained 200 acres and ran in a rectangle from the ocean to Reynolds Channel. Of this area the golf course occupied 115 acres, part of which between the beach and upland to the south of the channel was, at the time of purchase, land literally under water. After the purchase the ocean front was protected by groins, the channel front was bullheaded, and the acreage was filled with 2,000,000 cubic yards of sand, at seven cents a yard (the present cost of such fill would be over twenty cents a yard), sucked by dredges from the bottom of the channel and piped over the acreage to the

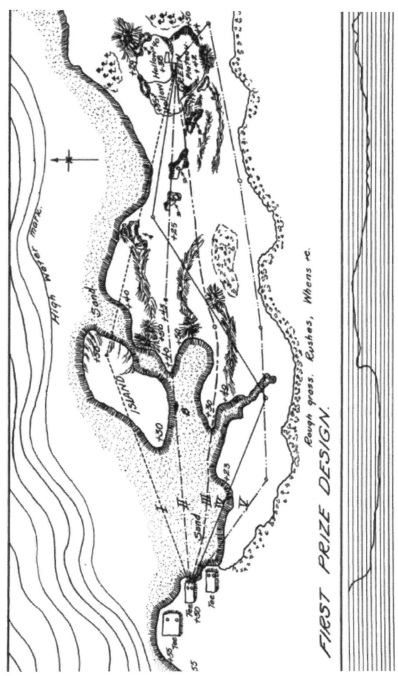

THE FIRST-PRIZE DESIGN IN THE *COUNTRY LIFE* COMPETITION
FOR THE LIDO TWO-SHOT HOLE.

various heights required by the necessity of meeting the grades laid out for the golf course to make the fairways rolling, to create the Alps, etc.

On top of the sand fill, to form the foundation for the fairways and the top soil, was placed meadow bog five inches thick in blocks 15 by 30 inches in size, and on this again was placed muck—both meadow bog and muck was taken from adjacent meadow land. A lagoon was built to create the island for the fairway of the fourth hole, with gates to let the water in and out of the channel.

Seth Raynor was invaluable in this work, seeing that the hills, the hummocks, and the undulations would fit in as well as possible with the plans.

After the course had been designed, the fill made, pleating of the fairway by meadow bog finished, then dressed heavily with muck, top dressed with lime, and a seed bed of topsoil and manure spread, it became essential to secure a first-class greenkeeper. I asked the well-known golf champion, J. H. Taylor, of Mid-Surrey, if he could help me out, and he strongly recommended Peter W. Lees, with whom I made a contract for $3,000 a year, to attend to the seeding and general upkeep of the greens. He proved an excellent man for the work, and the putting greens and fairway developed with little or no trouble.

Visiting the Lido course recently for the first time in two or three years, I was quite surprised and disappointed to find it had been permitted to run down. The original land purchase was made and the work started in 1914, about a week before the World War broke out, and the course did not reach playable condition until just about the time we went into the war, 1917, and it is true that the outbreak of the war and our entering it interfered substantially with the interest which would have been taken at another time by the founders of the club. Moreover, no club house was ever provided for until after the situation had passed out of the hands of those originally interested. But after the great flourish of trumpets by the original organizers as to the future of this course, to find they had all left it and permitted it to fall into the hands of a real-estate development company—people who knew little about golf and cared less, but who simply held the club together to further real-estate ventures—was a bitter disappointment to me.

Owing to high tides washing part of it away, the eighth hole has been entirely changed, and this made necessary the alteration of the ninth.

THE SECOND-PRIZE DESIGN IN THE *COUNTRY LIFE* COMPETITION FOR THE LIDO TWO-SHOT HOLE.

THE FOURTH HOLE AT THE LIDO GOLF CLUB.

Various alterations of a minor nature have been made which did not add to the excellence of the course. There had been no one there to watch the run of the ball and adapt the alterations which would be suggested under such circumstances. The finest holes, namely, the fourth, fifth, seventh, twelfth, fifteenth, and eighteenth, are still marvellous exhibits of golfing architecture, but they are not kept up. An ideal golf course must be controlled and developed by men who love and are devoted to the game without any possible emolument.

The fourth hole at the Lido I consider the finest two-shot hole in the world of golf, but fully 90 per cent of golfers will have to play it as a three-shot hole. I absorbed the idea from the sixteenth hole at Littlestone, but the Littlestone Club never took advantage of the remarkable natural opportunity they had there of making a separate fairgreen among the dunes, where there was a perfect setting for it, a fairway set in the dunes some thirty to thirty-five yards in width and 100 yards long, with a carry from the tee of 190 to 200 yards. Heaven knows when a player would get out of the rough if they didn't make this narrow fairgreen among the dunes, but once they did they had a wonderful driving iron or brassie shot to the green, which was on an eminence some fifteen to twenty feet

Regular Course										LIDO COUNTRY CLUB										(STYMIE)		
PAR	4	4	3	5	4	5	5	3	4	37	4	4	4	3	4	3	5	4	35	72	HANDICAP	NET SCORE
DISTANCE YARDS	361	398	160	505	354	477	455	150	350	3210	389	393	412	200	129	387	548	405	3152	6362		
HANDICAP	9	7	17	1	11	5	3	15	13	OUT	10	8	4	14	18	12	16	2	6	IN	TOTAL	
HOLES	1	2	3	4	5	6	7	8	9		10	11	12	13	14	15	16	17	18			

WON + LOST − HALVED 0

DATE_____

SCORER_____

ATTEST_____

SCORE-CARD OF THE LIDO COUNTRY CLUB.

above the fairway, with a deep bunker across the face of the green some forty yards from the hole. The bunker at Littlestone was about fifteen feet deep.

The charm of this hole at Lido is accentuated by the lagoon which encircles the entire fairway and which must be carried off the tee and also carried in the approach to the green, the back of the lagoon being about eighty yards short of the centre of the green.

Altogether my pilgrimage to the Lido brought only sadness to me, and I returned home feeling as if it were love's labor lost. To make matters more depressing, it was intimated to me that the present owners of the property intend abandoning the holes on the ocean front, developing for residential sites some sixteen to twenty acres.

One unfortunate development of the Lido situation has been the fill to the east, which now is somewhat higher than the Lido fill, which checks the drainage, making the bunkers in time of rains full of water and the low spots very wet. This will necessitate more thorough drainage in the future.

Charles Blair Macdonald

YALE

Although the students of various colleges and universities in the United States have been devoted to the game of golf, in 1925 there was no college which had an outstanding golf course. Strange as it may seem, St. Andrews has been the only university in the world that can boast of one.

In February, 1923, Mrs. Ray Tompkins presented to the Yale University the Griest Estate, to be known as the Ray Tompkins Memorial, consisting of 700 acres of land immediately adjoining the Yale Athletic Field, a few hundred yards west of the Yale bowl, to be used for encouraging outdoor sports among the undergraduates. To-day Yale has a classical course which is unexcelled in comparison with any inland course in this country or in Europe. The building of it was about as difficult an engineering problem as that of the Lido or the Mid-Ocean.

The land was high, heavily wooded, hilly, and no part of it had been cultivated for over forty years. There were no roads or houses upon it. It was a veritable wilderness when given to Yale. Although I had renounced having anything to do with building another golf course, I succumbed to the solicitations of numbers of Yale graduates to whom I had always been devoted. George T. Adee and Mortimer N. Buckner were the committee that waited upon me. So with Raynor we went over the land.

When in the timber one could not see fifty feet ahead, the underbrush was so thick. However, we found on that high land wonderful deposits of sea sand, indicating that the sea must have swept the land during the glacial period. In a bog some quarter of a mile long we found deposited some four to six feet of wonderful rich, black muck. These two deposits of sand and muck made it possible to build the course.

We first had a topographical map made of the property, then a relief plan. After a careful study we told the committee that it would cost between $300,000 and $400,000 to build the first eighteen-hole course (the intention is to build a second course). I did not think they would stand for so large a sum but, nothing daunted, they told us to go ahead.

Of the 102 acres cleared twenty-eight were swamps, forty-three stone ledges, and the cleared land was full of rock. After clearing the trees and underbrush it was possible to plow only twenty acres; then removing boulders, we plowed eleven more. Practically 75 per cent of the cleared area was ledge and swamp, necessitating blasting, filling, draining and

Scotland's Gift: Golf

THE FIRST TEE AT YALE.

covering with sand, earth, and humus to make grass-growing soil. The surface covering of leaf mold and black earth was very shallow, averaging only about one inch, and underneath was red clay and gravel.

It cost $70,000 to clear the course of trees and underbrush, and fully that amount to clear the property of stones. About 3,850 tons of manure and 190 tons of limestone were spread on the course and harrowed in with the black loam from the bogs.

Altogether the course when it was opened cost only a little less than $450,000. To-day there is no better test of golf than the Yale course anywhere, and as years go by it will become more attractive. The water holes are exceptionally fine; I know of no golf course where the water holes are as wonderful as those in New Haven.

The following is a letter of appreciation from the President of Yale University:

"Dear Mr. Macdonald:

"I write to express to you the deep appreciation of Yale for your generous willingness to assist in the laying out of our new golf course. There is no one in whose judgment we should have so great confidence and we regard ourselves as extraordinarily fortunate in securing your interest and assistance.

"Again with sincere appreciation, believe me
Yours very truly,
(Signed) F. R. Angell."

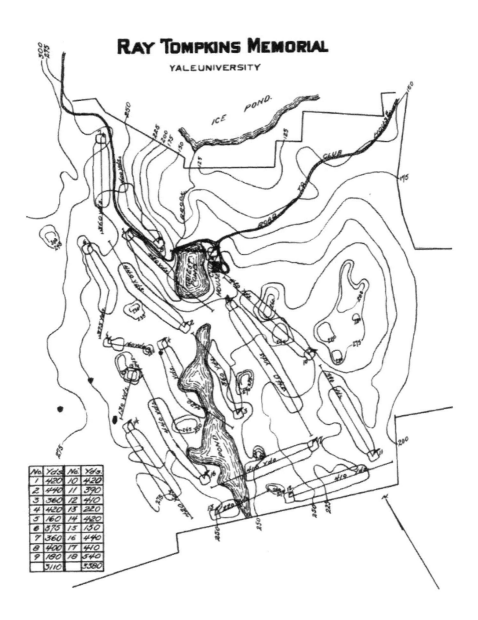

RAY TOMPKINS MEMORIAL YALE GOLF CLUB

Self ....
Op'nt ....

HOLE	CHAMPIONSHIP COURSE	REGULAR COURSE	SHORT COURSE	PAR		SELF	OP'T	SELF	OP'T
1	410	399	379	4					
2	365	349	338	4					
3	380	370	310	4					
4	440	426	309	4					
5	135	131	117	3					
6	350	342	318	4					
7	368	348	289	4					
8	415	409	372	4					
9	225	210	190	3					
	3088	2984	2622	34	OUT				
10	405	373	342	4					
11	375	320	320	4					
12	406	340	340	4					
13	190	190	190	3					
14	372	335	320	4					
15	188	170	135	3					
16	476	430	420	5					
17	425	382	382	4					
18	608	575	506	5					
	3445	3115	2955	36	IN				
	6533	6099	5577	70	TOTAL				

Date .... Attested ....

SCORE-CARD OF THE RAY TOMPKINS MEMORIAL YALE GOLF CLUB.

Chapter XIII

Activities of U.S.G.A., 1911-1927

It is interesting to note that since the establishment of the U.S.G.A. in 1895 the Executive Committee of the Association has amended the by-laws nearly every year. From 1913 to 1927 they were amended eleven times, and about nine times in the previous seventeen years.

After the burning question of centre-shafted clubs was settled in 1911 there was no further divergence in the method of playing the game, and the ruling bodies, the Royal and Ancient and the U.S.G.A., were entirely in accord, I think largely as the result of Silas Strawn's conference with Captain W. H. Burn, Chairman of the Rules of Golf Committee, in the spring of 1911.

I think the Royal and Ancient were not entirely satisfied with the reception their ruling regarding the "Form and Make of Golf Clubs" had met. It was tentatively agreed, Strawn stated to the Executive Committee of the U.S.G.A. upon his return, that the U.S.G.A. recognized that there was no obligation on the part of the Royal and Ancient to confer with the U.S.G.A. before making any changes in the rules, but that the U.S.G.A. would appreciate it if an understanding might be brought about to the effect that the Royal and Ancient in enacting any new rules or changing existing rules would furnish the U.S.G.A. with copies of the proposed changes a sufficient length of time in advance of any action thereon to give them an opportunity to make such suggestions as they might see fit.

The activities of the U.S.G.A. were then centred on home troubles. The amateur rule was most prominent, and then there was the ever-present threat of the Western Golf Association to play a different game which the U.S.G.A. took seriously. The Western broke distinctly away from the U.S.G.A. in 1917 when they barred the stymie.

In 1915 Frank L. Woodward was elected President, the second Western man in twenty-two years of its organization. Both Western Presidents, Strawn and Woodward, were stanch supporters of the U.S.G.A., believing in unification, but primarily for playing the Royal and Ancient game as it was played in Scotland.

In April, 1915, at the meeting of the U.S.G.A. the amateur ruling was referred to the Executive Committee to report January, 1916. When the ruling was adopted it debarred Ouimet, Sullivan, and Tewksbury as amateurs owing to their handling of golf supplies; in other words, commercializing their skill and making money out of golf.

At the meeting in January, 1917, the Woodland Club, of which Ouimet was a member, objected to the ruling, and an effort was made to alter the constitution, but a committee consisting of Wheeler, Strawn, Whitney, and others, vetoed it, and the ruling was upheld. Frank Woodward, who was president of the U.S.G.A. in 1915-1916, made a very impressive speech in 1917 at the U.S.G.A. meeting, supporting the Association. The Woodland Club had many legal guns to fight their case, but it was soon seen that the Boston contingent were out of it by the imposing array of attorneys which stood ready to defend the Association, including John M. Bowers, of New York; Austen G. Fox, of New York, and Silas H. Strawn, of Chicago.

The motion voted on was the Woodland Amendments to my original amendment which asked the meeting to concur in the report of the Executive Committee restating its position regarding the golf goods business and debarring golf architects. The amendment was for nonconcurrence, and the vote for the amendment was a vote against the Committee. The final vote was 13 for Ouimet and against him 33.

The outstanding features deciding the vote were: first, a letter of Committeeman Crosby to Ouimet informing him of his impending disqualification if he opened his store; second, a letter from Ouimet acknowledging receipt of the warning; and, third, invitation by Crosby to the Woodland Club to visit New York and consult with the members of the Executive Committee.

JEROME D. TRAVERS HOLING FINAL PUTT TO WIN THE OPEN CHAMPIONSHIP, JUNE 18, 1915, AT THE BALTUSROL GOLF CLUB.
The referee was the late Howard F. Whitney.

Tewksbury was reinstated in 1917 and Francis Ouimet in January, 1918. At the Annual Meeting of the U.S.G.A. in 1918, held in Philadelphia, President Perrin read the following resolution:

"Whereas, Francis Ouimet upon entering the service of the United States severed his personal connection with the management of the firm of Ouimet and Sullivan and thereby discontinued the practices which were decided to be in violation of the amateur rule of the U.S.G.A.,

"Therefore be it resolved, by the Executive Committee of the U.S.G.A. that he be, and thereby is, reinstated as an amateur golfer."

The month after Ouimet was reinstated he wrote an article in *Golf Illustrated* in which he acknowledged having received a letter asking if he cared for reinstatement, and saying that thinking of his true friends in the Woodland Golf Club and their efforts in his behalf, he finally decided he owed it to them to apply for reinstatement. He also states in this article:

"I want my reinstatement without a condition or not at all. I have never done anything connected with golf that I have regretted yet, and I

hope I never shall....Amateur restoration as I received it means nothing. If I am to be reinstated, then my partner must be. We will both come back together without any 'ifs', 'ands' or 'buts' or I don't come at all....I am not the least bit enthused as I have already said, and it may be narrow-mindedness and so forth, but those are my feelings."

And he winds up his article by saying:

"If I have to sever my connections with the firm Ouimet and Sullivan, to play golf as a lily-white amateur, then I must count myself out and suffer the consequences."

A former President, J. Fritz Byers, told me Ouimet expressed himself on the steamer going to Europe to play in 1921 that his disqualification turned out to be the best thing that ever happened to him.

Other than discussions of the amateur ruling there was very little doing of interest in the golfing world until after the war. The U.S.G.A. championships were resumed in 1919.

The Association originally confined itself to the championships. Gradually they assumed greater functions until finally, besides running the amateur, open, and ladies championships, they undertook to father a public links' championship and an amateur championship for juniors; they appointed a Membership and Reinstatement Committee, Amateur Status and Conduct Committee, Committee on Implements and Ball, International Matches and Relations Committee, Committee on Plan, Committee on Sectional Affairs, Selection of Course Committee, Committee on Green Section, Public Links Section, Publicity Committee, Finance Committee, and General Counsel. They have shouldered a responsibility that is very far-reaching, but so far the Association has been able to carry it out. I fear they are assuming too much responsibility, and in time it will become onerous and difficult to get men of ability who will devote the necessary time to carry on the Association successfully. Of course, when that time comes they will have to engage capable men to do the work. Now that they charge admission fees to witness the championships no doubt they will have sufficient funds to carry out their program if they cease extending it.

FRANCIS OUIMET

The financial position of the U.S.G.A. is now excellent, as shown by their statement of November 30, 1927:

Receipts for year ending November 30, 1927 . . . . . $73,334
(of which $24,159 came from gate receipts)

Assets:
    Cash $15,886
    Investment . . . . <u>59,841</u>
                                                   $75,727

I believe in building up a reserve and not trying to cover too much ground.

The enlarged scope of the Association has already made it necessary that they open an office and appoint an executive secretary with an assistant, and they have fortunately secured a very capable man in T. J. McMahon.

The third Western man, George H. Walker, became President in 1920. Harmony was the keynote of his administration.

There had been much discussion about Rules—the stymie in particular—standardizing the ball, and the amateur status. At the annual meeting, January 9, 1920, the following resolution was passed:

"Resolved, That the President of the Association be authorized and directed to appoint a Committee of Members of Active Clubs of the United States Golf Association to confer with the Rules of Golf Committee of The Royal and Ancient Golf Club of St. Andrews on the subject of the amendment of the rules of the game of golf, to conform to the accepted wish of the players of the world."

In accordance with the authority given the President by the above Resolution, the following Committee was appointed: Messrs. George H. Walker, Howard F. Whitney, J. Frederick Byers, Frederick S. Wheeler, and Robert A. Gardner. The Committee sailed in July, 1920.

Upon President Walker's return from St. Andrews he stated that the members of his Committee found the members of the Rules of Golf Committee alive to the importance of uniformity and equally ready to modify their views to that end.

The stymie presented the greatest difficulty, perhaps, Walker stated in his report, because, broadly speaking, the popular opinion here is against the stymie, while the opposite is true in Great Britain. There was some compromise here, and the U.S.G.A. amateur championship at the Engineers' Club was played under the following rule adopted by the U.S.G.A. but not the Royal and Ancient:

"When either ball is on the putting green the player may move the opponent's ball. The opponent shall then be deemed to have holed his next stroke."

At the September meeting of the Royal and Ancient they refused to make a rule which would abolish the stymie. Eventually the U.S.G.A. conformed with the Royal and Ancient ruling, as did Canada also.

Next in difficulty came the question of standardization of ball, and while the Royal and Ancient were more or less in favor of a floater, again the Americans stood for the heavier ball. Eventually it was agreed to accept a maximum limit of 1.62 ounces for weight and a minimum limit of 1.62 inches in diameter for size. This rule went into effect May, 1921.

In discussing the amateur rule the Royal and Ancient stood for "making a profit out of skill in the game is a test of professionalism." Bona fide golf architects had their amateur standing restored. I was heartily in favor of this latter ruling, although during my lifetime I never cared to accept any emolument for whatever I had done in the way of golf. At the same time, the attitude I took was by no means a criticism of my friends who have been architects and honorable devotees of the game; in particular, among others, Devereaux Emmet.

I do not think the term "golf architect" can be found in golf records previous to 1901, the time I formulated the idea of copying the famous holes, sometimes not in their entirety; at times taking only some famous putting green or some famous bunker or some famous water hazard or other outstanding feature which might be adapted to particular ground over which one wanted to build a golf course. I believe this was the birth of golf architecture. Now golfing architecture has really become an art, and is so recognized, being akin to science. As artists, architects certainly should not be classified as golf professionals. A golf architect must be a student of agriculture, understand nature, have a knowledge of soils, knowledge of implements, drainage, and above all the particular character of the lay-out which tantalizes a lover of the game and holds him spellbound.

The fourth question had reference to a lost ball and ball out of bounds, and it was definitely decided that the rule for lost ball, unplayable ball, and out of bounds should in the future be the same; loss of stroke and distance.

In 1921 Howard F. Whitney was elected President and the recommendations of the Walker Committee were adopted at the Annual Meeting, January 7, 1921.

So much had been said for some fifteen years regarding the U.S.G.A.'s class of membership that at the Annual Meeting in 1921 it was proposed that the Executive Committee send a letter to all allied clubs asking them to indicate whether or not if the U.S.G.A. created but one class of membership at $20 per annum they would seek that membership rather than the other. If 51 per cent of the allied clubs so indicated the Executive Committee proposed at their next Annual Meeting to submit an amendment to the Constitution covering that point, creating one class of membership only and making the dues $20 per year for all. Fifty-one per cent of the allied members did not indorse this proposition; hence it fell to the ground, and it was not until 1927 that the Association had a one-class membership.

Howard F. Whitney, when President, stood firmly for a uniform code which he emphasized in all his attitudes. In conferences with officials of the W.G.A. to establish uniformity the U.S.G.A. agreed to enlarge the Association's committee so as to include members of the boards of sectional associations throughout the country that had heretofore not had representation; further, to allow the allied clubs to become active members.

The W.G.A. on their part were to subscribe to the U.S.G.A. Constitution and play the same game. The U.S.G.A. fulfilled their agreement, but the W.G.A. did not. Their rules conflicted with those of the U.S.G.A., notably lost ball, unplayable ball, ball out of bounds, and stymie. The special rules regarding cleaning of ball, ball imbedded in mud, and ball on wrong green were justly local rules, but the other rules were a distinct departure from the agreement they made to abide by the U.S.G.A. code of rules. As a result the breach grew wider.

In the summer of 1921 W. C. Fownes, Jr., captained eight American golfers to cross the Atlantic and play in the British championship to be held at Hoylake. There was a team match with eight of the British golfers. The American team consisted of Fred Wright, Guilford, "Chick" Evans, Ouimet, Platt, Fownes, Paul Hunter, and Bobby Jones. The Americans won this match, but they failed to make a good showing in the British Amateur Championship, none of them reaching the semi-finals.

In 1922, during the first year of J. Fritz Byers' presidency, it was determined to charge a gate admission fee to witness the play of the amateur championship with the exception of the ladies. This action was deemed imperative owing to the ever-increasing activities of the Association—but particularly to defray the expense of the Walker Cup team abroad, estimated at $10,000, and entertaining the visiting team from Great Britain. This expense, coupled with that of the Green Section, demanded funds other than dues from member clubs. This was a departure from precedent, and while as much as one might regret gate money there was no other way out once the Association assumed certain responsibilities.

Fritz Byers was re-elected in 1923 and in his annual message referred to the "unfortunate and disagreeable misunderstanding" between the U.S.G.A. and the W.G.A., which "threatened to disrupt the unity of golf in this country," concluded by saying "that to-day the golfers of the country are in absolute accord." Unhappily that did not prove to be the case.

The dissension between the organizations became very acute, so much so that at an Executive Meeting held at Flossmoor at the time of the amateur championship in September, an effort was made to change the name of the U.S.G.A to that of the American Golf Association and to alter the constitution. Apparently, the majority of the committee agreed to it, supported by the Westerners.

Had it not been for the firm stand taken by J. Fritz Byers I fear a very grave mistake would have been committed by acceding to the demands of the W.G.A.

Perusing the letters of the Committeemen in 1923 apropos of the unification of the U.S.G.A. with other sectional associations, I think there were some misled committeemen. They totally failed to sum up the feeling in the East against a change in name in order to satisfy the recalcitrants.

The Executive Committee could never have delivered the U.S.G.A. to the W.G.A. without the liveliest fight ever witnessed at an annual meeting. The original membership of the U.S.G.A. to a man would have taken umbrage and possibly have disrupted the organization. The Havemeyer Cup and the U.S.G.A. meant something to the old guard and they would have resented selling their birthright for a "mess of pottage."

I understand the Executive Committee was almost stampeded into voting for changing the Constitution as well as the name at the executive meeting held at Flossmoor, but J. Fritz Byers, almost alone, stood adamant. Pleading for two weeks' time to consult his advisory committee, the officials of the W.G.A. graciously granted the request.

Scanning the letters from the members of the committee at that time I am surprised to find the General Counsel, James Francis Burke, had already drawn up a constitution to be adopted headed "American Golf Association."

It appears there was a majority of the Committee with him. Limist and Ward desired a change of name as well as constitution. Gardner, Vanderpoel, Burke, Wilson, and Standish sanctioned a change of name. Connie Lee, sailing for Europe, stated he did not favor a change of name, but would consent if the Committee deemed it essential. The following associates of the U.S.G.A., forming the Advisory Committee, stood staunchly to the contrary: Byers, Wheeler, Whitney, E. S. Moore, and the old presidents of the U.S.G.A, such as Lawrence Curtis, Bob Watson, and Herbert Windeler. Strawn also was against altering the name and called the demand of the W.G.A. "capricious." Curtis called it "puerile."

Finally the Advisory Committee reported that it had not had sufficient time to fully consider the proposals which might be far-reaching in their effect, and being desirous of cooperating with and assisting the Executive Committee it was unanimously agreed to make the following recommendations:

"*First: That a change of name of the Association be not considered.*

"*Second: That the proposed new constitution as submitted be not adopted.*

"*Third: That the Advisory Committee, if desired by the Executive Committee, will submit to it amendments to the U.S.G.A. constitution which will tend to broaden its scope and meet any fair requirements of the present situation.*

"Fourth: That the Advisory Committee will take pleasure in meeting the Executive Committee at any time in the near future that the two committees can be gotten together for the purpose of discussing general matters of policy and procedure."

Here the matter dropped.

The Annual Meeting in 1924 and the year passed uneventfully.

Regarding the amateur championship, the Association has now tried some half dozen methods and the number of golfers knocking at the door to compete is ever on the increase. It occurs to me that the experiment of conducting the open championship might be adopted by the Committee in the amateur championship. I understand that last year there were 898 competitors for the open, but by having sectional competitions they eliminated all but 150, thirty of whom did not have to compete owing to their record in the previous championship. Why not have sectional competitions for qualifying in the amateur championship and then run it off in thirty-six-hole matches, sixty-four qualifying? This could be done in one week.

The great objection to the medal play qualifying rounds is that the competitors must play under such varying conditions. Half the players are apt to be out in a storm and the other half in sunshine. Another objection to it is the time it takes, forcing your first two days to eighteen-hole matches only, which scarcely tests out the superior golfer.

Chapter XIV

Standardization

In searching the annals of golf from the time of the adoption of the oldest surviving code in 1754, I can discover no reference where the authorities in Scotland ever tampered with the Rules respecting the implements of the game. It was traditional to play with any ball you liked or any club you cared to. Standardization has violated tradition.

Standardization was first discussed when the Haskell ball was introduced in Scotland in 1902, and in that year the view was taken by the Rules of Golf Committee that the Haskell ball spoiled the game. A motion was duly drafted and approved empowering the subcommittee to draft a motion for the General Meeting with the object of standardizing the gutta ball. Referring to the above, here is a letter from W. H. Burn, Chairman of the Rules of Golf Committee in 1911, in which he says:

"For two reasons this was abandoned. Firstly, because we were unable to frame a definition which would meet the case, and, secondly, because, as you are aware, the voting power of a club is in the hands of Members who, as a rule, were in receipt of considerable handicaps, and who were so delighted with their performances with the new ball that the Committee was aware that the motion would be defeated by a large majority. The Committee therefore thought that the time was not ripe to bring the matter forward. I suggested a definition of a golf ball that it should be 'homogeneous' but was disappointed to find that the gutta-percha ball was not 'homogeneous' but was made of a mixture of sub-

stances, because gutta percha, pure and simple, was too soft a substance to make golf balls."

In 1911 at the Amateur Championship Meeting at Prestwick a memorial was presented to the delegates of the clubs intrusted with the management of that competition by a number of the players in which it was suggested that some limit should be placed by legislators on the power of the ball. The memorial was referred to the Rules of Golf Committee which did not then see its way to take action.

From 1909 to 1912 there was scarcely an issue of London *Golf Illustrated* that some one did not have something to say about the standardization of the ball. Finally in 1912 it came to a head. A letter was issued to all the leading golfers in Great Britain as follows:

"There is a pretty consensus of opinion among first-class players that the time has come when something should be done to check the excessive length to which the golf-ball can be driven. Ballmakers are vieing with each other in producing balls of ever-increasing driving capacity, and as most of the best courses have now been stretched to their utmost limits, it is obvious that holes and courses are speedily being ruined as tests of the game. Green committees and golf architects have been struggling for some time to maintain the normal rate of scoring by multiplying hazards, by rendering the approaches to holes more difficult, and even by increasing the difficulties to putting, but it is clear that a point has been reached at which such devices are destroying the balance and character of the game which make it enjoyable and worth playing. Moreover, expert opinion is practically unanimous that the long-driving balls are in themselves not sufficiently reliable for the finer strokes to afford a proper test of play, or to provide a sufficiently constant standard by which the merits of players can be measured.

"It is desired that the list of signatories should be increased by the addition of names of other distinguished amateurs, and I shall be glad to know, at your early convenience, whether I may add your name to them.

"*Yours faithfully,*
(Signed) Garden G. Smith."

It resulted eventually in replies from some 152 amateurs, of which 141 were in favor of the following requisition:

"The undersigned suggest to the delegates of the clubs governing the Amateur Championship, that they consider the question of whether it is possible to ordain that all entrants for the Championship use balls of the same material and structure."

At this time, April 22, 1912, I wrote Captain Burn the following:

"Captain W. H. Burn, Chairman,
Rules of Golf Committee,
Royal and Ancient Golf Club,
St. Andrews, Scotland.

"Dear Sir:—

"Irrespective of the sentiment in this country, my own personal feeling is that at the present time there is no necessity to standardize the ball. I realize that the old gutta made the game more interesting to the adept, and for my part I regret the advent of the rubber-cored ball. At the same time, I am confident that nine-tenths of the men who play golf—or speaking more broadly, nine-tenths of the men who support the golf clubs of the world—would never be content to go back to the old ball, because they would not get the pleasure out of the game.

"To my mind there has been a great deal of nonsense written about the superiority of the rubber-cored ball in breaking records and in length of game. Young Tom Morris did a 77 at St. Andrews in 1869 with guttas which were then not perfected, with golf clubs which had not been improved, and on a golf course not ironed out as usual now in present upkeep. True, St. Andrews has been lengthened, but at the same time the whins have been eliminated.

"A great advantage that the rubber-cored ball has over the gutta is that a badly hit ball goes pretty nearly as far as a well hit ball; but on the other hand, when one is in a bunker and the ball must be lifted over a steep bank, the gutta is infinitely easier to get out than the rubber-cored ball because the rubber-cored jumps too quickly from the club.

"On general principles, I am sorry to see any standardization enter into the game.

*"Yours faithfully,
(Signed) Charles B. Macdonald."*

The matter then was held in abeyance and did not become a moot question again until 1919 when at a fully attended meeting of the Rules of Golf Committee, held at St. Andrews on September 22nd prior to the business meeting of the Royal and Ancient Club, the members of the Committee after a lengthy discussion passed this resolution which was then reported to the meeting:

"The Rules of Golf Committee is of the opinion that in order to preserve the balance between the power of the ball and the length of the holes, and in order to retain the special features of the game the power of the ball should be limited."

The Committee proposed to consult the U.S.G.A. before submitting a definite proposal to the Club. A subcommittee, consisting of J. L. Low, A. C. M. Croome, A. V. Hambro, Captain C. K. Hutchinson, and J. Stuart Paton, was appointed to communicate with the U.S.G.A. and the other bodies specially interested. It was finally determined to standardize the ball.

As the result of several meetings between the Rules of Golf Committee and the delegates of the United States Golf Association, and after consultation with representatives of Canada and South Africa, it was unanimously agreed to submit the following resolutions for adoption to the Royal and Ancient Golf Club and to the Executive Committee of the U.S.G.A.:

"That on and after 1st May, 1921, the weight of the ball shall be not greater than 1.62 ounces and the size not less than 1.62 inches in diameter. The Rules of Golf Committee and the Executive Committee of the United States Golf Association will take whatever steps they think necessary to limit the power of the ball with regard to distance, should any ball

of greater power be introduced, and that the Rules of Golf be amended accordingly."

Once standardization was discussed, it naturally spread to golf clubs as well as balls. When the new rules were framed in 1908, a very innocent innovation was injected into the code of Rules called "Form and Make of Golf Clubs," reading as follows:

"The Rules of Golf Committee intimates that it will not sanction any substantial departure from the traditional and accepted form and make of golf clubs which in its opinion consists of a plain shaft and a head which does not contain any mechanical contrivance such as springs."

Here is the rock which was to render asunder unification, and no wonder. Certainly no one would believe that the above could be interpreted as it now reads:

"The Rules of Golf Committee will not sanction any substantial departure from the traditional and accepted form and make of golf clubs which in its opinion consists of a plain shaft and a head which does not contain any mechanical contrivance such as springs. It also regards as illegal the use of such clubs as those of the mallet-headed type or such clubs as have the neck bent as to produce a similar effect."

Why was not the original clause made clearer?
After the fight over the Schenectady putter in 1911 the ribbed club question was settled in 1923, and on January 1, 1924, the following rule became effective:

"Club faces shall not bear any lines, dots or other markings, made for the obvious purpose of putting a cut on the ball, nor shall they be stamped or cut with lines exceeding 1-16 inch in width, nor less than 3-32 inch apart, measured on their inside edges. Dots on the faces of the club may be used provided all rough or raised edges are removed. Both line and dot markings may be used in combination within the above limitations."

Next steel shafted clubs were barred, but in 1925 they were finally accepted as regular by the U.S.G.A., another break from unification. How far this standardization will carry the Rules of Golf Committee it is difficult to conceive. Personally, I do not think any of the centre-shafted clubs or any of the club faces with varying lines, dots, or other markings, or steel shafts make an iota of difference in the general play of a golfer, and I don't believe it is possible for a man to buy his golfing shot in the shop.

The outlawing of the Schenectady putter was supposed at the time to be aimed at Travis, but as all know, the change was not made until some seven years after Travis' win at Sandwich. It really was made because certain Englishmen tried playing with croquet mallets. But anyhow, what was all this enormous fuss worth? Who plays with the Schenectady now? A Schenectady won't help a bad putter to putt.

As to markings on the faces of clubs, here again it was generally supposed that the objection to markings came because Jock Hutchinson, in 1921, won at St. Andrews in dry, slippery weather and he could pitch where others couldn't. As a matter of fact, he won because he did the eighth hole in one and the ninth in two, and even then he only tied with Roger Wethered, who lost because in stepping back he moved his own ball. And what is probably more important—Horace Hutchinson told Jim Whigham that the greens were not fast. It happened to be very dry weather and therefore the Green Committee had made a special effort to water the greens, and the greens, for St. Andrews, were slow rather than fast, and any good player could pitch on to them.

Can any standardizer point to any freak club that is supposed to make it easy for the bad player to equal the good players that has survived? And has there not always been a change in the form and make of golf clubs? All the old timers remember when people approached with a baffy. We all can remember the first mashie played with by Willie Campbell and Johnnie Laidlay, and when the first bulger was played with a little later, and so forth. There has never been any accepted form.

It is generally thought that the Americans are the great patentees of Golf innovations. In *Golf Illustrated* it is stated that from September, 1892, until March, 1894, there were some seventy-six golf patents issued in Great Britain; thirty-four of them applied to clubs.

The standardization of the 1.62 x 1.62 golf ball has not been entirely satisfactory, and there is now a distinct demand for a more satisfactory standard ball.

In 1924 when the British Walker team were playing over the National Golf Links of America there was tested out a larger and lighter ball, 1.68 inches in diameter and 1.55 ounces in weight. The driving tests were made from the fifth tee and also from the seventeenth tee. There was a favoring wind of approximately fifteen miles an hour blowing at the backs of the drivers from the fifth, and from the seventeenth they played downhill into the wind. Tolley drove with wind, 274 yards with standard ball, and he drove 264 yards with the proposed new ball; and at the seventeenth 270 yards with the old ball, but downhill. A. W. Biggs, of Cherry Valley, out-drove Tolley on the fifth tee with wind, getting 280 yards with the new ball and 292 with the standard ball. As a result of the day's driving, on an average the test showed only six yards difference in the driving power of the two balls. Tests were also made at the Pine Valley and Morris County Golf Clubs, and the results were the same.

The driving test is not the one and only important element of the game. There are only about fifteen or sixteen wooden driving strokes in the game of golf for good players. The other fifty-five or sixty-five strokes are what tell the story. The adoption of the 1.68 x 1.55 ball question coming up before the Royal and Ancient Fall Meeting in 1924, the proposal was overwhelmingly defeated. The situation to-day is about as follows:

W. C. Fownes, Jr., president of the U.S.G.A., at the annual meeting, 1927, stated in reference to the standardization of ball:

"The driving power of the present ball is about 70 per cent of perfect resilience; and the people who have studied the matter from an unbiased standpoint believe that it is quite within the range of possibility that the manufacturer by improved methods can raise that resilience to 85 per cent.

"Now, what that would do to our courses and to the game it is easy to picture, because the difference between the present ball of the higher grade, like the Dunlop and Spalding, and some old-time balls that we have picked up lying around the club house of ancient vintage, is about 12 per cent, so that if it were possible to increase the resilience over the present balls by 15 per cent, we would absolutely ruin the game. The con-

soling element is that this step does not come at once. It comes on gradually from year to year, and as the people get accustomed to using longer driving balls, it is a little bit like anybody taking a cocktail before dinner. You do not like to do it. You like to see that long drive go out there, so that it seems to the committees of both countries that it is of the greatest importance to absolutely stop this competitive effort on the part of the manufacturers to continually obtain a more resilient ball."

Personally, I cannot concur in the above statement, though I am aware that Fownes is entitled to speak with more or less authority. But is the above statement a fair argument, taking as a test "old-time balls that have been picked up lying around the club house of ancient vintage." We all know old balls lose their resilience; that was true even of the guttie and much more so of the wound ball. I do not believe a 1.62 x 1.62 ball can be manufactured that will go 15 per cent farther than the present ball which *under normal conditions* is driven about 230 to 250 yards by fine drivers on an average. Fifteen per cent would be thirty-five to forty yards farther.

When the Haskell first came into life and was more or less perfected, say 1903 or 1904, it went about seventeen to eighteen yards farther off wood on an average than the gutta. In the last twenty-five years there has scarcely been a year that some golf ball maker has not advertised a ball to go five to ten yards farther than the ball of the previous year. If we take five yards per year for the last twenty-five years, to-day's ball should then go 125 yards farther than the old ball. After the driving matches at the Prestwick Open Championship and the driving with the gutta and hard balls at Woking, it was stated that there was only about twenty-five or thirty yards' difference between the gutta and the hard balls, a gain of only about twelve yards in twenty-two years (1904-1926). Consequently, it is impossible for me to believe a 1.62 x 1.62 ball can be manufactured that will go thirty-five to forty yards farther than the present ball. It sounds like T. N. T. I think we are all following a will-of-the-wisp. My judgment is we should at once go to a floating ball and give the makers carte blanche to do what they can so long as they conform to the one restriction, the ball must float. Naturally, the manufacturers do not want a floater, but if it fills the bill, certainly the players do, as it will save them many boxes of balls a year, and the approaching and putting will be much more interesting. It certainly would be a great boon to the undergraduates of Yale, where they have wonderful water hazards.

A goodly number of fine players are to-day playing with a floater and contend their scoring is better, for the few yards they lose on the drive is made up in approaching and putting.

Here is a partial list of rubber-cored golf balls which was on the market in 1911, with their weight, size, and buoyancy arranged according to weight. The reader will be surprised to note that over 50 per cent of them are floating-balls:

Name	Weight Grains Troy	Diam. Sixteenths of an Inch	Buoyancy
St. Mungo Water Core	615	27	Floats
White Colonel	618	26 ½	Floats
The Colonel	619	27 ½	Floats
Jolly Junior	629 ½	27	Floats
Black and White Dimple	638 ¾	27	Floats
Little Colonel	642	26 ½	Floats
Red Dot (white)	647	27	Floats
Haskell Streak	649	27 ¼	Floats
White Diamond	650	27	Floats
Black Diamond	653 ½	27	Floats
Jack Rabbit	654	27 ½	Floats
Diamond Chip	665	26	Sinks
Baby Dimple	671	26 ¼	Sinks
Glory Dimple	672	27 ¼	Floats
Zodiac	708 ¼	26 ¾	Sinks
Midget Bramble	719 ¼	26	Sinks
Black Circle	721 ¾	26	Sinks

Name	Weight Grains Troy	Diam. Sixteenths of an Inch	Buoyancy
Domino Dimple	723 ¼	27	Sinks
Heavy Colonel (Green Star)	727 ¼	27	Sinks
Diamond King	728 ¼	27	Sinks
Midget Dimple	737	26	Sinks
Bunny	753	26	Sinks

Finally, it being discovered that the small and heavier ball which sinks had the greatest run, the manufacturers concentrated on them, and, of course, profited by the balls that were lost in the water.

I was under the impression Hilton played the short holes with a guttie in 1911 and 1912. Asking him about it, the following is his reply:

"*October 28, 1927*

"*Dear Charles:*

"*Kindly excuse delay but your letter was wandering around for a time. No, you are not quite correct about the gutty, I had not one with me. I changed the ball to a big light ball with pimples on it. I did the same at Prestwick in that year in the amateur championship.*

"*Quite recently I was playing in a species of test match gutty or so called gutty and rubber-cored ball and I noticed that the short tricky lofting approaches were much simpler affairs to handle with the solid than with the rubber core. What I fail to understand is the ever recurring argument about the present day ball spoiling courses, why they do not make it a floating ball with no restrictions as to size. We would all be happy in three months.*

"*In five rounds at St. Andrews Bobby Jones only played ten wooden club shots through the green.*

"*Yours sincerely,*
H. H. Hilton."

In London to-day there is a club known as the Guttie Ball Club, of which Robert Harris, British champion in 1925, is captain. It seems that the press and ball-makers are quite mystified over their competitions. It is not propaganda, but the men are playing with the old ball because they believe they get the old-time pleasure out of the game.

Harris, writing to a friend lately, stated:

"We disclaim all thoughts of propaganda towards restriction, but it is wonderful how the theory has grown with momentum, while the makers are embarrassed by large orders for gutta balls. I do not think for a minute that a revolution is at hand, nor do I hope for one to the extreme extent, but undoubtedly we are creating an atmosphere."

The London *Times* of the 18th of November, 1927, reported a match of the Guttie Club versus the Seniors, who were armed with the ordinary rubber core. The Guttie Club won the singles by six matches to one, and halved the foursomes, winning in the end comfortably enough. The tees were placed well back.

Being interested in these competitions, throwing as they do a sidelight on ball standardization, I wrote my trustworthy friend, Bernard Darwin, asking him what it all meant. Following is his reply:

"December 6, 1927

"Dear Mr. Macdonald:

"Many thanks for your letter. There seems to be, I am glad to say, a feeling slowly growing up in this country in favor of some limitation of the ball, though the average golfer does not want it and looks with suspicion on any restriction of his driving power.

"You may possibly have seen that there is a small body called the Gutty Club, (of which I am an unworthy member) containing some highly distinguished pros, Taylor, Braid, Herd and Ray, and we have played a couple of matches with a solid ball and these have attracted some attention. The ball is not really the old quality but a solid, homogeneous ball made of the stuff which is used in making the covers of the present rubber cored ball. I don't think that anybody but a complete fanatic deems it

possible ever to have a solid ball again, but these matches have made a good many people think that a floating rubber core is the right ball to standardize. If this reform ever came then it would be by the championship authorities making it obligatory to play a floater in the championships, and then the rest of the world would follow.

"The most hopeful thing is this—though at the moment I believe it is more or less of a secret—J. H. Taylor who is the big noise in the professional world is going to bring up at the next meeting of the Professional Golfers Association a resolution that the Championship Committee be requested to make a floating ball obligatory in the Open Championships. He believes he can get it through. If he does that would be a great step because the average golfer here is far more impressed by what the pros say than by what leading amateurs say. Of course, I don't know what the Championship Committee would do, but in any case it would be a great step. I am sure that the floater is the thing to go for as a practical measure of reform.

"The ball you heard about Harris and Gillies playing with is no doubt the solid ball which I mentioned in the earlier part of this letter. It is a pleasant ball to play with on a shortened course. A modern full-length course is a bit too long for it. I should reckon it is four or five strokes a round worse than the modern rubber core. The matches played suggest that that is about the handicap required.

*"Always yours sincerely,
Bernard Darwin."*

Here is the last word on this subject in a letter from John L. Low, one who has unfalteringly stood by the highest conception of the game born of our Scotch forebears and handed down to us through the ages from generation to generation:

*"Little Dunkeld
Hook Heath
Woking.
Jan. 4, 1928.*

"Yes, the ball question keeps coming up; and I do not think we have the best ball to bring out the full science of the game, with its varying

strokes. The ball has been developed entirely by the manufacturers, and they, of course, cater entirely for distance and ease of play. The ballmaker always comes to the player and says, 'Now here is a ball which makes the game easier for you to play. You may not be a good player, or skillful, but it will bring you nearer to the good and skillful players.' That is of course the proper way to sell a golf ball; but you and I have to fight for the game (who else will fight for it?) not for the gain of the ball maker....These ball makers and the other venders of clubs, will always give wrong information if they think it is to benefit their sales. I remember in 1914 being told by the experts that the last hickory tree had been cut down in America, or would be cut down in a few weeks. To-day, in this country, we have the best supply of first class shafts that man can remember.

"But to go back to the ball, I think that a solid ball would have no chance of gaining general consent (unless it was very cheap) and even then people will always buy distance if they can. The floating ball was what I favored in 1920 when the Americans were in consultation. I give you a very abridged extract from my printed Report to the General Meeting at St. Andrews, Sept. 1920....

" 'Your subcommittee were in favor of a specific gravity scheme, which would ultimately have meant a floating ball. I was personally of the same view but feared that general consent could not be obtained. This proved to be the case; for we found both the American and Canadian opinion strongly opposed. We had therefore to fall back on the limitations by a maximum size and maximum weight, which in the ordinary means of definition in ball games:—Regarding the question of Distance as secondary to that of Quality of Stroke, your representatives desired a lighter ball; the American delegates favored a heavier; it became therefore a matter for compromise.'

"As a matter of fact, Charlie, the Americans were not empowered to lower the weight below the most popular ball in America at that time, which was supposed to weigh 1.62 oz. avoir. Well I believe that after these years that people are coming to see that there is something in what I said about Quality of Stroke.

"This little, heavy ball only produces two strokes; a drive from a high wooden tee with a deep faced bludgeon, and another shot with a deep faced iron mashie niblick.

"I have an idea you are right, and that the 'floater' would improve the game as a game of skill; and I think that the professionals in this country have come to see that people won't bother to watch them playing exhibition matches, and playing the same shot all the time. If I live to see another two years, I believe we shall see the 'floater' for competitions: but the Americans will have to go with us this time.

"Yours ever,
John L. Low."

The above letters confirm my view that we will come to a floater. In a letter from Fownes, in reply to one of mine, he makes some very sound and pertinent remarks. Following is an extract:

"It is a very difficult matter to decide what is best to be done on the ball question. There are, however, certain phases of the problem which to my way of thinking admit of little argument. For example, a standard, if adopted, should be the result of agreement between the R. & A. and the U.S.G.A., and action when taken should be simultaneous in both countries. And further, no action should be taken which will not be supported by public opinion. The U.S.G.A. got itself into this unfortunate position in regard to the steel shaft. For two or three years the Association opposed the steel shaft, whereas in all play, excepting the National Championships, steel shafts were being used in increasing numbers. In other words, the prohibition was not supported by public opinion and as a result the authority and prestige of the U.S.G.A. suffered accordingly."

I agree with this statement of Fownes, but I think his apprehension regarding the public following is hardly justified should a floater be adopted.

Eighty per cent of the men who play golf, or, speaking more accurately, 80 per cent of the men who support the golf clubs of the world, would never be content to go back to the gutta. These 80 per cent do not average a 160-yard drive. With a floater they would not lose more than five yards, which would not worry them. Consequently, I believe the handicap men would be perfectly contented. But to go back to the gutta—never! Some years ago—I think it was in 1923—when the question was being debated the handicap men declared: "Why should we be denied the fruits of science and invention, because a few professionals and certain amateurs hit the ball out of sight? Besides, who keeps the game alive? Who provides the vast sums of money that are annually spent on golf? Why, the handicap man; in most cases the man with double figures to his name."

This is all very true, and one can sympathize with the vast army of handicap players. But is it for the general good of the game that a few distinguished persons endowed with great skill, the necessary physical powers, and helped by ingenious manufacturers, should contrive to make golf courses look silly? The manufacturers must be curbed; otherwise all the finer elements of the game will be eliminated.

At one time it was intimated that the Rules of Golf Committee was going to standardize the tee. The well-known golfer, Major H. D. Gillies, used a tee nine inches high, known as the Gillies "skyscraper," which consisted of five inches of rubber tubing affixed to a stick of wood four inches long, at the bottom of which is a nail which enabled the tee to be stuck firmly in the ground. His driver had an enormous head and a face two and a half inches deep. Gillies used this tee in the amateur championship at St. Andrews in 1924. After playing the first round the following official notice was posted by the Royal and Ancient Club as an obvious protest against the use of the Gillies tee:

"The Rules of Golf Committee hopes that golfers, before making use of abnormal methods of play or of abnormal implements, will earnestly consider whether they are acting in the spirit of the rules of golf and in particular with the spirit of the regulations governing the form and make of golf clubs.

"The committee considers that it is much to be deplored that players, instead of trying to master the use of golf clubs, should endeavor to overcome the difficulties of the game by using implements which have never been associated with it."

Gillies used the nine-inch tee at every hole except the two short holes and two others at which he preferred an ordinary small sand tee. Taken all round, no one believed he gained any great advantage in his driving.

It was not until Gillies finished that afternoon that he saw the notice issued by the Royal and Ancient Club, and he then said that if it applied to him he would submit the club, the use of which is essential with the high tee, to the Rules Committee for decision as to its legality. No further action was taken.

It is my opinion golfing authorities have already gone much too far trying to standardize the implements of the game. Confine themselves to the ball and in doing that don't play into the manufacturers' hands; let the players exercise some judgment in the kind of floater they will play with and also determine if the ball is self-centred and absolutely true by testing it in water, watching if the same side of the ball always turns up. If so it will prove to be not self-centred. This will give the manufacturer something to think about.

Jim Whigham tells me he agrees about the floater, but mainly because it will stop the standardizer talking. It is the most practical solution.

So much has been said about the rubber-cored ball burning up the courses. One has but to turn to the British open championship records and he will not find this contention supported by the scores since 1903. Following are the scores:

1903	Vardon	at Prestwick	300	strokes
1904	Jack White	" Sandwich	296	"
1906	James Braid	" Muirfield	300	"
1908	James Braid	" Prestwick	291	"
1909	J. H. Taylor	" Deal	295	"
1910	James Braid	" St. Andrews	299	"
1912	Edward Ray	" Muirfield	295	"
1921	Jack Hutchinson and Roger Wethered (tie)	" St. Andrews	296	"
1922	Walter Hagen	" Sandwich	300	"
1923	Arthur Havers	" Troon	295	"
1926	Bobby Jones	" Lytham and St. Ann's	291	"

The above shows no marked burning up of courses—nothing to become alarmed about.

The rubber-cored ball is inclined to favor the slipshod, careless player, yet it still remains a game of infinite scientific possibilities. The loss it has suffered in scientific play (mainly concerning the expert) is more than compensated for by its comparative simplicity by making it a boon and blessing to the multitude, many of whom otherwise would not have persevered in the game.

Chapter XV

Architecture

"To the solid ground of Nature trusts the mind that builds for aye."—Coleridge.

To my mind every aspirant who wishes to excel in golf architecture should learn by heart and endeavor to absorb the spirit of the following lines, copied from "The Art of Landscape Architecture," written by the great Humphrey Repton in 1797:

"If it should appear that, instead of displaying new doctrines or furnishing novel ideas, this volume serves rather by a new method to elucidate old established principles, and to confirm long received opinions, I can only plead in my excuse that true taste, in every art, consists more in adapting tried expedients to peculiar circumstances than in that inordinate thirst after novelty, the characteristic of uncultivated minds, which from the facility of inventing wild theories, without experience, are apt to suppose that taste is displayed by novelty, genius by innovation, and that every change must necessarily tend to improvement."

Viewing the monstrosities created on many modern golf courses which are a travesty on Nature, no golfer can but shudder for the soul of golf. It would seem that in this striving after "novelty and innovation," many builders of golf courses believe they are elevating the game. But what a sad contemplation!

Motoring to Southampton, I pass a goodly number of new courses. As I view the putting greens it appears to me they are all built similarly, more or less of a bowl or saucer type, then built up toward the back of the green, and then scalloped with an irregular line of low, waving mounds or hillocks, the putting green for all the world resembling a pie-faced woman with a marcel wave. I do not believe any one ever saw in nature anything approaching these home-made putting greens. Then scattered over the side of the fairway are mounds modeled after haycocks or chocolate-drops. The very soul of golf shrieks!

It is true that a group of golfers cannot always find an ideal terrain where they can build a fine golf course, but let the property be ever so flat, one may construct an interesting course.

The right length of holes can always be adopted; after that the character of the course depends upon the building of the putting greens. Putting greens to a golf course are what the face is to a portrait. The clothes the subject wears, the background, whether scenery or whether draperies—are simply accessories; the face tells the story and determines the character and quality of the portrait—whether it is good or bad. So it is in golf; you can always build a putting green. Teeing-grounds, hazards, the fairway, rough, etc., are accessories.

T. Suffern Tailer's nine-hole golf course at Newport was built upon flat pasture land, but by building up the greens and bunkering them after classical models the course is a most interesting one, as evidenced by the great interest best golfers take in Tommy Tailer's annual Gold Mashie Tournament.

I shall not attempt to write a treatise on building golf courses under all conditions of climate, character of soil, character of undulations, and all that is incident to varying situations; I only have space to suggest that which one should strive to attain on whatever land may be given. Any kind of golf is better than no golf at all, so we must strive to get the best possible.

To my mind there is much nonsense preached regarding golf courses. It is not in my province to lay down the law—what is right or wrong—but so long as I am writing this story I am going to tell you what I think is best, regardless of any criticism there may be of it. Criticizing a golf course is like going into a man's family. The fond mother trots up her children for admiration. Only a boor would express anything else than a high opinion. So it is a thankless task to criticize a friend's home golf course. "Where ignorance is bliss 'tis folly to be wise." It is natural one

T. SUFFERN TAILER'S "OCEAN LINKS," NEWPORT.
Macdonald has laid his second dead to the hole for a "birdie" 3; Bourne, having sliced his drive (with a carry of over 200 yards), is about to play his second. He holds the green, but loses the hole in par 4. The figures from left to right are: Macdonald, Tailer, Bourne, Frank Crocker, Ford Johnson, and Bert Walker. From a water-color presented to the author by Mr. Tailer.

should love his home course. He knows it, and with golf holes familiarity does not breed contempt, but quite the reverse.

This is best exemplified by experiences I have had in improving various holes on golf courses that I have fathered. Usually there is much objection to any alteration by the rank and file, but once done, when the club members become accustomed to the hole, they admit the justification for the alteration, which reminds one of Pope's lines:

> *"Vice is a monster of so frightful mien*
> *As, to be hated, needs but to be seen;*
> *Yet seen too oft, familiar with her face,*
> *We first endure, then pity, then embrace."*

I do not believe any one is qualified to pass on the merits of any one hole, let alone eighteen holes, unless he has played them under all the varying conditions possible—varying winds, rain, heat, frost, etc.

Wind I consider the finest asset in golf; in itself it is one of the greatest and most delightful accompaniments in the game. Without wind your course is always the same, but as the wind varies in velocity and from the various points of the compass, you not only have one course but you have many courses. Experts at the game temper their shots to the wind and learn how to make the most of it, pulling or slicing at will into the wind or hitting a low ball into the face of the wind. It is here that the true golfer excels. Low says: "A good player always prays for a windy day, but he must not pray too earnestly."

In designing a course try to lay out your holes so that they vary in direction. In this way a player gets an opportunity to play all the varying wind shots in a round. The National is noted for this. There is no wind from any point of the compass which favors a player for more than four or five holes.

A golf hole, humanly speaking, is like life, inasmuch as one cannot judge justly of any person's character the first time one meets him. Sometimes it takes years to discover and appreciate hidden qualities which only time discloses, and he usually discloses them on the links. No real lover of golf with artistic understanding would undertake to measure the quality or fascination of a golf hole by a yardstick, any more than a critic of poetry would attempt to measure the supreme sentiment expressed in a poem by the same method. One can understand the meter, but one cannot measure the soul expressed. It is absolutely inconceivable.

I read much about ideal and classical courses; I used both these terms when I dreamed of the National, but I should like to make this distinction—no course can be ideal which is laid out through trees. Trees foreshorten the perspective and the wind has not full play. To get the full exaltation playing the game of golf one should when passing from green to green as he gazes over the horizon have an unlimitable sense of eternity, suggesting contemplation and imagination. This does not mean that a classical course cannot be laid out where trees are or where there is not the Atlantic, the Pacific or the North Sea to contemplate; but there is a vast difference between the ideal and a classical course. Yale is classical; St. Andrews, the National Golf Links and the Lido, the Mid-Ocean are ideal.

In speaking of trees, when I was in that lovely valley, White Sulphur, where they have two exceedingly fine golf courses, the leaves fall like

PRINCE PAUL TROUBETZKOY AT WORK ON HIS STATUE OF CHARLES B. MACDONALD, AUGUST 2, 1915, IN MRS. WILLIE ASTOR CHANLER'S STUDIO.

snowflakes over the greens. Thornton Lewis told me it cost them $500 a year to clear the putting greens of leaves in the fall. The price of clearing the greens of leaves, of course, doesn't change the character of the hole except that it requires an effort to pick them up or brush them aside in the line of one's putt or through the green when they are within one club-length of your ball. Many times your ball is hidden under a leaf, causing a search for it and delaying the game.

There are many moot questions argued by noted designers of golf courses. The character and placing of hazards has always been a bone of contention. Why I cannot quite understand, because one has only to study the great holes which the world concedes are unexcelled. There should be every variety of hazard. Variety is not only "the spice of life" but it is the very foundation of golfing architecture. Diversity in nature is universal. Let your golfing architecture mirror it. An ideal or classical golf course demands variety, personality, and, above all, the charm of romance.

The undulations and the run of the ball tell the story as to how the hazards should be placed. Don't place them without experience. Generally speaking, as stated above, they should be of great variety, the greater the better, but always fair. By fair I mean where a player can extract the ball in one shot if reasonably well played in some direction.

Errors in play should be severely punished in finding hazards, but now the golfer wants his bunkers raked and all the unevenness of the fairway rolled out. A player does not get the variety of stances or lies that in olden times one was sure to have. A hanging lie or a ball lying in any position other than level is a blemish to the modern golfer. The science and beauty of the game is brought out by men having to play the ball from any stance. To play the game over a flat surface without undulations leaves nothing to the ingenuity of the player, and nothing is presented but an obvious and stereotyped series of hits. To-day there seems to be a constant endeavor to make golf commonplace, to emasculate it, as it were, of its finer qualities.

Sand mounds are excellent grouped not where one has to climb up ten or fifteen feet, but say three to six feet, planted with sea bent so that the mounds will not blow away, but hold the sand in strong winds. The bent prevents lies where an expert player can take an iron club and easily make 100 to 140 yards recovery. Sand mounds can be created to conform truly with nature, but pot bunkers rarely do if on flat ground; never if they are not on the side of a mound or hill can they be made to look natural, and when building a course this should be borne in mind.

I do not believe in deep-ditch hazards; they always have long pass, usually very long in the bottom, are generally muddy and frequently have casual water, involving rules not generally understood. Water hazards should always be well defined. An arm of the sea can be wonderfully utilized, as can also a brook or stream; the former is much to be desired. I think Brancaster has one of the finest holes I know, where there are two arms of the sea running diagonally between the tee and the hole. Bushes never should be placed on the line of the hole, but can be so utilized on a dog-leg hole, where they are excellent, as they give severe punishment if they are not properly negotiated; also bushes say thirty yards from the middle of the course on the side, as rough similar to what St. Andrews used to be when it was at its best with the whins of some fifty years ago. Bushes, if placed too close, entail searching for one's ball, which is often lost. In such instances they should be thinned out. Searching for a lost ball is not a pleasant vocation, but since golf was first played a lost ball has always been a part of the game. So reconcile yourself to tradition.

Paths or roads should never be built introducing them as part of the course. If established before the course is laid out, leave them as natural hazards, but see that they are fair in their position.

I think there should be two holes which have fine large cross-bunkers protecting the green, both long two-shot holes; one, a hole resembling the Alps at Prestwick 410 to 430 yards in length; the other placed in a punch-bowl, say from 420 to 440 yards long. The cross-bunker in the latter case should be severe and very difficult, placed quite close to the green, for the reason that if one carries over the bunker he is home and protected on all sides. Holes of this character are of the very finest. Only the good golfers can reach these greens in two strokes; the others must play short so that the cross-bunker is no punishment to them unless they top their third shot. Ninety per cent of the players cannot reach a 420-yard hole in two strokes, while the scratch men have to make really fine seconds, and if the wind is against them, the second will be a very difficult second. Fine drives and fine long second shots give the finest emotion or thrill in golf. That is why two-shot holes are the best in golf.

I do not like cross-bunkers directly across the entire fairway to be carried from the tee unless built so that a player has his choice to "bite off as much as he can chew" by making them diagonal A few such bunkers are excellent, diagonal or en echelon. Why a player should condemn the placing of any bunker I fail to comprehend. Any bunker properly placed is excellent.

Johnny Low has stated that there is hardly such a thing as an unfair bunker. He is right. Variety is what one wants in a hole properly laid out. Long carries should not be compulsory, but if taken, the player should have a distinct advantage. Where there are bunkers at varying distances from the tee, the player has the option of going around or over according to his judgment. Bear in mind that a course must be absorbing and interesting, and not built for crack players only. Don't sacrifice accuracy for length.

A golf architect should endeavor never to construct what is known as a "trick green"; otherwise he will be suspected of being a card sharp. Don't seek an original idea in building a golf course. John La Farge somewhere has said if "an idea were an original one it is safe to say it would not be a good one."

I should like also to suggest that the construction of bunkers on various courses should have an individuality entirely of their own which should arouse the love or hatred of intelligent golfers. Rest assured such holes are far too complex for one's absolute condemnation or absolute approval. Bunkers of this character are much to be desired on any golf course.

Golf architects should make use of ground sloping in toward the bunkers as a means of enlarging the scope and peril of the bunkers. An appreciation of this is very valuable in constructing bunkers.

Always bear in mind that golf courses are not laid out for scoring competitions, and as long as a good player can get out in one stroke, either forward, backward, or to one side, that bunker is not unfair. The risk of going into a bunker is self-imposed, so there is no reason why a player should condemn a bunker as unfair. If there were not more or less luck in a game it would not be worthy of the name, and a risk should be taken commensurate with the gravity of the situation which brings out the ideal factor, luck, and raises it above a mere record-breaking competition.

The principle of a dog-leg hole can be made a feature of several holes advantageously, usually from the tee, but there is no reason why one hole should not be featured by a dog-leg for the second shot.

In laying out the National here is a bit of advice I received from Charles F. Whigham, a very fine golf player:

"I. Don be in a hurry to make many bunkers through the green until the course has been played on for a bit. Until you have played on a course a good deal in all winds and at all seasons, both wet and dry, it is impossible to gauge the length that good shots will get. This does not apply to bunkers round the greens. You can't have too many of these, as, granted that you have a fair sized good green, a good player ought to be able to put his ball upon it no matter how many bunkers there are round about.

"II. Don't make great big bunkers, but groups of small deep bunkers after St. Andrews' style. A big bunker is the flukiest thing I know. If you

lie clean you are not punished at all, while if you lie in a bad hole, the strongest man can't hit the ball hard enough to get out."

Where I have large bunkers at the National, such as at the second hole, I plant sea bent. This prevents the sand from blowing and prevents the player from getting a full shot from the hazard.

I should always advise a place for three tees; one the championship tee, which would probably give pleasure to less than 5 per cent of your club membership; then the regular tees, which two-thirds of your club membership really care to play, leaving about 30 per cent of your club membership to play from the short tees, which means men who can drive only about 120 or 130 yards. This gives all your members a fair game and you do not take the joy out of their life.

I have not touched upon one fundamental in golf course construction, and that is, the necessity of having an abundant supply of water with good pressure to sprinkle the fairway from 150 to 270 yards from the tee and also the putting greens and the approach thereto. If the various courses in this country would water their fairway as above, you would hear very much less about 250 to 280-yard drives. Secondly, do not fail to have the low spots well drained.

In expressing my opinion on architecture in this chapter the reader must bear in mind I am assuming the golf course is being constructed on a desirable terrain. I have known a number of men of means with large estates who desired private eighteen-hole golf courses. I have always endeavored to deter them from building a private course of that character for the reason that they are very rarely kept up and it is difficult to get people to come and play. On a private course it is seldom that there are more than three or four playing, so it is more or less lonely.

I tried to deter Otto Kahn from building eighteen holes, but he thought he would like to have a fine lawn in front of his beautiful Long Island house. Of course, that in itself is worth while.

When Payne Whitney proposed building an eighteen-hole golf course on his property at Manhasset the land was not adapted to it, and I persuaded him to build a nine-hole course and to build it on some twenty or thirty acres immediately back of his home. I grouped three classic holes in the centre of the land which had to be played to at different angles. In this way it was perfectly simple to get nine good holes on a small

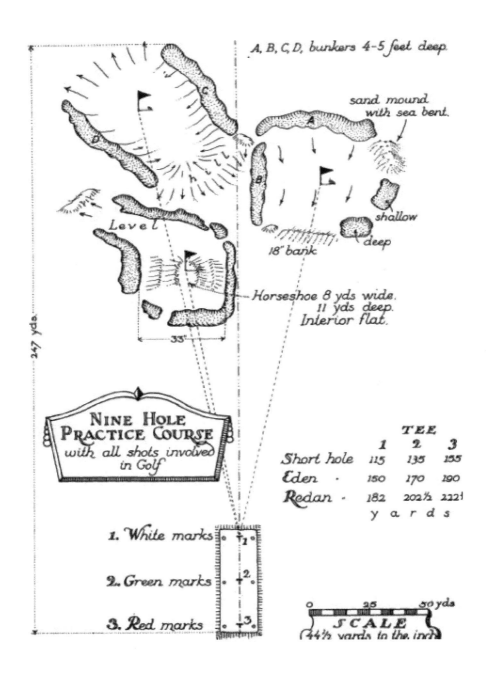

acreage. It could easily take care of ten or twelve men playing, and I doubt very much if there were ever more than that number golfing over his course. It was beautifully kept up and one had as many fine golfing shots as he could have had on any golf course. This suggested to me the building of a practice ground on six acres by grouping three well-known classical greens, namely, a short hole, an Eden hole, and a Redan. By making a tee forty-two yards long by fifteen yards in width one could go to the front tee and play a ball to each green, then go to the middle tee and play a ball to each green, and then go to the third tee and play a ball to each green—that is, nine balls in all—then walk to the different greens and play them out. Having done this, take the balls back to the tee again and instead of teeing them drop them so you will get the fairway practice the same as if you were playing through the green.

I am appending herewith a sketch of this situation. Any one in the vicinity of New York can, I am sure, at any time run down to Eddie Moore's place at Roslyn and see holes patterned more or less on this idea which I laid out a year or two ago.

I read a golf article not long since in which the writer called a "fetish" the copying of holes from the classical courses of Great Britain, holes which have the testimony of all the great golfers for more than a century or two past as being expressive of the best and noblest phases of the game.

Architecture is one of the five fine arts. If the critic's contention is true, then architecture must be a "fetish," as the basis of it is the copying of Greek and Roman architecture, Romanesque and Gothic, and in our own times among other forms, Georgian and Colonial architecture. One must have the gift of imagination to successfully apply the original to new situations. Surely there is nothing "fetish" about this.

I believe in reverencing anything in the life of man which has the testimony of the ages as being unexcelled, whether it be literature, paintings, poetry, tombs—even a golf hole.

Perhaps it may be apropos to close this chapter by quoting another great landscape architect, Prince Puckler:

"Time is not able to bring forth new truths but only an unfolding of timeless truths."

Chapter XVI

Rambling Thoughts: The Physiological and Psychological Aspect

"Know then thyself. Presume not God to scan, The proper study of mankind is man."—Pope.

The Banffshire *Journal* states that the earliest reference to golf in the burgh of Banff (Scotland) is in the year 1637 when Francis Brown, "ane boy of ane evil lyeff," was hanged on the Gallows Hill of Banff for *inter alia* stealing "Some Golf Ballis," two of which he confessed "he sauld to Thomas Urquhartis."

Again, in the fall of 1910 a magistrate in Birkenhead, England, fined a man who picked up a golf ball on the links one pound, and the man who bought it was fined five pounds.

At the present time the habit of caddies losing balls on the links purposely and then going to find them later, and the practice of pilfering balls from a man's bag, caused Robert Watson, while president of the U.S.G.A., to write a pamphlet endeavoring to make this offense punishable. But it takes more than an edict from a golf committee to change human nature. Golf balls still disappear mysteriously.

The only solution as far as I have been able to discover is to have each man's ball marked with his name and have the professional, when the ball is returned to him, give the boy a small reward and return the ball to its owner. No unmarked balls should be allowed to be bought.

* * *

It is bewildering the number of books that are published to-day by various golfing enthusiasts who have attained some proficiency in the game and by some who do not know how to play well but try to instruct other people how to play and how a golf course should be constructed. To my mind there is a wealth of stupidity in this, and while I apologize for my own, I wish to say that I am not trying to teach anything but simply reminiscing, endeavoring to express what I have sensed in the game, hoping to present some sidelights on which the uninitiated have not pondered.

There are two kinds of golfers who attain exceptional proficiency; one, the natural golfer; the other an acquired golfer by infinite pains. The natural golfer acquires his own style, his swing in addressing the ball, etc., etc. No two of the great golfers play alike—stance, swing, and follow-through. Much depends on a man's physique, which must determine his style of play. The acquired golfer follows the tenets of teachers, practices incessantly, and usually has a laborious style. There is little that can really be taught by precept in golf; the game itself is beyond all that.

It is perfectly simple to tell a beginner, after showing him how to hold his club and how to stand, that he must keep his eye on the ball, he must go slowly back, he must not sway his body, he must keep his head down, he must follow-through, and all the other guiding admonitions. Yet a perfectly good, well-formed, strong, and healthy man with a keen eye may do all this and yet never really learn to play the game well, try as he will. In getting all these injunctions synchronized comes the real test of a man's inherent ability to excel; primarily there must be concentration, and further, there must be coordination with the subconscious self, strength applied with extreme delicacy.

There is no game I know of where the mind so often influences the body as in the game of golf. Concentration every one knows is essential to accomplish the best in you when playing the game. That being admitted, the obvious corollary is that any deviation of the mind influences the body, usually causing more or less disaster. Some one moving or talking when you are addressing your ball diverts your mind and influences your stroke. Your ball falls off the tee, concentration is interrupted and it becomes an effort to reassume your attitude of mind. I remember quite well when I played golf in Scotland in the seventies no Scotchman would re-tee his ball on the same spot where his ball had fallen off the tee. He was convinced that it presaged a bad shot.

I always thought this rank superstition, but after years of golfing experience I believe psychologically the Scotch were right, for one never seems to get back the same attitude of mind that he had when he stepped up to the first ball, confident of striking it. He wavers between himself and the superstition of his opponent.

I can well remember Harold Hilton at the time he won the amateur championship of the United States at Apawamis beckoning me to speak to him, and then he requested me to ask the U.S.G.A. officials not to permit any one to approach him, explaining that he was so determined and so concentrated on winning his match he did not wish to have his mind diverted. He explained further that he would be only too happy after the game was over to grant an interview to any one and answer anything he was capable of replying to. That was *psychic.*

Again I can recall in 1920 motoring out with Charles E. Mitchell to Southampton. We stopped at the Engineers' Club where the amateur championship was being held. Following Bobby Jones for one or two holes we witnessed him putting out. He had a downhill putt some twelve feet from the hole when a bee hovered about his ball. He brushed it away again and again, but the bee was so persistent that finally he chased it around the putting green like a whippet after a hare. The bee was finally hived and Bobby went to his ball. He putted and overran the hole about one yard, and coming back he missed the putt. Ordinarily he would have holed the first putt once out of three times. I turned to Charlie Mitchell, saying: "Mark my words, he will not win. He lacks concentration."

In his book just published Bobby Jones says that his first win in a U.S.G.A. championship was at Inwood in 1923. In the previous seven years he had played in eleven national championships and had never won one. He states he was becoming discouraged, but in those years he went through the ordeal of learning to know himself and control himself, overcoming the feeling that if he missed a shot it wasn't necessary to throw his club as far after the ball as his dubbing shot justified. He tells us it required a tremendous effort to acquire self-control. He says he still has the same feeling, but his only way of showing it is by becoming red behind the ears. All this is *psychic.* After conquering himself and winning the open in 1923 Bobby Jones won five national championships in the next four years. To attain self-knowledge there is no place more likely to give one an insight into his own character and enable him to find himself

BOBBY JONES

than on the golf links, and there one should go if he desires to acquire that knowledge of himself.

A really fine golf player, as his record demonstrates, but one who never could control himself, was Fred Herreshoff. However, he always played in the best spirit of the game. I can remember in one of the championships before Fred went out to play, Travis and myself were standing with him when he was taking a strong glass of brandy. I remonstrated with him, but Travis turned to me and said: "Don't do it. He is of such a nature that he must awaken his subconscious self to accomplish some of the wonderful shots he pulls off." To my mind that was rank heresy then, and it is heresy now.

It is curious how well we play against certain opponents and how badly against others. It can only be explained by psychology. Herein lies the unfathomable fascination of the game. Attempting wholly to possess it is like attempting to square the circle, to capture perpetual motion or discover the fourth dimension. Nor can any one teach you to control yourself; it is a battle with yourself, you alone must conquer yourself.

This aspect of golf was brought out very well in an article by Henry Chellew, lecturer on psychology at the University of London:

"All games which demand skill, foresight, concentration and undivided attention are matters which involve both psychology and philosophy. In other words, they call for wisdom, caution and care on the part of the players, and these virtues are not created in a moment, but they may be regarded as the children of experience. Whatever braces the wits and sharpens the faculties may be regarded from the standpoint of philosophy—i.e., the wise way of looking at things. 'Keep your eye on the ball' contains as much philosophy as the tag 'Festina lente,' and is quite as important. When walking up the fairway after the ball we are in Nature's great scheme, out of doors, giving rein to our pent-up energies and mental complexes. Indeed, we endow our minds with wings, uplift our hearts with the zest of the game, and expand our lungs with life-giving energies. This is not the so-called philosophy of the Lyceum and the Academy, but it is rather the wisdom of the Book of Life itself, wherein we drop the artificiality of the life of the city, and we become awhile real human beings. Golf enables us to advance in the great business of being a human being. The man who regards golf as a matter of 'card and pencil' is not a golfer at all, for he has lost his soul in arithmetic, whereas the true golfer puts his soul into the game for the love of it, and not because it amounts to a mere matter of mathematics as he wends his way back to the club house."

Apropos of the slowness of players which is caused by four-ball matches more than anything else, unless it be the abominable scoring

FRED HERRESHOFF

habit, it is interesting to note that Jim Whigham and myself, when playing a single, usually went around in an hour and forty to an hour and forty-five minutes. Commenting upon this after two rounds of golf at Garden City, one evening Jim Whigham offered to bet he could go around the course in fifty-five minutes under 100 strokes and never go off a walk. Wagers being placed, he started out about six o'clock the same evening. He did the first nine holes in 42 strokes, which was his usual score when deliberate. Coming in he was not so fortunate, and took 49 strokes, making a grand total of 91, covering the course in forty-nine minutes and twenty seconds.

Another story that I think is worth recording is of a well-known member of the Garden City Golf Club, the National, and a number of other leading clubs, who was noted for his excessive deliberation and holding up the field. Going out late one afternoon with Fred Herreshoff and Jim Whigham to have a round at Garden City we found our slow friend had been waiting all afternoon for a game, and he asked Fred if he might join us. I told Fred no—that we were out to have a pleasant game and could not wait on him, having only two hours of daylight. Fred came back and told me that the slow friend said he would agree to keep up with us, so we assented. Extraordinary as it may seem, although his usual game was about 85, he made a 79, the lowest score he ever made around the Garden City course. Sometimes he fairly ran between the shots.

* * *

In 1924 and 1925 Bobby Jones won the amateur championship. Consequently, his home club, the East Lake Club, of Atlanta, Ga., became the custodian of the Havemeyer Cup. Unfortunately, this club house was destroyed by fire on December 22, 1925, and with it the Havemeyer Cup.

For some reason or another, the U.S.G.A. did not favor having a replica of it made. Edward S. Moore, who was then a member of the Committee, offered the Association a very handsome gold cup which had much more room for the names of future winners of the amateur event. Eddie Moore insisted that it should be called the Havemeyer Cup, and requested that his name should not be placed on it, and it was without his consent that his name appeared.

The Havemeyer Cup had a far-reaching sentimental value. It was to many of us the genius of the game in America, pledged, as it was, to be played for under the rules of the Royal and Ancient Golf Club.

* * *

While studying the various courses abroad Jim Whigham and I visited La Boulie at Versailles in 1906, where Arnaud Massy was the professional. Going around the course to see if there was any outstanding golf hole, Massy played the best of Whigham's and my ball. We were quite impressed by his play, and concluded that he had an excellent chance of

JIM WHIGHAM

winning the open in Great Britain, which he did at Prestwick in 1907. He also tied with Vardon in 1911, but lost in the play-off.

Yves Botcazon, the one-armed player, was at La Boulie when we visited the course. He was capable of giving Massy a good match, and it is recorded that he made the La Boulie course in 72, which is a remarkable score.

* * *

Scotland's Gift: Golf

After Bobby Jones won the United States open championship in 1923, the same year that Roger Wethered won the British amateur championship at Deal, a dinner was given Bobby Jones at Atlanta, and Harry Atkinson, a friend to whom I am devoted, who presided, asked me to send a message. Following is the message:

"To my mind no two events have ever occurred in any one year in golfing history which have done so much for the honor, dignity and purity of the game as Roger Wethered's victory in Great Britain and Bobby Jones' victory in America. Cleaner, finer sportsmen do not exist, and this example should prove a great incentive for fair and honorable practice among everyone who plays the game.

"Extend to Bobby Jones my keen appreciation of his win and what it means to golf."

One of the most delightful sensations I have experienced in a long time was when I learned of Bobby Jones renunciation of the wonderful tribute paid him by his friends and admirers in Atlanta who gave him a $50,000 house. His refusal of it had nothing to do with his amateur status—that was secure—but he was keenly sensitive about the welfare of the game in its highest significance, and, like a true nobleman, stood by his convictions.

So many people preach equity in golf. Nothing is so foreign to the truth. Does any human being receive what he conceives as equity in his life? He has got to take the bitter with the sweet, and as he forges through all the intricacies and inequalities which life presents, he proves his metal. In golf the cardinal rules are arbitrary and not founded on eternal justice. Equity has nothing to do with the game itself. If founded on eternal justice the game would be deadly dull to watch or play. The essence of the game is inequality, as it is in humanity. The conditions which are meted out to the players, such as inequality of the ground, cannot be governed by a green committee with the flying divots of the players or their footprints in the bunkers. Take your medicine where you find it and don't cry. Remember that the other fellow has got to meet exactly the same inequalities. Johnny Low says it is this idea of equity with which the brains of so many golfers are obsessed, and at the bottom of it all is the outcry against the stymie.

* * *

BOBBY JONES AND THE AUTHOR AT ATLANTA, GEORGIA, 1926.

I do not like to refer to people who are always trying to tinker with the rules of the game. They are to me heretics. One group of men make an effort to increase the size of the hole; another group think putting too important, and desire to call a stroke on the putting green one-half stroke. God forbid!

If you have a good sporting game, for heaven's sake don't try too much to improve it. Your business is not to improve the game *but to improve your play.*

The scoring habit of American golfers is a pernicious habit, much to be deplored, and if persisted in will result in the destruction of the eternal conception of the game in its highest sense. As Johnny Low has stated:

"The beginner wished to know his own worth as a player day by day, and conceived the plan of writing his autobiography on small pieces of paper planned for the purpose. Golf became for him of interest only in so far as his own total of hits and misses was concerned....In this selfish struggle it is little wonder that the position and very life of golf as a game is assailed."

* * *

Scotland's Gift: Golf

I have read many times golfing writers who support the statement that golf is a sport and not a game. I was brought up to call it a game, and I have examined a number of the leading dictionaries and I cannot see where the difference comes in, but if there is a difference here is the nicest distinction I have found:

"Sport is defined as a recreation where man pits himself against Nature, and with his wits endeavors with his skill to anticipate and overcome the unknown. A game differs from a sport in that the natural element involved is already known, as billiards, croquet, baseball, racquets, tennis, and cricket."

From my point of view it matters little whether it is a sport or game. It is all the same to those who love it. I suppose some one will come along and write chapters on this distinction, but what matters is when we go out into the open with our friends to follow one of the most delightful, absorbing, and intelligent pursuits that has ever been conceived.

* * *

When one considers how golf has been introduced on virgin soil 3,000 miles from the fountain-head, among people who had been taught from the time of the Revolution that they were a law unto themselves and resented any enthrallment which might be dictated by the mother country, it is really extraordinary how well the game has established itself in harmony with most that was best in it in its Scotch home. Here and there there have been dissentions, but when all is said and done there are only a few unimportant diversions from the established game as fathered by the Royal and Ancient Golf Club of St. Andrews; notably, the use of the Schenectady putter and steel shafts, both of which are infinitesimally unimportant. There are a few rules of which the interpretation varies somewhat, but this also matters little. In the matches played when the Oxford and Cambridge team was here in 1903 and since in the various Walker Cup Matches there never has been one question of difference between the players. Everything has been harmonious. They played one game, a game of noble hearts and noble minds, its one end success honorably attained.

I personally contend that any section of the world may play any game which it desires and possibly call it golf, though it will not be golf. There is no reason why one section should dominate another, but there is every reason why a community desiring to play golf should abide by the guiding spirit of St. Andrews. Wait, and in time the prodigal son will surely return home.

The Royal and Ancient Golf Club of St. Andrews never attempted to dominate the English who had ten times the number of golfers that Scotland could muster. St. Andrews simply said:

"We are going to play the game as it was handed down to us by our forefathers. We will tell you how it was handed down, and we will give you our interpretation of the rules and endeavor to convey to you all the spirit of the game, but do as you like, much as we desire to see you play the game that has been played for so many centuries in Scotland."

The result is that the Royal and Ancient has been universally accepted as the parent of the game, and its influence has prevailed over Great Britain and Ireland. St. Andrews had nothing to gain but only to give, which it has done freely, generously, and ungrudgingly.

I am absolutely confident from my experiences in my boyhood days that the game to-day, if anything, is not quite as fine in its character as it was when I first played it. The game was played more on honor, without bickering; when you played you played conscientiously, with your strength, with everything good in you, and it was inconceivable your opponent would try to cheat or deceive you. It didn't take long to find out if some opponent was not doing the right thing. When discovered he was quietly sent to Coventry and ostracized. In a community like Scotland this could be done, and the punishment was far greater than any Board of Governors could inflict.

When one studies the past history of golf he marvels that so many types of men with their multitude of interests and occupations should have concentrated on this game as their chief form of recreation, and it would seem to prove its democracy in the highest sense as meaning a conception of culture, not so much as striving after intellectual knowledge, such as that which tends to make artists, philosophers or saints.

THE HONORABLE MORGAN J. O'BRIEN AND THE AUTHOR, 1924.

In August, 1926, after eighteen years of service on the Rules of Golf Committee of the Royal and Ancient Golf Club I resigned—Howard F. Whitney was appointed to fill the vacancy, unhappily, only for less than a year, when to the regret and sorrow of the entire golfing community he passed away. J. Fritz Byers was then appointed to fill his place.

* * *

Finally reminiscing over the fifty-five years of my golfing experience, I am impressed with deep feeling that the most compelling force in the joy I have taken out of life from youth to three-score and ten years and has made life worth living for me and led me to contentment has been golf. It is best expressed in poetry. Here is something that was written by Edward Dyer the last half of the sixteenth century:

> "My mind to me a kingdom is,
>   Such present joys therein I find
> That it excels all other bliss
>   That earth affords or grows by kind:
> Though much I want which most would have,
> Yet still my mind forbids to crave.
>
> "Content to live, this is my stay:
>   I seek no more than may suffice;
> I press to bear no haughty sway;
>   Look, what I lack my mind supplies:
> Lo, thus I triumph like a king,
> Content with that my mind doth bring.
>
> "Some have too much, yet still do crave;
>   I have little and seek no more,
> They are but poor, though much they have,
>   And I am rich with little store:
> They poor, I rich; they beg, I give;
> They lack, I leave; they pine, I live.
>
> "My wealth is health and perfect ease;
>   My conscience clear my chief defense;
> I neither seek by bribes to please,
>   Nor by deceit to breed offense;
> Thus do I live, thus will I die;
> Would all did so as well as I!"

As I dedicate this book to my grandchildren and to golfing posterity, I should like to commend them in their leisure moments to pursue the game of golf for diversion, for health, and for companionship, forever endeavoring to find the soul of golf, for possibly if they do they may discover their own souls.

Appendix

LINKS, *s., pl.*

1. The windings of a river, *s.* "Its numerous windings, called links, form a great number of beautiful peninsulas, which, being of a very luxuriant and fertile soil, gave rise to the following old rhyme:

    > "The lairdship of the bonny Links of Forth,
    > Is better than an Earldom in the North."
    > —Nimmo's "Stirlingshire," pp. 439, 440.

2. The rich ground lying among the windings of a river, *s.*

    > "Attune the lay that should adorn
    > Ilk verse descriptive o' the morn;
    > Whan round Forth's Links o' waving corn
    >   At peep o' dawn,
    > Frae broomy know to whitening thorn
    >   He raptur'd ran."
    > —Macneill's "Poems," ii. 13.

3. The sandy flat ground on the seashore, covered with what is called bent-grass, furze, etc., *s.* This term, it has been observed, is nearly synonymous with downs, *e.* In this sense we speak of the Links of Leith, of Montrose, etc.

"Upoun the Palme Sonday Evin, the Frenche had thameselfis in battell array upoun the Links without Leyth, and had sent furth thair skurmischears."—Knox's "History," p. 223.

"In his (the Commissioner's) entry, I think, at Leith, as much honour was done unto him as ever to a king in our country.—We were most conspicuous in our black cloaks, above five hundred on a brae-side in the Links alone for his sight."—Baillie's "Letters," i. 61.

This passage, we may observe by the way, makes us acquainted with the costume of the clergy, at least when they attended the General Assembly, in the reign of Charles I. The etiquette of the time required that they should all have black cloaks.

"The island of Westray—contains, on the north and southwest sides of it, a great number of graves, scattered over two extensive plains, of that nature which are called links in Scotland."—Barry's "Orkney," p. 205. "Sandy, flat ground, generally near the sea." Note, ibid.

4. The name has been transferred, but improperly, to ground not contiguous to the sea, either because of its resemblance to the beach, as being sandy and barren! or as being appropriated to a similar use, *s.*

Thus, part of the old Boroughmuir of Edinburgh is called Bruntsfield Links. The most probable of the designation is, that it having been customary to play at golf on the Links of Leith, when the ground in the vicinity of Bruntsfield came to be used in the same way, it was in like manner called Links.

* * *

THE OLDEST SURVIVING CODE
Articles and Laws in Playing the Golf
(St. Andrews, May 14, 1754)

I. You must Tee your Ball within a Club length of the Hole.

II. Your Tee must be upon the ground.

III. You are not to change the Ball which you strike off the Tee.

IV. You are not to remove Stones, Bones, or any Break-club for the sake of playing your Ball, except upon the fair Green, and that only within a Club length of your Ball.

V. If your Ball come among Water, or any watery filth, you are at liberty to take out your Ball, and throw it behind the hazard, six yards at least; you may play it with any club and allow your adversary a stroke for so getting out your Ball.

VI. If your Balls be found anywhere touching one another, you are to lift the first Ball till you play the last.

VII. At holing, you are to play your Ball honestly for the Hole, and not to play upon your Adversary's Ball, not lying in your way to the Hole.

VIII. If you should lose your Ball by its being taken up, or in any other way, you are to go back to the spot where you struck last, and drop another Ball, and allow your Adversary a stroke for the misfortune.

IX. No man, at Holing his Ball, is to be allowed to mark to the Hole with his Club or anything else.

X. If a Ball be stop'd by any person, Horse, Dog, or anything else, the Ball so stopped must be played where it lies.

XI. If you draw your Club in order to strike, and proceed so far in the stroke as to be bringing down your Club—if then your Club shall break in any way it is to be accounted a stroke.

XII. He whose Ball lyes farthest from the Hole is obliged to play first.

XIII. Neither Trench, Ditch, nor Dyke made for the preservation of the Links, nor the Scholars' holes, nor the Soldiers' lines, shall be accounted a Hazard, but the Ball is to be taken out, Teed, and played with any iron Club.

* * *

RULES FOR THE GAME OF GOLF AS IT IS PLAYED BY THE ROYAL AND ANCIENT GOLF CLUB OF ST. ANDREWS OVER THEIR LINKS
(May 5, 1858)

I. Mode and Order of Playing the Game

The Game of Golf is played by two persons, or by four (two of a side) playing alternately. It may also be played by three or more persons, each playing his own ball. The game commences by each party playing off a ball from a place called the tee, near the first hole. In a match of four, those who are opposed to each other, and to play-off, shall be named at starting, and shall continue so during the match. The person entitled to play-off first shall be named by the parties themselves; and although the courtesy of starting is generally granted to old captains of the Club, or members, it may be settled by lot or toss of a coin. The hole is won by the party holing at fewest strokes, and the reckoning of the game is made by the terms odds and like, one more, two more, etc. The party gaining the hole is to lead, unless his adversary has won the match, in which case the adversary leads off, and is entitled to claim his privilege, and to recall his adversary's stroke should he play out of order. One round of the Links, or 18 holes, is reckoned a match, unless otherwise stipulated. If, in a double match, one person shall play twice in succession, he loses the hole.

II. Place of Teeing

The ball must be teed not nearer the hole (either in front or side of the hole) than six club lengths, and not farther from it than eight, and after the balls are struck off, the ball farthest from the hole to which the parties are playing must be played first. When two parties meet on the Putting Green, the party first there may claim the privilege of holing out, and any party coming up must wait till the other party has played out the hole, and on no account play their balls up lest they should annoy the parties who are putting. No player may play his teed ball, till the party in front have played their second strokes.

III. Changing the Ball

The balls struck off the tee must not be changed, touched, or moved before the hole is played out (except in striking, and the cases provided for by Rules VIII., XVIII., and XIX.); and if the parties are at a loss to know the one ball from the other, neither shall be lifted till both parties agree.

IV. Lifting of Break-Clubs, etc.

All loose impediments within a club length of the ball may be removed on or off the Course, when the ball lies on grass (see Rules VI. and XII.). When a ball lies in a bunker or sand, there shall be no impression made, nor sand or other obstacle removed by the club, or otherwise, before striking at the ball. When a ball lies within a club length of a washing-tub, the tub may be removed, and when on clothes the ball may be lifted and dropped behind them.

V. Entitled to See the Ball

When a ball is completely covered with fog, bent, whirs, etc., so much thereof shall be set aside as that the player shall merely have a view of his ball before he plays, whether in a line with the hole or otherwise. A ball stuck fast in wet ground or sand may be taken out and replaced loosely in the hole it has made.

VI. Clearing the Putting Green

All loose impedimenta, of whatever kind, may be lifted on the Putting Green or Table Land on which the hole is placed, which is considered not to exceed twenty yards from the hole. Nothing can be lifted either on the Course or Putting Green, if it is to move the ball out of its position.

VII. Lifting Balls

When, on any part of the Course, or off it, or in a bunker, the balls lie within six inches of each other, the ball nearest the hole must be lifted till the other is played, and then placed as nearly as possible in its original position—the six inches to be measured from the surface of the balls. In a three-ball match, the ball in any degree interposing between the player and the hole on the Putting Green, must be played out.

VIII. Ball in Water, or in the Burn, and Place of Re-teeing

If the ball is in water, the player may take it out, change the ball if he pleases, tee it, and play from behind the hazard, losing a stroke. If the ball lies in any position in the burn across the first hole, the player may take it out, tee it on the line where it entered the burn, on the opposite side from the hole to which he is playing, and lose a stroke; or he may play it where it lies, without a penalty. However, should a ball be driven into the Eden at the high hole, or the sea at the first hole, the ball must be placed a club length in front of either sea or river, the player or party losing a stroke.

IX. Rubs of the Green

Whatever happens to a ball by accident, such as striking any person, or being touched with the foot by a third party, or by the fore-caddy, must be reckoned a rub of the green, and submitted to. If, however, the player's ball strikes his adversary, or his adversary's caddy or clubs, the adversary loses the hole; or, if it strikes himself or his partner, or their caddies or clubs, or if he strikes the ball a second time while in the act of playing, the player loses the hole. If the player touch the ball with his foot, or any part of his body, or with anything except his club, or if he with his club moves the ball in preparing to strike, he loses a stroke; and if one party strikes his adversary's ball with his club, foot, or otherwise, that party loses the hole. But if he plays it inadvertently, thinking it his own, and the adversary who plays the wrong ball, it is then too late to claim the penalty, and the hole must be played out with the balls thus changed. If, however, the mistake occurs from wrong information given by one party to the other, the penalty cannot be claimed; and the mistake, if discovered before the other party has played, must be rectified by replacing the ball as nearly as possible where it lay. If the player's ball be played away by mistake, or lifted by a third party, then the player must drop a ball as near the spot as possible, without any penalty. Whatever happens to a ball, on a Medal day, such as a player striking his caddy, or himself, or his clubs, or moving the ball with his foot or club, or his caddy doing so, or the player striking it twice before it stops motion, the player in such case shall lose one stroke only as the penalty.

X. Ball Lost

If a ball is lost, the player (or his partner, in a double match), returns to the spot, as near as possible, where the ball was struck, tees another ball, and loses both the distance and a stroke. If the original ball is found before the party has struck the other ball, the first shall continue the one to be played.

XI. Club Breaking

If, in striking, the club breaks, it is nevertheless to be accounted a stroke, if the part of the club remaining in the player's hand either strike the ground or pass the ball.

XII. Holing Out the Ball

In holing, no mark shall be placed, or line drawn, to direct the ball to the hole; the ball must be played fairly and honestly for the hole, and not on your adversary's ball not being in the way to the hole; nor, although lying in the way to the hole, is the player entitled to play with any strength upon it that might injure his adversary's position, or greater than is necessary honestly to send your own ball the distance of the hole. Either party may smooth sand lying around the hole. but this must be done lightly and without pressure, or beating down with the feet, club, or otherwise.

XIII. Unplayable Balls

In Match playing every ball must be played, wherever it lies, or the hole to be given up, excepting when it lies on clothes, in water, or in the bed of the burn, (see Rules IV. and VIII.), or in any of the holes, or short holes, made for golfing, in which latter case it may be lifted, dropt behind the hazard, and played with an iron, without losing a stroke. In Medal playing a ball may, under a penalty of two strokes, be lifted out of a difficulty of any description, and teed behind the hazard, and if in any of the golfing holes, it may be lifted, dropt, and played as above, without a penalty. In all cases where a ball is to be dropt, the party doing so shall front the hole to which he is playing, standing close on the hazard, and drop the ball behind him from his head.

XIV. Medal Days

New holes shall always be made on the day the medals are played for, and no competitor shall play at these holes before he starts for the prize, under the penalty of being disqualified for playing for the medal. On medal days, a party starting off from the tee, must allow the party in front to cross the burn, before they strike off. All balls must be holed out on medal days, and no stimies allowed.

XV. Asking Advice

A player must not ask advice about the game, by word, look, or gesture, from any one except his own caddy, his partner's caddy, or his partner.

XVI. Disputes

Any dispute respecting the play shall be determined by the captain, or senior member present; or, if none of the members are present, it shall be settled by a committee appointed by the parties interested; or by the captain and his annual council for the time, at their first meeting.

XVII. Parties Passing Each Other

Any party having lost a ball, and incurring delay by seeking for it, shall be passed by any other party coming up, and on all occasions a two-ball match—whether by two or four players—may pass parties playing three or more balls. Also, parties having caddies may pass those carrying their own clubs.

XVIII. Balls Splitting

If a ball shall split into two or more pieces, a fresh ball shall be put down in playing for a medal, without a penalty, and likewise in a match, on the penalty of one stroke.

XIX. Breach of Rules

Where no penalty for the infringement of a rule is specially mentioned, the loss of the hole shall be understood to be the penalty.

XX. Repairing the Links

The person appointed to take charge of keeping the Links, shall make new holes every Monday morning, and in such places as to preserve the Putting Green in proper order.